THE
DIRECTOR'S VISION

Play Direction from Analysis to Production

LOUIS E. CATRON

College of William and Mary

Mayfield Publishing Company
Mountain View, California

Library of Congress Cataloging-in-Publication Data

Catron, Louis E.
The director's vision.

Bibliography: p.
Includes index.
1. Theater — Production and direction.   I. Title.
PN2053.C35   1989   792′.0233   88-32582
ISBN 0-87484-760-5

MANUFACTURED IN THE UNITED STATES OF AMERICA

10 9 8 7 6 5 4

Mayfield Publishing Company
1240 Villa Street
Mountain View, CA 94041

Sponsoring editor, Janet M. Beatty; production editor, Gwen Larson;
copy editor, Loralee Windsor; text and cover designer, Joan Greenfield.
The text was set in 10/12 Garamond Light by Compset Inc. and
printed on 50# Finch Opaque by R. R. Donnelley & Sons Co.

Cover photograph: Jack O'Brien, Artistic Director of the
Old Globe Theatre, San Diego. Mark Hiss, photographer.

This book is dedicated with respect and gratitude to the directors, actors, playwrights, students, and colleagues who so willingly gave of themselves and their talents in my productions and classes.

PREFACE

One of the purposes of the Directors Unit [at the Actors Studio was] to familiarize the young directors with . . . what [Lee] Strasberg calls the "basic procedure" for attacking a play, namely, visualizing it, analyzing the text, and translating it into the kinds of directions that facilitate the actor's responding as the director requires.

— DAVID GARFIELD
The Actors Studio

Each time we direct we express our definition of good theatre. Using our vision we marry imagination and discovery. Play direction involves a continual search for answers to two basic questions: *What is "good theatre"? What basic procedures does the director follow to create good theatre?*

This book offers procedures that will help beginning and more experienced directors create an accurate and imaginative view of the script — "the directorial vision." Throughout are guides to an organized methodology — "thinking like a director" — that will bring that vision to life on stage.

Many lay people and even some theatre workers believe play direction is relatively easy, albeit time-consuming: One gets good actors together, rehearses the cast, incorporates technical effects, and waits for the show's opening. But that view ignores the director's research into the play and the many complicated preparations before auditions; it also overlooks the director's leadership tactics and problem-solving processes during rehearsals.

Good theatre productions have superior craftsmanship, but that is a by-product of the more important aspect of direction, *the director's vision,* which is the ability to use a lively sense of theatricality to express the truth one sees in the play. Ansel Adams makes a helpful distinction between mechanics and vision: "The beauty of a photograph by Weston does not lie in the assortment of facts about negative, material, papers, developers — it lies in the realization of his *vision.*" So, too, must the theatrical director be comfortable with the "assortment of facts" about auditioning, blocking, and the like; but good theatre depends on the director's vision.

Creativity flourishes with discipline. The director can create good theatre by following a disciplined, logical, step-by-step procedure. Careful preparation is essential, starting with an accurate play analysis that will lead to a viable interpretation. From that base, the director creates a vision of the whole and then works with designers and actors to bring that vision to life for an audience. Careful pre-production preparation gives the director freedom to create spontaneously during rehearsals. This book guides the director through preparation procedures and creative rehearsal strategies.

As we accumulate experience we learn that there is no single way to direct, no set of iron-clad rules that guarantee we will achieve a quality production, and no assurance that what satisfied us with our last production will be satisfactory with the next. But with experience we learn a methodology, which is one essential focus of this text.

Organization of the Text

As directors, we have a basic responsibility to search for definitions of good theatre. This book urges directors to establish a conceptual foundation by considering those definitions before undertaking any aspect of the directorial process. *Part One* begins an examination of fundamental definitions and the director's responsibilities, an examination that will occupy much of our careers.

The play director seeking to achieve good theatre must begin with accurate play analysis. *Part Two* offers a logical method for analyzing a play: individual chapters discuss plot, character, thought, diction, music, and spectacle. These chapters contain concrete examples of how the director uses these important elements on stage.

Careful pre-planning is crucial to good theatre. We need an organizational methodology that we can depend on to lead us — and thereby our casts and crews — in the pursuit of perfection. *Part Three* discusses aspects of pre-planning such as preparing a well-researched and richly detailed prompt book, planning auditions and casting, and constructing a day-by-day rehearsal schedule. Pre-planning helps us consider problems in advance, outside rehearsals (when the pressure is off), and seek alternatives so that we are better prepared when questions arise. My goal is to help directors learn good habits and procedures that will be valuable for a life's career in theatre.

Part Four describes working with actors, establishing guidelines for rehearsals, and helping actors solve problems. Problem-solving techniques are discussed, including how to identify the problems, consider all possible alternatives, and provide appropriate answers.

Special Features

After a quarter of a century of teaching and practicing play direction, playwriting, and acting, I continue to marvel that these three arts have greater commonalities in approaches and purposes than differences in vocabulary and techniques. As a result of those years of experience, this book for play directors contains many resonances of acting and playwriting. I am convinced that the more one learns about acting and playwriting, the better one's directorial efforts can be. Throughout this text, I have encouraged readers to make inter-connections between directing, acting, and playwriting.

Beginning students might start with either scenes or plays; more experienced students probably will be working on whole plays. On the premise that most readers will be primarily interested in applying their study to a one-act or full-length play or musical, references in this book are to "the play you are directing," not "the exercise or scene you are developing"; but of course all references are as applicable to scenes as to plays.

Quotations begin and end each chapter, and many enrich the body of the text as well. Students who find these citations interesting should be encouraged to read the books from which the quotations are drawn. Directors can never stop learning, and certainly books provide one excellent source for our continued education.

Exercises conclude each chapter to help students apply the ideas discussed. For maximum benefit, readers should approach them with a willingness to commit the necessary time and energy to develop answers fully.

Theatre necessarily discriminates in terms of talent, dedication, imagination, intelligence, dependability, and pure continued hard work, but it must not discriminate in terms of race, creed, sex, or color. In this book I have chosen my words to reflect that belief, avoiding sexist references that would seem to exclude any group. I have often elected to use the word "performer," rather than become involved in awkward constructions such as "he/she," and I use "actor" to refer to both sexes, just as "director" does.

Using This Book

Every instructor necessarily brings personal experience and concepts to a play direction class. You will want to shape this book to your particular theories and approaches. The following thoughts are intended to be suggestions, not prescriptions, and are based on my use of various drafts of this manuscript in my classes.

Experience indicates that my students require most time to master play analysis, and therefore, I plan to spend a great deal of class time with the chapters in Part Two.

Although most of my students are highly vocal people (or perhaps because of that characteristic), I insist that exercises be *written*. Further, to ensure that the students carry over knowledge from chapter to chapter, I require that students include many of the exercises, especially those dealing with analysis, schedule, and problem-solving, in the prompt book.

Because play analysis is difficult to grasp, and more difficult to apply to specific plays, instructors may wish to spend additional time with exercises in the chapters that make up Part Two (Play Analysis). I have found that students benefit from doing many analysis exercises twice. First the class works as a group, applying the exercises to one particular play. (After experimentation I have found that the following widely-read plays are especially suitable for this purpose: *Medea, Macbeth, Ghosts,* or *Streetcar Named Desire,* though many others could also be used.) Then ask students to go through the exercises again individually, to analyze their individual plays. They write the exercises, turn them in to me, and then report orally to the class. Spirited discussions illuminate the analysis process.

My advanced students, who have directed full-length plays such as *Bent, The Romancers,* or *Extremities,* are required to do not only the play analysis exercises in Part Two but also many other exercises focused on scheduling, problem-solving, actors' exercises, prompt book, and the like.

Acknowledgments

I am deeply indebted to the many people in my classes and productions who have contributed to this text and, indeed, to my own continuing education as a director.

I am especially thankful to those students who taught me the lesson all of us in theatre need to keep foremost in our minds: Art, like love, turns tiny when it is used selfishly; it grows best when it is warmly given without concern for repayment.

I thank the College of William and Mary for granting me a semester research leave to pursue this project.

I sincerely appreciate the many directors and others who made suggestions to improve this manuscript; I would like to acknowledge my appreciation to the following reviewers of the text for their many excellent suggestions: Carole Brandt, Pennsylvania State University; Timothy D. Connors, Northern Arizona University; Sidney Friedman, Boston University; Michael McLain, University of California at Los Angeles; Christian H. Moe, Southern Illinois University at Carbondale; Alan A. Stambusky, University of California at Davis; Jack Sydow, University of Washington.

To the people at Mayfield Publishing Company, my deep gratitude for their consistent drive for excellence and, equally, their ability to treat authors as individuals. While any weaknesses in the book are the author's responsibility, this book is richer because of the countless contributions of editor Janet Beatty, production manager Gwen Larson, permissions editor Pam Trainer, product manager Jil Wood, and copy editor Loralee Windsor. Somehow they maintain personal warmth and a sense of humor even during the most hectic problems. Working with them has been a distinct pleasure.

In particular I wish to thank two colleagues at William and Mary. I must express my appreciation for Jerry Bledsoe's contributions to the illustrations in this book. And I am most especially grateful to Richard Palmer for his active support, encouragement, criticisms, and suggestions during the writing and revising of this text.

I must acknowledge with gratitude the generous assistance of the many theatrical companies who supplied the photographs.

CONTENTS

Part Two:
Play Analysis

Part Three:
Preparing for Production

Part Four: Rehearsing the Production

Appendices

THE DIRECTOR'S VISION

PART ONE

Introductory Concepts

CHAPTER ONE

Developing Your Directorial Vision

[Lee Strasberg at the Actors Studio] made me think differently about what a director does, as well as about how and why he does it. He made me consider not just the lines of a play but the life of the play, out of which the lines spring. A play, he taught me, is like an iceberg, eight-ninths of which never rises above the surface of the water; but the size and shape of that one-ninth that does rise above the surface are always determined by the eight-ninths that remains below.

It was not until Lee asked me a simple question, "From where has that character come?" that I began to think properly as a director. It seems ridiculous to me now, but I had never consciously asked myself that. And it led to two million other questions: What does the character want? What happens to that character in the scene? What had happened to all the characters in the scenes that were not in the play? And, most important of all, what is "dramatic action"? The answer to that question, by the way, might best be summed up as "a change of relationship." That is the single most valuable discovery I have been able to make as a director. . . .

—ALAN SCHNEIDER
Entrances: An American Director's Journey

"Vision," writes Jonathan Swift, "is the art of seeing things invisible." In art vision creates life and meaning. For example, a sculptor faces a block of granite and "sees" in it a shape that must be set free; a poet perceives an intense human experience and fashions a poem to express a vision of life's meaning; and an actor's vision turns a dramatic character into a lifelike, dimensional human. Equally the director's imaginative powers create a vision of what Alan Schneider calls "the life of the play" — in a manner of speaking, the full iceberg — and from that vision fashions the entire theatrical production that will transform the script from the inanimate page to the living stage. Directorial vision provides artistic unification of the production.

All of us who direct, whether we are beginners or veterans, must continually work to enhance our abilities to think like directors and to develop our visionary powers. We know we must read as many plays and see as many stage productions

Richard Bauer in *Accidental Death of an Anarchist* at
Arena Stage, Washington, D.C., a multimedia
production that exemplifies Douglas Wagner's
directorial vision. — *Photograph by Joan Marcus*

as possible, and when we have selected a play we wish to direct, we must study
it with the dedication of other artists.

Key to the creation of the director's vision is a process of using a theatre in
your head, imaginatively *hearing* the performers speaking and *seeing* the stage
full of action and movement. On your imagination's stage can appear any performers you wish to cast, and your settings can disregard all financial or practical
limitations. The playscript is to the director as the block of granite is to the sculptor, materials containing the essential life that the director must set free.

Directorial art begins with seeing the "invisible" in the playscript, and directorial craft devises the performance and staging techniques that will best communicate the directorial vision to the audience. Where do you start? Some
directors find that their artistic vision is stimulated by the play's characters in
conflict as they make plans and react to obstacles; other directors begin with the
play's basic intellectual concept or meaning; still others respond first to the play's

Collaboration in action: Director and designers discuss
a model of the basic set for two Guthrie Theater
productions, *Cyrano de Bergerac* and *The Taming of
the Shrew*. Working with talented designers during
production meetings enhances the director's vision.
Left to right: Desmond Heeley, codesigner of sets and
costumes; Gil Wechsler, lighting designer; and Michael
Langham, Guthrie artistic director and director of the
two productions. — *Photograph by Joe Giannetti*

action and plot. In all cases the director's vision brings life where before only
script pages existed.

The director's primary motivation is a desire — no, more than a desire, a
compelling *need* — to share his or her vision with the audience. In the process
the director seeks the collaboration of theatrical colleagues — performers, designers, technicians, and management. All contribute their own art and become
part of a communicative team to create a theatrical experience, artistically unified
by the director, that reaches out to touch the audience. Just as a playwright is
driven to tell a story illustrating his or her view of the world, a director is com-
pelled to communicate the story through the stage.

The director is not satisfied with just any vision; he or she must have a valid,
logical, and theatrical vision. The initial step to finding that vision is careful anal-

ysis and sound interpretation of the play. After successfully analyzing and interpreting the play, the director initiates carefully planned, logical production steps — preparing a thorough prompt book, conducting auditions, casting the play, constructing a rehearsal schedule that will achieve specific goals, working with actors to construct dramatic characters, blocking the action, and using the music and spectacle of the stage — to bring the vision to life.

To paraphrase Robert Frost, the director is the dreamer of things that never were, envisioning a production that never was. No matter how often the play has been produced, the director with a vision sees each production as fresh and new. Armed with a powerful vision, the director can create in cast and crew a sense of optimism that the production will achieve excellence, the director's and the theatre's constant albeit elusive goal.

The theatre is the direct descendant of fertility rites, war dances and all the corporate ritual expressions by means of which our primitive ancestors, often wiser than we, sought to relate themselves to God, or the gods, the great abstract forces which cannot be apprehended by reason, but in whose existence reason compels us to have faith.

—TYRONE GUTHRIE
A Life in the Theatre

Three Fundamental Concepts of Theatre

Directorial vision is built on a firm understanding that three essential qualities are inherent in all good theatre: conflict, emotion, and entertainment. The directorial vision that does not include these three basics can all too easily result in a failed production. Careful study will lead you to perceive the play's dramatic conflict, emotional projections, and entertainment factors.

CONFLICT

Conflict is essential for drama. Without conflict, there is no tension; without tension, there is no drama. Conflict exists in the play's subject and theme, in the dramatic characters, and in the plot. Playwrights learn to develop a dramatic event by starting with a basic conflict of forces that grows steadily scene by scene; performers learn to develop characters by emphasizing the conflict that arises from obstacles interfering with goals; and directors learn to develop dramatic movement in the entire play by emphasizing those conflicts.

Drama is the art of the showdown, expressed as well in the great western movie *High Noon,* which shows the marshall alone in the streets as the gunslingers approach, as in the classic drama *Hamlet,* which shows a son so confused about the reported murder of his father that he stages a mock murder before his stepfather-uncle to test the man's guilt or innocence. Conflict is eyeball-to-eyeball confrontation, force against force, individual against individual or group. It can

The dueling scene from *Hamlet* encapsulates theatrical
conflict, emotional involvement, and entertainment.
This is the well-known "modern dress" *Hamlet*
directed by Tyrone Guthrie to open the Guthrie
Theater, Minneapolis, in 1963. George Grizzard (left)
played Hamlet and Jessica Tandy (center) played
Queen Gertrude. The production was designed by
Tanya Moiseiwitsch. — *Photograph courtesy of the
Guthrie Theater*

be interior or exterior, personalized or abstract. This basic theatrical proposition is so important to the director that it deserves repetition: No force against force, no conflict; no conflict, no drama.

As a director you continually search for ways to present the basic conflict in vivid theatrical terms. Think of a three-act play as a fifteen-round prizefight. For the fight to last the full fifteen rounds, the fighters must be relatively equal. At first one appears to be winning, but then the other rallies; one fighter is down but gets up and manages to knock the other to the ropes; there are feints, tricks, tactics, and strategy; and the fight is touch-and-go all the way. So, too, your direction of a play should equalize forces.

If one fighter is clearly stronger than the other, the fight is over in round one. If one character dominates too strongly in Act One, the struggles during Acts Two and Three are boring and without suspense. Imagine, for example, a production of *A Streetcar Named Desire* that begins with Stanley so aggressive and hostile to Blanche (even in the opening section where Williams shows Stanley as relatively hospitable to the unexpected visitor) that she has no chance to achieve her goal. The struggle would be eliminated from the play. A director might make such a crucial error by looking only at the play's ending instead of considering the basic conflict that starts the action and leads to its ultimate conclusion.

As a director you should encourage performers to find the conflict in their characters. Imagine a Hamlet never reacting to the conflicts he faces: if he never came to grips with those obstacles, the audience would never see into his tortured soul. Your role as a director is first to find the play's conflicts, then to help actors discover effective, stageworthy ways of playing those moments of high dramatic tension.

I believe that a theatre, where live actors perform to an audience which is there in the flesh before them, will survive all threats from powerfully organized industries which pump prefabricated drama out of cans and blowers and contraptions of one kind or another. The struggle for survival may often be hard and will batter the old theatre about severely. Indeed, from time to time it will hardly be recognizable; but it will survive. It will survive as long as mankind demands to be amused, terrified, instructed, shocked, corrupted and delighted by tales told in the manner which will always remain mankind's most vivid and powerful manner of telling a story.

—TYRONE GUTHRIE
A Life in the Theatre

EMOTION

Emotion is a core ingredient of drama. Emotions range from the heights of ecstasy to the depths of despair, creating the play's action, the character's complex motivations and drives, and the captivating intensities that bring the audience into the universe of the play. Knowing that emotionless characters are bland and uninteresting, the playwright fashions characters who are alive because of their emotions; performers bring characters to life by showing first what they feel and only

Seeking to free his wife who is unjustly accused of witchcraft, John Proctor (standing, left) attempts to convince the judges that her accuser, Abigail Williams (standing, right), is immoral. Only if the actor conveys Proctor's emotions will the audience empathize with the electric vitality of this dramatization of the Salem witch hunts. James Blendick is Proctor and Blair Brown is Abigail in this production of Arthur Miller's *The Crucible* directed by Len Cariou at the Guthrie Theater. — *Photograph courtesy of the Guthrie Theater*

then what they think. The director's plan of attack during rehearsals should encourage performers to mesh with the playwright's emotional challenges.

One of theatre's most potent tools is not a stage technique but is inherent in the audience, which, assuming proper emotional stimuli from the stage, will empathize with the characters in the play. Empathy is a psychological phenomenon directors call "feeling in"; the empathic audience member experiences the feelings of the theatrical character, virtually living within the character's psyche and soul.

The audience's empathic emotional connection to the characters leads to intellectual involvement with the choices the character faces. First, however, there must be an emotional link between audience and character. For example, the existential dilemma John Proctor faces at the end of *The Crucible* — whether to sign his name to a confession and thereby imply that everyone should sign such documents or refuse to sign and face dire consequences — makes a powerful intellectual dramatic statement. But if audiences don't care for Proctor — if, for example, the director leads the actor to create an arrogant Proctor — that dilemma and its meaning would be of little concern to the audience. An emotional connection to Proctor is necessary to make the play's intellectual concept clear to the audience.

As directors our job is to discover the characters' emotional ebbs and flows, charting their rhythms and developing a sensitive empathic response to them. We then need to cast performers capable of projecting the characters' emotions and, during rehearsals, create a working environment that encourages the actors to display those emotions. We devise techniques to enlarge, enrich, and focus audience attention on the emotions.

Art is the response to the demand for entertainment, for the stimulation of our senses and imagination, and truth enters into it only as it subserves these ends.

—GEORGE SANTAYANA
The Sense of Beauty

ENTERTAINMENT

Theatre must first entertain if it is to appeal to the audience, but that is not to say theatre must only entertain. Theatre can inspire, exhort, lecture, amuse, satirize, and decry; it can create tragedy with man against the gods or comedy with the earnest pursuit of important trivia; it can challenge intellectual concepts and thereby force a confrontation of ideas; it can angrily denounce or proudly hail, point with pride or view with alarm. The possibilities are virtually endless, but theatre can achieve those communications only if it is entertaining.

Entertaining is used here in the sense of diverting attention from daily concerns, creating involuntary concentration on the stage, and causing the "willing suspension of disbelief" that Coleridge says is so essential for theatre. Entertainment does not necessarily mean pie-in-the-face comedy, although only snobbery would make us dismiss low farce or any other particular form of theatre. Slapstick is entertainment; so is *King Lear*. You may prefer one to the other, but both can fulfill theatre's basic need to entertain.

Entertainment requires a knowledge of the audience. We cannot entertain in a vacuum; we entertain people who, even when combined into an audience, have distinct individual qualities. Just as there are many "theatres" (educational, children's, Broadway, realistic, musical, dinner, and more), there are many audiences, and to entertain we need to know the personality of those we would entertain. Children will laugh at a farcical event that barely evokes a smile from their mothers; a businessman may delight in a "twenty girls, count 'em, twenty" dance that his wife finds offensive or merely boring; there are audiences for Shakespeare and Simon, *Carousel* and *Fool for Love,* Aristophanes and Stoppard. If you have

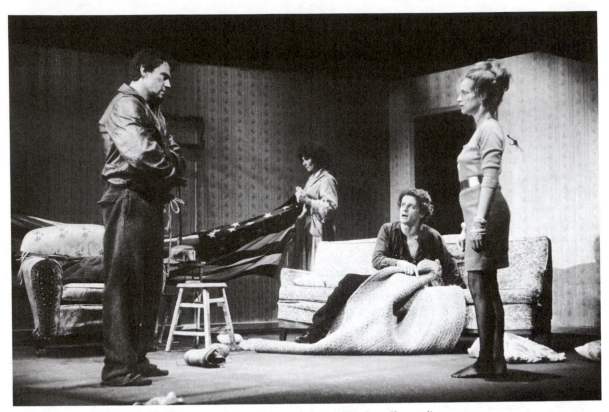

Theatre is entertainment. Whether a tense psychological drama like Sam Shepard's *A Lie of the Mind* (above, New York production directed by the playwright) or an explosive, spectacular musical like *Cats* (opposite, New York production directed by Trevor Nunn), theatre must entertain its audience. One hallmark of quality theatre is its

the good fortune to work with a theatre company that has earned a reputation for good theatrical productions, your audiences will accept all forms of theatre.

Our operational premise is clear: All audiences want entertainment. It may be entertainment of the sentiments or of the soul, of the mind or of the heart; it may help audience members relax in a world of order and morality or force them into the tension of chaos and anarchy. Humanity hungers for entertainment. If this premise were not true, theatre would not have been created.

So many things in the theatre are discouraging that any man of sense would give up. But the theatre is a *femme fatale,* and for those who feel her fascination the question: what is to be done? has perpetually to be asked and perpetually to be answered affirmatively.

—ERIC BENTLEY
The Playwright as Thinker

ability to capture audience interest — whether with simple sets and costumes or elaborate staging, realism or romanticism, large casts or small — with excellent scripts excellently presented. — *Left photograph copyright 1986 Martha Swope — Right photograph copyright 1984 Martha Swope*

Exercises

Each chapter concludes with exercises designed to help you understand and apply the points discussed. As in any book, class, or theatrical activity, you will benefit most from applying imagination, insight, and sensitivity to these exercises, always approaching them in good faith, determined to receive all possible benefits.

These exercises apply to the play you are preparing to direct or to a play you are studying to enhance your awareness of the directorial process.

To examine these questions thoroughly you should write your answers in detail. All exercises can become part of your "director's prompt book," discussed at length in a later chapter.

CONFLICT

Your first steps are to find and chart the conflict that creates the action of the play. To help you envision the conflict in the play you will direct, work through the exercises below.

1. Give the name of the play, the playwright, and the date written.
2. Describe the play's basic conflict in an abstract sense (for example, in *Medea* the abstract conflict is between justice and revenge). Identify the opposing forces.
3. Describe the play's basic conflict in a concrete sense (again in *Medea* the concrete conflict is between what Medea wants and what Creon wants). Be detailed. Your answer may take several pages.
4. Identify the specific characters in conflict. What motivates each of them? Quote lines that indicate characters' motivational drives.
5. What action before the play begins (the "inciting incident") has led to the present conflict?
6. At what precise point in the play does the conflict begin (the "point of attack")? Quote the lines that show the conflict's beginning.
7. Who are the characters intimately involved in the conflict? What does each want, and how does the other oppose those desires?
8. List each step of the conflict, scene by scene. Describe how the steps accumulate, piling tension on tension like building blocks. Are some scenes designed to allow the tension to relax?
9. At what point does the conflict reach its highest point?

EMOTION

1. What is the play's overall emotional tone? Be as definite as possible, seeking the single tone that best describes the play.
2. Who is the central character? What is the central character's primary emotion throughout the play? Be precise.
3. Follow the central character throughout the play, describing each emotional change. What stimuli cause the changes? Your answer may require a detailed chart of the character through the play's scenes.
4. Who is the next primary character? What is this character's dominant emotion throughout the play?
5. Follow that character throughout the play, again charting the character's emotional changes and identifying stimuli that cause emotional responses.
6. Repeat exercises 4 and 5 for each additional major character in the play.
7. Describe the primary and secondary emotions of each minor character.
8. Describe the emotional connections and interplay between the major characters.

ENTERTAINMENT

Analyze devices the playwright uses to involve the audience by working through the exercises below.

1. What writing techniques does the playwright use?

	The playwright uses the element to hold audience attention. . .		
	A Great Deal	Moderately	Little
Plot, the play's action	_____	_____	_____
Character	_____	_____	_____
Intellectual concept	_____	_____	_____
Diction, the play's language	_____	_____	_____
Music, the play's sounds	_____	_____	_____
Spectacle, the play's visuals	_____	_____	_____

2. Specify the storytelling devices the playwright uses to entertain the audience. Consider such aspects as suspense, comedy, unique characters, word play, visible emotional displays, and the like.
3. Specify, in order of importance, the major qualities that attract you to the play. Explain.
4. In order of importance, what will the audience find most entertaining in the play and its production? Explain.

A theatre, in the widest sense of the word, is the general term for all places of amusement through the ear or eye, in which men assemble in order to be amused by some entertainment presented to all at the same time and in common.

—SAMUEL TAYLOR COLERIDGE
Progress of the Drama

CHAPTER TWO

The Director's Functions and Responsibilities

I know of one acid test in the theatre. It is literally an acid test. When a performance is over, what remains? Fun can be forgotten, but powerful emotion also disappears and good arguments lose their thread. When emotion and argument are harnessed to a wish from the audience to see more clearly into itself — then something in the mind burns. The event scorches on to the memory an outline, a taste, a trace, a smell — a picture. It is the play's central image that remains, its silhouette, and if the elements are rightly blended this silhouette will be its meaning, this shape will be the essence of what it has to say.

—PETER BROOK
The Empty Space

Just what is a director? What does a director do? What are directorial functions and responsibilities? Why does theatre need the director? The more we direct, the more we hear such questions. Indeed, all of us who direct are wryly aware that as we accumulate experience we repeatedly ask these questions of ourselves. Perhaps we can best understand our complex directorial roles by perceiving how, and especially why, the modern director emerged.

Emergence of the Modern Director

In the theatrical hierarchy the director is the new kid on the block, what Stella Adler calls "a baby in the theatre," because the position of director, as we understand it today, is merely a century old. Granted, from theatre's earliest origins some individual — a playwright, an actor-manager, a star — was responsible for putting together a package of performers, playscript, and playing space, but traditionally that person sought merely to get the show on the boards. Only relatively recently has theatre needed someone to ensure that the complex production is organically and artistically whole. The need for a director originated in the many

The pinball machine finally pays off — a triumphant
victory of "man against machine" — in the last act of
William Saroyan's *The Time of Your Life*. Above, the
original New York production codirected by Eddie
Dowling and William Saroyan. — *Photograph courtesy
of the Library of Congress*

theatrical and nontheatrical movements that took place around the mid-
nineteenth century. We can describe those evolutions briefly here.

Prior to 1850 the popular writing style was romantic. It reflected an optimistic
view of the world and focused on aristocrats who lived in distant lands and times.

The wing and drop set was the generic environment for all plays from comedy to tragedy, and performers had their personal costumes, chosen not for particular roles but to enhance their personal appearance. Actors were cast by type: This young lady always played the ingenue and therefore would have memorized ingenue roles for a large number of popular plays, that man always played the leading male and would have memorized those roles. To prepare a production the brief rehearsals typically consisted of the production's star telling other performers, "I shall enter here, move to center, and exit there: Stay out of my way." Actors were evaluated by their vocal and physical, almost gymnastic, skills. The standards called for them to *act,* not *be,* the character.

Then came sweeping changes. By the mid-nineteenth century worldwide repressive political movements, accompanied by the industrial revolution, turned humankind's focus from romanticism's idealization and optimism to more somber truths about the relationship between society and the individual. An explosion in scientific methodology focused on what could be experienced by the five senses (sight, hearing, taste, smell, touch), again making romanticism an inadequate mode of expression. Charles Darwin's *On the Origin of Species* in 1859 proposed a new way of thinking about humanity's place in the world, just as Sigmund Freud's psychological studies of the subconscious advanced a new view of mankind's innermost secrets.

Theatre practices were also evolving drastically during this period. Starting around 1850 with Emile Zola authors developed a new realism and naturalism, often focused on contemporary social issues, environmental influences, and psychological understanding. Such playwrights as Henrik Ibsen, August Strindberg, Gerhart Hauptmann, and Maxim Gorky, followed by John Galsworthy, Anton Chekhov, and George Bernard Shaw, quickly made the new style popular. Because the new style stressed environmental influences, scene designers replaced the wing and drop set with the more complicated box set (thus establishing the fourth wall concept), which could create unique environments for individual plays. A fascination with antiquities outside the theatre led to theatrical productions featuring historically accurate costumes even when the plays did not require such details. Within the context of such realism the excessive bombastic vocal pyrotechnics of the star performer became increasingly unacceptable.

Someone had to take control and combine all these theatrical elements into a meaningful whole. The modern director emerged to fill that role. Most theatre historians agree that the first modern director was Georg II, Duke of Saxe-Meiningen, whose acting troupe, the Meiningen Players, was active in the latter part of the nineteenth century, beginning what came to be known as a director's theatre. The duke's major contribution was his integration of the playscript with all the theatrical arts, including scenic effects, costumes, and performers. The star system disintegrated under his highly disciplined regime; his actors would play a leading role in one production and a walk-on in the next. To help the performers work within the influences of the play's environment, the duke insisted that all rehearsals take place on the completed set, a practice many directors today wish they could achieve. He was particularly careful to work with every member of the production, especially members of crowd scenes, directing each performer to be a unique character.

In a fascinating coincidence, a number of individuals around the world began at the same time to evolve the modern director, working to create new "free theatres." In France André Antoine founded the Théâtre Libre; in Germany Otto Brahm started the Freie Buehne; in England J. T. Grein began the Independent Theatre; and in Russia Constantin Stanislavski and Vladimir Nemirovich-Danchenko started the Moscow Art Theatre. Each helped define the director as the artistic leader responsible for ensuring that the playscript was properly interpreted, integrating each individual production unit into one artistic entity, and working with performers in long, intense rehearsal periods to discover the internal motivational drives of the characters.

This brief description shows us that the modern director was created to pull together the disparate units of a theatrical production into a cohesive whole, unified and brought to life by the director's artistic vision. This perspective allows us to understand the functions and responsibilities of today's director.

A director can do a brilliant job in one play and fall apart in the next if he's not clear on what a director does.

—LEE STRASBERG
cited in S. Loraine Hull, *Strasberg's Method*

The Director's Five Functions

To help us understand the director's role in the theatre, and to indicate how directorial vision shapes production, we will now seek to define the director by five functions. All are interwoven, and each has complex subdivisions. Although all are crucial, they are discussed here in a relative order of importance starting with the prime directive.

ARTISTIC UNIFICATION

The most important single function of the director is to ensure artistic unification of every aspect of the production. Theatrical experience leads us to understand the significance of this function. For example, we have seen productions with a number of different acting styles, as if the performers were not all in the same play; productions with costumes or scenery that were jarringly incongruous for the interpretation of the playscript; or productions of tragedy that evoked continual audience laughter. Productions such as these exemplify the negative side of directorial work, and we who direct must take a number of steps to avoid such errors by achieving an artistic unification.

Analyze and interpret the play. Artistic unification is impossible unless the director first has a solid, theatrical, valid analysis and interpretation of the play. Others contribute opinions, but the director alone shapes the final interpretation of the play leading to production. Directorial analysis and interpretation must be

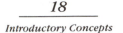

accurate because they are the principles guiding designers' creations and performers' characterizations, as well as the director's decisions regarding style, tempo, and pace; use of the stage, and all other aspects involved with bringing the script to life.

Analysis and interpretation must also be theatrical. A play is written not to be read but to be staged; the director sees the script not as literature but as an inanimate object to be brought to life in a staged production. It is not enough for the directorial interpretation to have literary or intellectual validity, although of course those qualities are necessary; first the interpretation must be stageworthy.

Guide performers' interpretations. Performers' interpretations of characters must fit within the directorial interpretation of the play. Each actor has artistic freedom to create a living, breathing character, and the director must not inhibit that wondrous creative process. At the same time, however, each performer's character must be an integral part of the play's whole. The production's unity cannot afford characters who deny the operational interpretive premise of the play.

To a novice director this may sound like a potential confrontational situation between director and actors. In practice, however, problems seldom occur. The director avoids confrontations by clearly establishing each character's basic parameters at the beginning of rehearsals. "Here are the dimensions of each character," you say, directly or by implication. "Based on my interpretation of the play, this particular character lives within these clear-cut walls and therefore contributes to the playscript's overall effect in such-and-such a manner." Within these parameters the performer has freedom to bring the character to life.

Unify designers' interpretations. All aspects of design must fit within the basic interpretation of the play, so production design must also be part of the director's vision. Again there is no conflict of interest or confrontation. On the contrary, as you work with talented designers, your insight into the play and its production grows sharper.

The wise director carefully encourages design colleagues to exercise their creativity. Costumes, scenery, sound, lighting, properties, and makeup are elements that contribute richness to the whole production. Careful scheduling provides ample time for lengthy discussions with all designers, both in groups and individually. Initial meetings allow you to explain your vision of the production and invite insights from your colleagues.

REPRESENTING THE PLAYWRIGHT

As directors our second function is to think of the playwright as a working partner and the script as the inspiration that gives us a vision for production. We achieve our goal by thinking we represent the author.

Respect the script. Directors need to keep a sense of perspective about the contributions of the script to the production. We therefore direct the play as if the playwright is a respected colleague who will attend the production. Just as the director must unify the interpretive work of performers and designers, the playwright controls the interpretive work of the director. Helpful questions to keep in mind are — What would the playwright say about this directorial analysis and interpretation? How would the playwright respond if he or she saw this production? Am I serving the playwright's best interests?

Two schools of thought separate directorial attitudes toward the script. For discussion purposes here we can call them the "revisionist" and the "collaborative" schools. The revisionist school believes the director must actively search for fresh approaches to staging plays, especially classics that are frequently produced. Directors in this group believe they should freely change the script as necessary to give new views of standard works. They maintain that innovative changes improve the play by modernizing it for today's audiences or correcting the playwright's errors.

The collaborative school believes the playwright's work suffers when revised. Objecting to revisionism and "play doctors," directors in this school ask — Should a contemporary editor revise Emily Dickinson's poetry for a modern edition "to be sure those complex poems can be understood"? Should a museum director change the colors of Van Gogh's cornfields "to make the fields more meaningful to American midwestern farmers"? Should "photo doctors" add water colors to Ansel Adams photographs "because black and white pictures are so old-fashioned"? Members of this school believe in the sanctity of the script. They work on the premise that audiences deserve to experience the depth of the writer's work untarnished by directorial changes.

In actual practice most directors take positions more or less in the middle of these two extremes. Those who tend toward the revisionist school believe in ensuring that the audience will experience the riches the playwright has to offer, and those who incline more to the collaborative school are willing to consider making limited script changes.

Both schools tend to agree that no director has a right to exploit the script for self-serving reasons. *Exploitation* in this case means to select a play based on eagerness to build one's personal resume, without regard to the theatre's needs, or to corrupt the playwright's work by forcing an overlay of personal or political opinions on the script. Such practices can confuse the audience or make them conclude that the playwright wrote a confused play. Most directors believe such exploitation violates directorial ethics.

Work with the playwright. The director works with the playwright more closely than anyone else involved with the production. If the playwright is present, you mediate dealings between writer and theatrical company to maintain positive communications. Because few playwrights understand performers' psychology and methodology, it is seldom wise for the director to allow the writer to speak directly to performers during the rehearsal period. The playwright's direct explanation of a character may short-circuit a performer's own discovery process, and ill-chosen words of advice may confuse a performer still trying to grow in a role.

As a director you also filter performers' comments. Rather than encouraging performers' constant "suggestions" to the writer about this line or that charac-

Many directors find that working with a playwright on an original play can be exciting creative work. Director Charles Towers consults with playwright Deborah Pryor regarding her play, *Wetter Than Water,* presented by the Virginia Stage Company in Norfolk, Virginia. Towers and Pryor undertook a novel arrangement that allowed the author to revise freely following every night's performance; in the following productions performers either had new lines memorized or, if necessary, carried the new script pages. The result of such cooperative collaboration is vibrantly alive theatre for director, playwright, performers, and audience. Such innovative theatres encourage new playwrights to learn the art and craft of playwriting.

ter — comments with potentially negative effects that once started are likely to grow — the wise director tries to prevent such statements from going uncensored to the playwright. As a sensitive director you can judge the validity of the comments and know how much the playwright can accept at any one time.

If the playwright is absent, you are his or her representative, operating on the basic principle that in the absence of the author there can be no substantial changes in the script that would not be made if the playwright were present. If exceptions are absolutely essential, you consider the author's viewpoint before approving changes.

REPRESENTING THE AUDIENCE

As directors we are motivated by a need to share our vision with an audience. Therefore our third function is to represent their interests. From the preliminary planning sessions through rehearsals and final dress, directors serve as "an audience of one," as Tyrone Guthrie says, seeking to bring the play to life on the stage in a way that is true to the script, correctly theatrical, and captivating to an audience.

Theatre exists neither to train participants nor, unfortunately, to give its people financial reward. The goal of theatrical production is to communicate the play to the audience. One crucial measurement of production success lies in the answer to the question — Did the audience members find that the production made the play more meaningful than it would have been had they read it quietly at home?

Clarify communication. As a director you continually examine the production's ability to communicate to the audience. Questions you should ask yourself include — Are we engaging audience emotions correctly? Are we evoking proper moods? Are we presenting the play's values clearly? Will the audience perceive the script's qualities with the appropriate emphasis? Are we distracting attention from the play's major thrust (by, for example, adding heavy-handed intellectual concepts to a light-hearted comedy or confusing notes of comedy to a tragedy)? If the play is designed to be ambiguous, will our production allow the audience to confront the play's questions without forcing answers on them? If the play is clear, are we showing that clarity to the audience without adding levels of confusion?

Eliminate distractions. One directorial guide is the belief that for every performance there is a slightly deaf person sitting in the last row. In the latter stages of rehearsal you will aim the production at that mythical person until you are confident that he or she can hear every aspect of the production.

You must also ensure that everyone in the audience can see all of the action on stage. Avoid watching rehearsals from one central location; make a point of observing the action from all audience seats. Walking to far corners of the auditorium during rehearsals will help you ensure proper sightlines.

You must also eliminate backstage distractions. Walk through the auditorium to ensure that the set properly masks the backstage areas. The dramatic illusion

Working with performers, director Peter Sellars
rehearses with (above) Priscilla Smith and (opposite)
Marianne Tatum during rehearsals for *Hang on to Me.*
Instead of the old-fashioned cliché of using a
megaphone to communicate from the back of the
auditorium, modern directors believe in one-to-one
director-performer communications. Such intimate
working relationships are, for many contemporary
directors, the most enjoyable of all directorial
functions. — *Photographs by Joe Giannetti*

will be destroyed if the audience is able to see past the disguise of the stage set
into the grim backstage area, crowded with technicians and out-of-character performers, or hear backstage noise. There are limits to an audience's "willing suspension of disbelief," and no performance should be forced to fight to hold
audience interest while technical activities compete for attention.

ORGANIZING A WORKING PROCESS

The director is the production's chief organizer. You are responsible for setting goals for everyone involved in the production and working out a viable
schedule that incorporates all production elements. You continually establish
priorities to be sure the production accomplishes goals.

Make decisions. As the director you have final responsibility for all decisions about your production. Fortified with a vision based on knowledge gathered from play analysis and research, you are the resident authority on the playscript and the production's interpretation. If you are well prepared, decisions will be relatively easy; many will be amalgams of input from your colleagues. Often your best course of action will be to delegate authority to others, giving them guidelines about how to approach the problem.

Oversee the production budget. In many theatrical organizations the director is responsible for keeping all aspects of the production within budget. If you are directing in a well-established theatrical organization that has evolved a system for handling budgets, everyone involved with the production will have worked out expenditures based on experience, leaving you little to oversee. On the other hand, if you direct in a new organization or one that has no established procedures for handling expenditures, you can expect to be involved in all budgetary decisions.

You must stay within the show's predetermined budget. Going over budget is harmful to your reputation, production, and theatre. If you work with other directors in an established organization, such as a community or university theatre, and your productions continually cost more than your colleagues', you should not be surprised if they begin to view you as selfish or exploitive.

Prepare schedules. One of the secrets of a good production is superior planning that uses time most effectively. As a director you need to construct an efficient and productive rehearsal and production schedule that will achieve its goals. Here, as in so many other instances, advance work pays off handsomely in more productive rehearsals.

Cast the show. In certain professional situations the producer may select leading performers, but in all other cases the director is solely responsible for casting. No director should accept casting decisions made by a community theatre board of directors or the university theatre artistic director.

WORKING WITH PERFORMERS

Most directors believe working with performers is the most enjoyable directorial function. Starting with a strong interpretation of the play based on careful play analysis, you work with performers to bring the play and its characters to life. It is exciting to observe creative performers go through the process of developing rich characterization. During the intensive rehearsal period, you and the performers work closely together, as they ask questions and gather insights not only about the characters and the play but also about themselves.

Moreover you have the good fortune to be present for the whole process, from the beginning, when performers are searching for character, to the final production, when they have created dimensional, living characters. You have an objective view of each individual performer's growth during rehearsals. For most directors observing that growth is the most rewarding facet of the entire directorial process.

The Most Important Function

Of the five functions discussed above, which is the most important? The question is valid, but sharply defined answers are difficult to find. On the other hand, while all five functions are vitally important, there are definite priorities. Most directors have had extensive previous acting experience and therefore are likely to believe that the director's prime function is working with performers. It is true that directors spend more time and creative energy working with performers than with any other function. It is also true that working with performers is often more enjoyable and rewarding than the other functions.

But directorial vision, based on careful play analysis and interpretation, takes priority over working with performers. If the directorial vision of the play is flawed, all work with performers — indeed, *all* the work preparing the play — will be at best equally flawed and at worst disastrous because in theatre errors tend to compound themselves. Thus your first function must be to ensure accurate play analysis and interpretation. Your second priority is to plan the production, allowing you and the performers the necessary freedom to work toward creation of the characters and the play.

Perhaps we should divide these five functions into two parts. The first part is "preproduction" and includes the work before the production gets under way — analysis, interpretation, and planning. The second part involves the actual production work — working with actors. If all steps of analysis, interpretation, and planning are successfully completed before auditions and casting, thereafter the director's primary function is working with performers.

Let me say something about ethics in the theater. [One] reason for the collapse of well-intentioned venture after venture is sloth and egomania. We must accept the fact that the theater is a communal adventure. Unlike the soloist we can't perform alone in the theater. . . . The better the play, the more we need an ensemble venture. We must recognize that we need each other's strengths, and the more we need each other's professional comradeship, the better the chance we have of making theater. We must serve the play by serving each other; an ego-maniacal "star" attitude is only self-serving and hurts everyone. . . .

We must aim for "character" in the moral and ethical sense of the word, compounded of the virtues of mutual respect, courtesy, kindness, generosity, trust, attention to the others, seriousness, loyalty, as well as those necessary attributes of diligence and dedication.

—UTA HAGAN
with Haskel Frankel, *Respect for Acting*

The Director's Responsibilities

The theatrical director is like a ship's captain in charge of an important voyage from point A to point B and responsible for the safety and well-being of the ship, the crew, its passengers, and other vessels that may be affected by the ship's maneuvers. Both ship captains and theatrical directors rule less by democracy than by what many view wryly as a benevolent dictatorship; they seek opinions of others, but final decisions rest with them. The decision-maker necessarily carries a number of responsibilities.

TO THEATRE AS AN INSTITUTION

Theatre's devotees, while blessedly fervent in enthusiasm, are regrettably few in number. We therefore must woo our fellow citizens to enter the theatre where we can prove to them the power of our art to entertain, challenge, amuse, divert, shock, educate, and, especially, satisfy their inherent hunger for the beautiful. As directors our challenge is to make theatre vital and alive for those who are indifferent or hostile to our art. Consider yourself a missionary in a strange land where not all the natives are friendly. Your assignment is to convert as many as possible.

Although you may not win all people to your cause, as a missionary you continue trying, just as pioneers before you dedicated their careers to making theatre a vital part of the lives of convicts and Puritans, school children and elderly, impoverished and wealthy. You must regret the loss of audience members who have attended poor productions, concluded that theatre has no standards or drive for excellence, and decided not to attend another production. Sad, too, is the loss of those who find theatre productions simply too inbred and full of in-jokes, pompously self-important, pseudointellectual, or artsy-craftsy. Such productions may be ever so amusing for the participants but just boring to spectators.

Your responsibility as a theatrical director is to build theatre audiences not only for your particular production but also for all theatre, not only for today but also for tomorrow. Like other arts theatre attracts audiences by presenting high-caliber artistic works. When theatre presents its best, audiences grow. Your concern, therefore, must be to achieve the highest possible quality.

Your obligation to theatre includes a responsibility to train and educate both participants and spectators. Give each playwright a fair and just hearing to help the living writers grow and the dead maintain their reputations; and constantly encourage new playwrights to replenish the font of dramatic literature. Actors should be better performers when they finish a production than they were when you began working together. Give audiences the opportunity to experience modern voices as well as the classics. Remain alert to new developments in writing and staging and continue to experiment and grow because it is an immutable law that when theatre becomes static it starts to fall.

TO A SPECIFIC THEATRE

As a director working within any given theatrical organization, you share with others in the organization a responsibility for that group's current and future growth and reputation. Just as the director rightfully expects loyalty from the cast, the theatrical organization has reason to expect loyalty from its director and other responsible workers.

The opposite practice would have the director exploit the theatrical organization, selfishly taking from it all that benefits him or her with no sense of obligation to make contributions in return. In your theatrical career you may encounter such harmful attitudes. Undoubtedly you will discover that though exploiters may profit from their grasping practices for several years, the process eventually damages an internal quality — one might call it "heart" or "soul" — and ultimately that damage becomes visible in their work. Art, like love, turns tiny when it is used selfishly; it grows best when it is warmly given without concern for repayment.

TO THE PLAYWRIGHT

As the playwright's representative in production, your responsibility to the author is a result of a number of factors, not the least of which is the fact that you and the playwright share common bonds. You are both communicators who use the stage to touch audience emotions and intellects, and you both think more of the broad panorama of the concept than of individual moments. Director and playwright share a deep interest in the play's basic concept and thought.

Chief of your responsibilities to the playwright is accurate analysis and interpretation of the author's play. Mistaken interpretations can create a blurred vision that damages the work of performers, designers, and technicians. Inaccurate interpretation causes a failed production.

Legal responsibilities. The playwright enjoys the strong legal protections of international copyright regulations, which prohibit presentation of a play without prior approval from the copyright holder, usually a play publisher/leasing agent such as Samuel French, Inc., or Dramatists Play Service. The law further says you are not allowed to make "substantial changes." This term is difficult to define precisely, but the principle is clear enough to understand in a broad sense. The director who deletes passages for the convenience of production — perhaps the director does not know how to bring them to dramatic life, or a performer is unable to cope with their artistic demands — may be breaking the copyright law. Before such laws were passed, directors had a strange penchant for changing the endings of plays. Ibsen's *A Doll's House,* for example, originally played in America with a "happy ending" that put Nora back into her husband's arms at the final curtain. Clearly that is offensive to the playwright's intention. Copyright laws forbidding "substantial changes" to the script have a clear moral imperative. You *know* it was wrong to change *Doll's House,* and you can apply that principle to proposed changes in any script.

Artistic responsibilities. Because your initial desire to select the play was based on the vision the playwright's creative work gave you, there are implied artistic responsibilities to the playwright as well as to the script. As a director you have a further responsibility to kindred theatre artists. A sense of artistic pride is involved: it is important that the production achieve the highest possible standards to reflect fairly on the playwright, as well as on production personnel.

TO PERFORMERS

The performer places a great deal of trust in the director, who in turn is obliged to live up to that faith. As a director you have a responsibility to cast the performer correctly and fairly, neither sharply above nor far below a just estimate of perceived talents. Casting a performer below his or her ability level can be both discouraging to the performer and wasteful of talent; giving the performer a demanding role in which he or she has no chance of succeeding is equally discouraging and wasteful.

A director must be concerned for the performer's physical well-being and safety. As the production's authority figure you may thrust a performer into potentially harmful situations: a staged sword fight without safety measures, movement on a high level or steps during a total blackout, or strenuous work or dance without proper physical warm-up. Performers' normal self-preservation instincts are often submerged by the desire to do well for the production; you must be careful to protect them from harm.

Just as you must be concerned about the performers' physical well-being, you are responsible for the performers' emotional, artistic, and mental condition. Rude and inhumane behavior is never acceptable; a director can do a great deal of damage by browbeating actors.

TO THE PRODUCTION TEAM

Production team colleagues have artistic needs that the director must respect. You want them to have full opportunity to express their talents while doing their best work for the production. Good teamwork produces exciting theatre. The wise director remembers that production personnel also hunger to achieve perfection.

TO THE AUDIENCE

The director has a responsibility to give the audience honest production values. Audiences attend our productions for numerous reasons. They need entertainment, they hunger to participate in an aesthetic experience, they seek theatre's emotional and intellectual stimulation, they want to be diverted from their own concerns and taken imaginatively to other worlds, or they desire insight into their personal situations. Your selection of plays must focus on the audience; you should ask yourself how you can serve the audience, not how you can benefit yourself.

If you are directing a play that may shock your audiences — and often a director deliberately allows audiences to confront a playwright's blunt truths — you owe them the courtesy of letting them know in advance what to expect. The motion picture industry wisely classifies movies with various ratings; we in theatre must also let our audiences know if we are presenting what is euphemistically known as "adult material," such as nudity, potentially offensive language, or controversial situations or themes.

TO YOURSELF

As a practicing artist, you have a responsibility to protect and nourish your art. Although the drive for excellence should be tempered by an awareness that perfection is elusive and seldom comes to mere mortals, you cannot afford to be satisfied with anything less than your best. Without rationalizations or excuses about the work of others, you should be able to say to yourself, "This production is the highest possible level I can achieve at this stage of my development."

To protect your art estimate what directorial challenges will best fit your specialized needs. Tackling a major production too early — a tragedy such as *Macbeth,* or a modern classic like *After the Fall,* for example — is likely to be harmful. It would also be harmful continually to expend your directorial talents on plays with neither substance nor challenge. Ask a trusted mentor or colleague to make recommendations about the directorial work you should consider.

To nourish your art be certain each directorial effort is an educational experience. Again the trusted mentor or colleague can provide major stimulation, and you should solicit his or her opinions about each production you direct. Opinions of such experts will help you set goals for self-improvement with future productions.

Early burnout is a genuine danger facing many beginning directors. Weigh your understandable eagerness to direct as many productions as possible, and thereby obtain valuable experience, against an objective measurement of personal stamina and endurance. An exhausting directorial schedule provides few benefits. Too often talented young directors explode forth only to burn out quickly, a skyrocket on the Fourth of July, marvelous in its moment but gone before the Fifth. Protect yourself by thinking of a lifelong career, not of continued one-shot efforts.

A style of performances arises only in response to a single guiding genius possessed of a unique view of the end result he seeks, the stage director.

—NORRIS HOUGHTON
The Exploding Stage

Exercises

These questions will help you increase your sensitivity to directorial functions. Answer by using your empirical observations of productions you know quite well, from your view as participant or audience member. (To avoid embarrassing the directors or yourself, you may wish to disguise the identity of the productions.) Your answers should be detailed; many will require several pages.

ARTISTIC UNIFICATION

1. Selecting a production you know well, discuss in detail what you believe to be its lack of artistic unification. Identify the failure(s) you observed. What specifically made you conscious of the lack of artistic cohesiveness? Were there jarring incongruous notes in performance or design? Were there flaws in interpretation by director or performers? Describe the problems. What effect did the lack of artistic unification have on your response to the production? What could the director have done to eliminate these problems?
2. Discuss a production that you believe was artistically unified. What made you aware of the artistic cohesiveness? Describe the effect of this production. What were the director's contributions to artistic unification?

REPRESENTING THE PLAYWRIGHT

1. Discuss a production that you believe made the playscript look muddy or weak. Would a lay audience member, with no prior knowledge of the script, have concluded this was simply a poorly written play? Why? What might the playwright have said about the production? What factors caused the production to appear muddy?
2. Discuss a production that you believe was an excellent showing of the playscript. What created the production's strength? What were the director's contributions in this regard? Describe the factors leading to the strong representation of the script.

REPRESENTING THE AUDIENCE

1. Describe a production that you believe failed in one or more of the following categories. If performers could not be heard, do you conclude that the fault lay with the performers or with the director? If significant action was not visible, how could the problems have been eliminated? If there were backstage distractions, what preventive steps could have been taken? What was the artistic effect of the production? Had you been this production's director, what steps would you have taken to ensure that the audience could see and hear the stage actions?

2. Describe a production that you believe had no problems in these areas. While you were in the audience, did you feel the performers were laboring to be audible, or did they appear completely natural? Was the director's blocking unobtrusive and smooth while ensuring that all action was visible? What was the overall artistic effect of this production?

ORGANIZING A WORKING PROCESS

1. Describe a production in which you participated, as crew or performer, that you believe was disorganized. In what areas did it lack organization? What were participants' responses to the lack of a thorough schedule? What were the results of the director's inability to make decisions? Had you been director, what steps would you have taken to lead participants to a satisfactory production?

2. Describe a production in which you participated that you believe ran smoothly with all technical and performance units organized to achieve a successful goal. Did participants have a sense of security that the director would lead them to the production without last-minute frenzy? What was the director's organizational approach? Was the rehearsal schedule communicated adequately to all involved? What organizational secrets did you learn from the rehearsal process, and which of them would you seek to incorporate when you direct a play?

WORKING WITH PERFORMERS

1. Selecting a production in which you participated, as performer or crew, discuss what you believe to be the director's inability to work successfully with performers. Did performers improve during rehearsals? If not, why not? What were the director's specific problems? What were the causes of those problems? Did the director seem unable to concentrate on performers? Why? Had you been the director, what would you have done to correct the problems?

2. Describe a production in which you believe the director worked extremely well with performers. Did performers improve during rehearsals? If so, why? What were the director's contributions to a positive atmosphere at rehearsals? Did the director seem to enjoy working with actors? When you direct, which of this director's processes do you want to emulate?

I tried to put myself in the author's shoes. I used to try to say: "I'm now speaking for this author." Each author is different. I said to myself: "I'm doing *Tea and Sympathy* by Robert Anderson — this should be like a Chopin prelude, light, delicate, without overstressing" or "I'm doing a play by Tennessee Williams: he's morally ambivalent, he admires the people who destroy him, he doubts himself, he is afraid of certain people and yet he is drawn to them. I must see life like he sees it." When I did a play by Arthur Miller, I said to myself: "This man deals in ethical absolutes (at least he did through the plays I directed), he is absolutely certain where he stands on issues. He is certain maybe because he is afraid of facing ambivalences, but I must not introduce ambivalences. I must keep it clear, forceful. I must save up force for the last part because he makes a final summation statement at the end of every play." And so on, and so on. In other words, I tried to think and feel like the author so that the play would be in the scale and in the mood, in the tempo and feeling of each writer. I tried to *be* the author.

—ELIA KAZAN
cited in Michel Ciment, *Kazan on Kazan*

PART TWO

Play Analysis

CHAPTER THREE

Introduction to Play Analysis

Without quibbling over which is the greatest of the arts, let us remember that the theatre makes its appeal on two levels, the aesthetic and the intellectual. On the aesthetic level the theatre, like music, painting, and dancing, makes its contributions to the emotional needs of man and to his hunger for the beautiful. On the intellectual level a tremendous proportion of the greatest ideas ever expressed by man have been expressed in dramatic form. We need only remember that students of philosophy study Aeschylus, Goethe, Ibsen, and Shaw as well as Plato, Schopenhauer, Nietzsche, and Dewey. No other branch of human learning can point with pride to a more impressive list of great names. No other field of literature can quite equal the drama in the total extent of its contributions.

—FRANK M. WHITING
An Introduction to the Theatre

The Goodbye Girl *Syndrome*

In Neil Simon's movie, *The Goodbye Girl,* Richard Dreyfuss played a stage actor cast in the title role of *Richard III* by a director who insisted that Dreyfuss act Shakespeare's Richard as a blatantly stereotypical homosexual with lisping talk and mincing walk. It is amusing to conjecture what Shakespeare would have said about that interpretation of his richly drawn character. "Now is the winter of our discontent," indeed.

The Goodbye Girl is a marvelous spoof of muddle-headed directors with wildly off-base analyses and interpretations of plays, playwrights, characters, and the theatre. The movie is great fun. But that sort of misinterpretation in real-life productions will make audiences retreat from the theatre bewildered and confused.

Many of us can relate grim stories of being forced to sit through productions (at least until one can decently leave at an intermission) that were equally off target, sad and dreary affairs that managed to exorcise the spirit of the playscript and left nothing but a confusing mystery for the audience to suffer through. "Not much of a play," I heard victimized audiences conclude after attending a production of *Waiting for Godot* that eliminated the clarity of Beckett's thought. "There's no mind in that playwright," they said of a slipshod production of Brecht's *Mother Courage* that deemphasized the stature of the major characters. "No sense going to the theatre," audience members decide after such experiences. Directorial misinterpretations can cause theatre to lose its very reason for existence: the audience.

One grants that playing Shakespeare's King Richard in such flaming disregard of the play sounds like a hilarious idea when discussed jokingly at a theatrical party, but we know it is totally — we can say unforgivably — wrong for a production. Was that simply movie slapstick, far removed from real-life theatrical practice? Sadly, no. You may have heard directors talk about ideas for comparable productions. One such concept I have heard discussed frequently for several decades asks — Wouldn't it be fascinating to have an all-female production of Edward Albee's *Who's Afraid of Virginia Woolf?* Fascinating? The playwright did not think so. Albee invoked his legal right as copyright owner of his play to prevent a theatre from opening its production of an all-female *Virginia Woolf.* At about the same time Samuel Beckett used legal means to prevent a different theatre from opening its all-female production of his *Waiting for Godot.* Both playwrights said something along the lines of, "If I had wanted those characters to be female, I would've written them that way." The reaction of the playwrights proved that the directors of those productions had missed the point of the plays. But who speaks for playwrights now dead?

All of us who direct can make such errors with dismaying ease. I still remember how easily a mistake infected a children's adventure play I directed when I was a college student. We took it on tour and opened in a grade school; after the show youngsters flocked backstage to get actors' autographs. Then a child asked one of those horribly penetrating questions that youngsters so easily ask: "But who was the good guy?" With a flash of delayed insight I saw the validity of the question. My vision of the production included using a great deal of physical activity, and because I simply had not properly analyzed the key scenes I had managed to mess up the production so that the protagonist was unidentifiable. For one example, during crucial moments of the protagonist's decisions, and his statements of goals, I kept him in this or that upstage corner while the animal characters frolicked down center. Winsome? Oh, indeed, and of course the children loved the animal scenes, but my overemphasis on those scenes destroyed the clarity of the script. My directing professor's criticisms were more detailed than the children's, but no more painful.

We learn from our mistakes. It is not enough to have a directorial vision. Our vision must be *valid.* Luckily we do not need to make painful mistakes in public performance to learn that the director must carefully analyze and interpret the play before forming a vision of the production.

If it is academic to see plays in the context of thinking, feeling, and doing rather than in the context of footlights and box offices, then there is much to be said for academicism.

—ERIC BENTLEY
The Playwright as Thinker

Given that the director's most important function is to create an artistically unified production, it follows that the first step toward that goal must be play analysis that leads to an accurate interpretation. Directorial vision must be built on a firm foundation of play analysis. From studies of the script spring dozens of important directorial decisions: character interpretation; scene, lighting, and costume design; tempo and key; stress to accent significant moments; blocking; and casting. If analysis and interpretation are erroneous, such decisions will be sorely flawed.

The connective links of play analysis to production can be summarized briefly:

- After play analysis comes play interpretation.
- With play interpretation comes concept and directorial vision.
- Interpretation, concept, and vision dictate casting and design.
- Interpretation, concept, vision, design, and casting develop performance.

Let us set up a hypothetical situation for the purposes of illustration. Let's assume that we can arrive at thirty different interpretations of a given play. We must not assume that all are acceptable; on the contrary, twenty-five of the thirty can be completely wrong; one of the twenty-five could lead, for example, to a production like the *Richard III* discussed at the beginning of this chapter.

If twenty-five of our hypothetical thirty interpretations are incorrect, what of the remaining five? If they are well-supported by careful directorial analysis, they can be valid. A work of art can be viewed from a number of perspectives (but not an infinite number of perspectives because that would open theatre to chaos and confusion).

Let's agree that reasonable and proper analysis of a given play might produce five different accurate and acceptable interpretations. All can lead to a directorial vision that would create a strong production. I like to think that only one of the five interpretations will be precisely correct for a specific cast, director, theatrical organization, and audience. If the director works from any of the five, the production has a fine chance of succeeding; if the director selects the one that is directly on target, the production will have a special richness that participants and audiences will remember for years thereafter.

Your job as a director is to ensure that you analyze the play correctly in order to avoid the twenty-five incorrect interpretations and select that one special approach to perfection. Properly conducted play analysis is not some free-wheeling indoor sport with flexible rules subject to directorial whim. It is a demanding craft that the director can learn with study and experience.

The playwright selects significant incidents from chaos and arranges them in a meaningful order that helps us better perceive our world. It follows that the director must understand those dual processes of selection and arrangement to stage a production of the play that clearly communicates the playwright's insight. Fortunately there is a time-tested approach that will lead you to the necessary understanding of what makes a play.

You start with an examination of the play from six viewpoints — plot, char-

Porgy and Bess (photographed here in its original 1935 production) exemplifies a rich combination of character, plot, music, spectacle, diction, thought, and style. Rouben Mamoulian directed the Gershwin classic. — *Photograph courtesy of the Library of Congress*

acter, thought, diction, music, and spectacle — and analyze each in turn. These six can be divided into logical patterns for the director's use.

- To derive an interpretation of the play you begin by examining plot, thought, and character, primarily the protagonist and protagonist's objective.
- To study the play as a production vehicle you look at character, music, and spectacle.
- To study the units in order of importance as they influence the play you focus on plot, character, and thought.
- Before you are ready to hold auditions, you must have a secure understanding of at least plot, character, and thought.

In the following chapters we examine each of these units. Armed with insight into all six, you can avoid such disasters as were mentioned earlier. Once you have grasped these units in a given play, you will be secure in knowing that your directorial vision is true.

To direct a production means serving the playwright with a devotion that makes you love his work. It means finding the spiritual mood that was the poet's at the play's conception and during its writing, the living source and stream which must arouse the spectator, and of which even the author is sometimes unaware. It means realizing the corporal through the spiritual. . . . the director must unite the stage and the auditorium, the spectacle and the spectators. . . . One could go on forever analyzing the work of the director but, in trying to define it, I only prove that it is easier to do a job well than to write well about it. To sum it up, the directing of a play is a turn of the hand, a turn of the mind and of the heart, a function of such sensitiveness that everything human can enter into it. No more, and no less.

—LOUIS JOUVET
"The Profession of the Director,"
cited in Cole and Chinoy, *Directors on Directing*

CHAPTER FOUR

Plot: How a Play Is Constructed

This quality of *shape* is very important to me. I have always entertained the profoundest respect for art, meaning "artefact," and for the suffix "wright" in the word *playwright*. . . . if a play irritates by seeming to be too well made, this surely means that it has not been well made enough: that the smoothness of the joinery is sealing the work off from the viewer.

—PETER SHAFFER
The Collected Works of Peter Shaffer

Directorial vision is a response to the play's basic shape, its story and plot. Your vision often consists of a comment or an attitude you wish to express about the action, and on your imagination's stage you see the play's actions, the rise and fall of the play's conflicts, and the pattern of complications. Some directors' vision allows them to "see" and "hear" the characters in major scenes; other directors make a mental graph of the play's peaks and valleys; and most perceive the play in terms of how they will play the significant events, in effect saying, "this happens, which causes that to happen, and I can see how I'll stage these actions in order to comment on the events."

The director's concern with plot can be explained by drawing an analogy between actor and director. Just as an actor is expected to decide what words or phrases to emphasize in speeches, the director is responsible for deciding what moments or scenes to emphasize throughout the play. Actors learn that stressing every word gives no emphasis at all; directors are aware that giving equal emphasis to all scenes also leads to no emphasis. Actors make their decisions based on study of the speech and the character; directorial decisions are based on careful analysis of the play's plot.

Death of a Salesman with Hume Cronyn as Willy
Loman, Jessica Tandy as Linda Loman, and John
Cromwell as Uncle Ben at the Minnesota Theatre
Company, directed by Douglas Campbell.
— ***Photograph by Marty Nordstrom***

Plot and Story

A story is a narrative of events; a plot stresses causality. E. M. Forster defines the
difference between story and plot with these short sentences:

"The king died and then the queen died" is a *story.*
"The king died and then the queen died *of grief*" is a *plot.*

The difference is causality. When we study a script, we search for the plot's
cause-effect relationships; when we direct, we ensure that the audience will perceive those relationships. Just as Shaffer says the playwright should not seal off
the work from the audience, the director must make the play accessible through
production.

Forster adds, "Or again, 'The queen died, no one knew why, until it was
discovered that it was through grief at the death of the king.' This is a plot with a
mystery in it." The plot pursues the question — *Why* did the queen die? But we

must not infer that the word *mystery* refers only to melodramatic detective plots. On the contrary, as Arthur Miller says, all plays seek to illuminate a certain basic mystery, perhaps about mankind's relationship to society or humankind's actions.

As a director you study a play's plot to recognize what should be stressed and what subordinated in the production, thereby illuminating the play's mystery and ensuring that major questions — Who? Why? How? — are, when appropriate, asked and answered. Recognition of the playwright's organization, what Shaffer calls the "shape" of a play, is the essential first step.

The director must learn the playwright's tools to ensure accurate stress of key plot elements. As you repeatedly read the play, you search for the various subdivisions of plot, such as exposition, foreshadowing, point of attack, complications, and climax. As a director you will use these tools to provide production values, stimuli for actors developing characters, and interest factors for audiences.

The following study does not examine all aspects of plot, but it includes the prime ingredients that shape our vision of the play and, where possible, concrete ways of playing these moments in production.

FIRST KEYS TO UNDERSTANDING PLOT

Plot is the structure of the play, the playwright's selection of a meaningful arrangement of events that shapes the story by creating conflict and complications to demonstrate the play's thought. It is the action of the play, presenting dramatic challenges to the characters, which cause responses that bring to life added facets of personality.

The MDQ and the protagonist's goal. Two keys help you unlock a given play's plot. One key is the major dramatic question (often abbreviated MDQ). The other is the protagonist's goal. These two keys interact enough to allow us to examine them together.

Most plays are centered on a major dramatic question that is raised in the audience's mind relatively early in the action. Can Blanche find the refuge she so desperately needs? Will Lear maintain his image as king by dividing his kingdom among his daughters? Can Willy recognize his flawed ethics (symbolized by the question whether he will accept Biff's own definition of himself)?

A play's twists and turns, the plot's complications, center on the major dramatic question. The protagonist's goal also centers on that question. Blanche's goal is to find a safe haven. Lear's goal is to absolve himself of the responsibilities of leadership but continue being treated like a king. Willy's goal is to avoid the confrontation with Biff and, thereby, with himself. When the major dramatic question is finally resolved, or the protagonist's goal won or lost, the play is over.

In *Macbeth* the major dramatic question is — What will Macbeth do when he suddenly achieves power? All the play's complications and reversals relate to that basic question. When the witches tell Macbeth he will be king, the protagonist's goal is established. Macbeth determines to be the ruler, and the rest of the play relates to that goal. At the play's climax the major dramatic question is resolved. Macbeth will do anything, even die, rather than surrender his power.

The major dramatic question in *Hamlet* is posed early
in the play when the ghost of Hamlet's father demands
revenge: What will Hamlet do? The rest of the play is
constructed around the MDQ. In this production of
Hamlet for the Folger Theatre in Washington, D.C.,
Frank Grimes is Hamlet and John Wylie is the ghost.
The production was directed by Lindsay Anderson.
— *Photograph by Julie Ainsworth*

Plot is constructed of many storytelling techniques, but at the core is one
driving force — the protagonist working to achieve the goal — that leads to an
inevitable conclusion. The entire play is tightly unified by the single major question.

The Inciting Incident

The inciting incident is the event that lit the fuse before the curtain goes up. Audience members learn of it through exposition, and foreshadowing causes them to worry about the ramifications of the problem. Soon that burning fuse causes an initial explosion (the point of attack); there are additional explosions (complications, obstacles, and reversals); and a final explosion (the climax) uses up all the combustibles so that there can be no further explosions.

In *Hamlet* there are at least two inciting incidents. One took place some time ago (the death of the king) and one happened just moments before the play begins (the appearance of the Ghost to the men on watch). There are even more inciting incidents in *Ghosts*: All the late Chancellor's infidelities cause the action in the play's present.

Why doesn't the inciting incident take place after the play begins? Moving the inciting incident from its location before the play to a place inside the play would change its structural contribution to the plot. It would become a stimulus to present action, making it a complication. For example, imagine revising *Hamlet* so that the king's death takes place after the play begins. Is it still an inciting incident? No. It is a complication.

Can a play exist without an inciting incident? Yes. However, most full-length plays have plots built on the inciting incident. On the other hand, some one-act plays operate so strongly in their present that often there is no need for inciting incidents.

What is the value of knowing the inciting incident? Knowledge of the inciting incident helps your play analysis because the incident is necessarily linked to the point of attack: When you identify the former, you are better assured that you have correctly identified the latter. Further, the tone of the incident influences the play: The death of Hamlet's father and the appearance of his ghost clearly suggest the play's basic mood. And because the inciting incident is communicated by exposition, the tone of that incident helps you decide how to play the expositional passages.

A Sense of Equilibrium

Think of a balance scale. When a play begins, all forces are in balance. It may be a happy balance, as in *The Importance of Being Earnest,* with characters focused on minor concerns such as proper dress, choice of sandwiches, or social activities. Or the balance may be uneasy, as in *Medea,* with ominous warnings of a forthcoming conflict between revenge and justice. If nothing happens, the forces will remain equal. The point of attack and subsequent complications upset the balance.

What is the value of finding the sense of equilibrium? If you identify the play's opening sense of balance, it helps you know how to play the beginning scenes. Identification of the opening equilibrium also helps you ascertain the point of attack (discussed below) because that is the moment the balance is thrown off and the active conflicts begin.

Exposition

Exposition is the presentation of information that the audience needs to enter the play's action. One prime use of exposition is to describe the inciting incident. In older plays exposition is often a "feather duster scene," with a butler and maid (the latter wielding a feather duster, hence the term) discussing the background of the masters of the house. Thornton Wilder's *The Skin of Our Teeth* opens with a delicious satire on those old-fashioned scenes.

Where do you find exposition? In older plays exposition is most frequently found in the opening scene. Today's playwrights usually weave short pieces of exposition into more scenes.

Is exposition limited to the beginning of the play or act? No. Imagine a three-act play with long passages of time between acts. When the new act begins, exposition is necessary to let the audience know that time has passed. "Well, Harry," says one character in the beginning of the second act, "I haven't seen you for . . . must be, what? Five years?" Harry replies, "Eight," and the other says, "Oh, that long? Eight years. Amazing, time's rapid wings."

Henrik Ibsen's *Ghosts* and Sam Shepard's *Fool for Love* both contain exposition throughout. In these plays a piece of necessary background is used to make the current action move forward. Most playwrights today use this technique.

Can a play exist without exposition? Yes. You may find plays with little or no exposition, either because that is the playwright's style (Harold Pinter writes exposition grudgingly as though he had to pay extravagantly for each use) or because the playwright envisions characters with unimportant backgrounds or with no mutual history.

How do you play exposition? Keep three points in mind regarding exposition and production.

1. It is possible that the playwright is focusing on communicating information to the audience and not on characterization. Because the writer's major concern is to pass facts to the audience, performers may find that expositional speeches appear out of character. This can happen if the playwright has, say, ten items of information to communicate and distributes those items in four speeches, not especially caring who says what. The performer should not base character analysis on such speeches.
2. Exposition passages are not expendable. Late in rehearsals you will understand all aspects of the play and exposition may seem pointless. Remember that the audience comes fresh to the play, with no knowledge of events, and exposition most often contains information essential for them to get into the action.
3. Exposition should not be played with so much emphasis that you have no room to stress subsequent action. For example, Euripides' *Medea* starts

with a very long scene of exposition between the Nurse and other characters. I once saw a regional theatre's production of *Medea* that had as the Nurse a fine performer who played the first scene so dynamically that Medea's entrance was anticlimactical, and the Medea-Creon encounter containing the point of attack was played with less vigor than the Nurse's exposition speeches. The director had allowed the actress to take over the play, resulting in a misshapen production caused by too much emphasis on a scene that, although containing nicely explosive lines for the Nurse, is of little actual importance to the whole.

Foreshadowing

Foreshadowing is a storyteller's device that indicates the direction of forthcoming action and awakens suspense and interest. It seizes the audience's attention and makes the story line easier to follow. In writing foreshadowing, the playwright typically thinks more of effect and less of character. For that reason, as with exposition, the director and performer should not be surprised if foreshadowing speeches do not appear quite within character.

Where do you find foreshadowing? The playwright usually places foreshadowing early in the play. It may simply help prepare for the entrance of a character — "I wonder where Suzie is? She promised she'd be here to see me before I leave, and she's already fifteen minutes late" — or it may warn of a whole series of problems to follow — "But never, never, *never* let them get wet or feed them after midnight!"

How often does foreshadowing appear? One can expect to find foreshadowing throughout the play in preparation for additional action. It is not restricted to the opening moments.

How do you play foreshadowing? Because foreshadowing creates suspense, it is highly important to the audience and requires appropriate directorial emphasis in production. Foreshadowing also has values for your analytical process. Because it predicts action, foreshadowing helps you analyze the play's plot. The playwright uses foreshadowing to indicate the salient action, so it also helps you differentiate between major and minor events.

The Point of Attack

The point of attack is the single most important aspect of the plot for you to identify because it begins the plot's action, allows you to perceive the plot line, stimulates the protagonist to start toward his or her goal, and introduces the MDQ. A complication is any force that changes the direction of the action; the point of attack is the play's first complication, destroying the existing sense of equilibrium. The point of attack begins the plot's action, and all future complications grow from it. When you understand the point of attack you can structure the production and see that appropriate stress and emphasis are given to key scenes as they relate to the point of attack.

Does the point of attack connect with the inciting incident? Yes, you should find a link between the two. The death of Hamlet's father and the appearance of the Ghost (two inciting incidents) are connected to the play's point of attack.

Is the point of attack always found in the first few minutes of the play? Not necessarily. In *Macbeth* the point of attack is remarkably early. In Euripides' *Medea* the point of attack is quite delayed.

Will the play's protagonist be involved in the point of attack? Yes. The protagonist is the character working toward a definite goal. Hamlet, for example, must ascertain the truth of the Ghost's horrible claim. Typically the point of attack is a motivating cause for the protagonist's decision to take action.

How do you find the point of attack? To find the point of attack, the director looks for: (1) a link between the inciting incident and a major happening in the play; (2) the event that motivates the protagonist to act; (3) the first movement in the plot or change in the direction of the action; (4) an event that changes the equilibrium; (5) an action that fulfills earlier foreshadowing implications; (6) a shock to the protagonist, in a scene in which the protagonist is active; or (7) an event that is interconnected with subsequent actions of the play.

How do you play the point of attack? Beginning directors, or careless experienced directors, are apt to ignore the point of attack, letting it go by without emphasis. If you were in the audience for such a production, you would not know the point of attack existed and most of the play's subsequent action would seem to lack cohesiveness and meaning. You would probably conclude that the playwright wrote a boring play with too little action. You might even be confused about the play's meaning.

On the other hand, a director properly sensitive to play construction emphasizes the point of attack, figuratively pointing a finger at the event, and stressing it more than all previous scenes. If you were in that play's audience, the point of attack would be crystal clear; you would see how subsequent events were part of a master plan, all set off by the initial explosive moment; and your attention would be focused on the play's meaning.

The Protagonist's Goal

We can see the protagonist's goal clearly in *Hamlet,* Act One, Scene 5. The Ghost tells Hamlet of the murder, saying "If thou didst ever thy dear father love, revenge his foul and most unnatural murder," and then exits saying, "Adieu, adieu, adieu! remember me." Hamlet, now alone on stage, speaks his goal.

HAMLET
O all you host of heaven! Oh earth! What else?
And shall I couple hell? O fie! Hold, hold, my heart!
And you, my sinews, grow not instant old,
But bear me stiffly up. Remember thee?

Ay, thou poor ghost, while memory holds a seat
In this distracted globe. Remember thee?
Yea, from the table of my memory,
I'll wipe away all trivial fond records,
All saws of books, all forms, all pressures past
That youth and observation copied there,
And thy commandment all alone shall live
Within the book and volume of my brain,
Unmixed with baser matter. Yes, by heaven!
O most pernicious woman!
O villain, villain, smiling, damned villain;
My tables, my tables! Meet it is I set it down
That one may smile, and smile, and be a villain;
At least I'm sure it may be so in Denmark.
(Writes)
So uncle, there you are. Now to my word:
It is "Adieu! Remember me."
I have sworn't.

For the director's play analysis, the protagonist's goal illuminates (1) the protagonist, (2) possible antagonists opposing the goal, (3) complications when the
goal is thwarted, and (4) climax, when the goal is finally achieved or forever
denied.

Character and plot are tightly married. The protagonist determines an objective, a statement of the play's action. The protagonist's goal is a road map that
indicates the direction the play will follow. Hamlet's goal is clear: "Remember
me," says the Ghost; Hamlet replies, "I have sworn it." The play's action is established by the protagonist's goal. In Act One the protagonist sets forth the play's
MDQ — How will Hamlet seek to avenge his father's death? All the play's action
stems from the answers to that question.

How do you play the statement of objective? Hamlet could be a confusing
play if the director muddied the statements of the protagonist's goals by, for example, putting Hamlet far up left on the stage, having some distracting action
down center, or causing the performer to make the speech casual instead of
intense. As a director you should stress the protagonist's statement of goals in
order to help the audience perceive the play's direction and the protagonist's
motivations.

Complications

We include in *complications* terms such as *reversals* and *obstacles* although in a
strict sense there are subtle differences between the terms. A complication is a
force that changes the course of the play. It may be an obstacle — a barrier the
character must overcome — or a reversal — a sharply disappointing setback. The
complication is a new twist in the plot, an interruption to the forward progress
of the protagonist, an unexpected event.

Are complications necessary? Yes. A play directed without complications is a blank page. Nothing happens. There is no conflict, no will pitted against will, no battle of self against self or self against others, no struggle of good versus evil. The audience may feel something significant must be happening, but all the play's action is hidden in mush. Weary of trying to find logic and meaning, the audience leaves the theatre disappointed, probably with the playwright; they complain about wasting time sitting through a nonevent.

A character in a play written without complications is dull, never stimulated to show changing aspects of personality. A performer in a production directed without complications is equally dull, never changing. Complications are stimuli for characters. The character may be figuratively relaxing when there comes a call of "Fire! Save the women and children!" How does the character respond? Selfishly? Angrily? Nobly? Does the character simply freeze? Just as the playwright must provide stimuli to make characters display dynamic dimensions of personality, the director must stress the stimuli to help performers see the need to change.

How many complications are found in a given play? There is no recipe for complications, and therefore the number of complications varies a great deal depending on the writer's approach to the story.

How do you play complications? Because each complication is a change in the course of action, the director must give each complication adequate emphasis to keep the play alive. You want to give appropriate snap and punch to the complications. Careful study will help you perceive the relative impact of each complication, and that will help you determine how much emphasis each requires. Usually the complications build in intensity as the action progresses.

THE BUILDING BLOCK THEORY

Drama is constructed of a series of events rising like building blocks. Those events are most often complications. Your job is to be sure each complication contributes to the building process. If the blocks remain level, the result is static theatre; if a dramatic production is static, it loses ground.

Climax

If one thinks of a play as a dramatic question, the climax is the final scene that answers the question. The climax pits protagonist and antagonist against each other in a final confrontation that settles all their difficulties. At the climax the protagonist makes a discovery about himself or about the state of the world: Macbeth sees what he has become and in *The Crucible* John Proctor sees that he cannot sign a confession and thus effectively dictate that everyone sign. The climax drives home the play's intellectual message or thought. The climax, then, is extremely important because in it all parts of the plot are resolved, the protagonist is enriched with special insight, and the play's thought is made clear.

How do you play the climax? You should examine the parts of the climax carefully and play each with a certain deliberate touch, not letting them merge messily. You want to achieve clarity; confusion here would be most unfortunate. Remember that to the audience, the climax brings a relief from the strain the plot has so carefully built.

Resolution

Before the point of attack, the universe of the play is in a state of equilibrium. The point of attack begins the action by throwing the universe out of balance. The climax, in this sense the exact opposite of the point of attack, ends the action by putting the universe back in balance. The resolution shows the universe of the play in a state of equilibrium.

The play's resolution puts the pieces together. The story is finished. Sometimes there is an implied continuation of action. In the resolution of *The Lesson*, for example, a new student enters who will repeat all we have just seen; in *A Doll's House* Nora continues out the door into a new life. But even in such cases this particular story is over. In the resolution, tensions are relaxed and conflict ended.

Divisions of a Play

A play consists of definable units that contain the action and hold it to a given course to make it part of the play's overall building block strategy. The function of the smaller units of a play can be seen by drawing an analogy with the organization of a book. A play's acts correspond to a book's parts. Scenes and French scenes are similar to chapters of a book; action units are roughly equivalent to paragraphs.

Just as the play itself is constructed with a beginning, middle, and end, that triad is often found in acts, French scenes, scenes, and action units. To return to the analogy of play and book, we know that writers customarily construct paragraphs that contain the development of a single idea, chapters that hold many ideas belonging to one theme, and parts that pull together all pieces of one concept. Each has its own structural development. In the same way playwrights construct action units, scenes, and acts to advance the play's action. Often each of these units can be removed from the play and examined as a sort of miniplay, a given scene seeming to contain all the elements of a play.

THE FRENCH SCENE

The French scene is defined as a unit of a play delineated by the entrance and exit of a major character. The term *French scene* originated with the seventeenth-century neoclassic French playwrights, who constructed developmental units of their plays around entrances and exits of major characters. Today's printed versions of those plays continue the tradition. For example, in Molière's

The Misanthrope, the scene divisions indicate the entrance-exit system. Listed below are the scenes of the first two acts; note who is in each scene. What is the change from scene to scene?

ACT ONE
> *Scene 1:* Philinte, Alceste (250 lines).
> *Scene 2:* Oronte, Alceste, Philinte (190 lines).
> *Scene 3:* Philinte, Alceste (10 lines).

ACT TWO
> *Scene 1:* Alceste, Celimene (85 lines).
> *Scene 2:* Alceste, Celimene, Basque (3 lines).
> *Scene 3:* Alceste, Celimene (20 lines).
> *Scene 4:* Alceste, Celimene, Basque (8 lines).
> *Scene 5:* Eliante, Philinte, Acaste, Clitandre, Alceste, Celimene, Basque (185 lines).
> *Scene 6:* Alceste, Celimene, Eliante, Acaste, Philinte, Clitandre, Basque (5 lines).
> *Scene 7:* Alceste, Celimene, Eliante, Acaste, Philinte, Clitandre, A Guard (30 lines).

All the scenes take place in Celimene's house — there are no changes of scene locales — and move cleanly from one into another without pause. The "French scene" divisions simply indicate entrances or exits of major characters.

Despite what at first appears to be a mechanical system of dividing scenes, the French scene technique suggests a valuable approach to establishing scene units. Today's director uses the basic concept of the French scene, that the scene changes when a character enters or leaves the action. For the modern director, the concept has psychological truths: People naturally behave differently when alone. There are changes in the dynamics of relationships. As a director you can borrow from the French scene to define the action unit.

THE ACTION UNIT

The action or motivational unit is a change in the pattern of events. The term refers to parts of a play divided by changes in action, as is suggested when we describe a play's action by saying, "This happened, and then this happened, which caused this to happen." Each "happening" is an action unit. An action unit may be a French scene or any similar change in the action; most often it is the introduction of a major idea or complication. Action units use the French scene concept and the complication-to-complication idea.

For example, in *Macbeth,* Act One, Scene 3, we see the following action units:

1. The witches appear.
2. Macbeth and Banquo enter and see the witches.
3. The witches make their prophesies.
4. Macbeth reacts, without words, the play's point of attack.

5. Banquo requests predictions regarding his future.
6. The witches disappear and Ross and Angus enter saying Macbeth is now Thane of Cawdor.

The rest of the scene emphasizes the prophesies.

Action units have varying lengths (short in the above illustration) and may overlap. Note that action units are easily defined when they involve a major plot movement, such as a point of attack or complication, or when there is an entrance or exit of a major character. In other instances, these units may be more difficult to ascertain, so individual directors may have differing lists of action units.

How do you play the action unit? Play analysis starts with the action unit because it is the smallest part of the plot. As a director your study of the play involves dividing the acts into action units.

In the early weeks of rehearsal, you do not run the entire play or act over and over. Working on the whole would prohibit in-depth study. Instead you rehearse small parts of an act, spending perhaps an hour on this scene or that unit, even though in production those parts will play in only ten minutes. The logical way to divide the play into small parts is the action unit.

Give titles to action units. Your play analysis should divide the play into its action units, giving each unit an accurate title describing the action. "The witches establish the mood of the play." "Macbeth meets the witches, who make predictions." You should not expect to find all the titles easily, but with experience you will discover the value of the process. Ask questions about each action unit, such as — Why did the playwright put this scene in the play? What is the major action of this scene? Whose scene is it? What single line or lines must the audience hear and understand, if this action unit is to make sense to them? Does this action unit build on previous units, or does it undercut so later units can build?

Within action units are beats, a performer's division of thoughts in a given speech. Each new thought is a beat shift; short speeches typically contain one beat and longer speeches may have several beats. We will discuss beats in detail in later chapters.

Exercises

Answer the following questions on the play you are to direct. Be as detailed and specific as possible.

1. What is the play's major dramatic question?
2. What is the protagonist's goal?
3. What is the play's inciting incident?
4. What elements of foreshadowing appear throughout the play? Use specific quotations.
5. What is the play's point of attack? Describe it in detail. When does it come in the play? What happens? Who is present? Who is affected?

6. What is the protagonist's goal? Use specific quotations when possible.

7. What is the play's second complication (following the point of attack)? Describe it in detail.

8. What is the play's third complication?

9. What is the fourth complication?

10. What are the rest of the play's complications?

11. What is the play's climax?

12. What is the resolution?

13. What are the action units in the play? Write the page numbers of each action unit. Give each unit a definitive title that describes what happens in that unit. List each character in the action unit, and describe how the action affects each character.

The actor must be disciplined. He must be so trained that he automatically carries out the director's orders. I expect my actors to do exactly what I tell them to do and to do it quickly, so I can see my own mistakes if I have gone wrong. I believe the director must know the play so well that he grasps every important moment of every scene. He knows — and he alone — when the action should rise and where it should fall. He knows where to place the accents. An individual actor may not see the logic of an action. I require him to do so, and he must do it, for if the director really knows the play there is a sound reason for that action. . . .

—LAURENCE OLIVIER
"The Olivier Method," The *New York Times,* Feb. 7, 1960

CHAPTER FIVE

Character: The People of the Play

When *A Streetcar Named Desire* was the sensation-hit of its decade, a Chicago company was formed and a long out-of-work character actor was selected to play the small role of the doctor. This character appears in the final minutes of the play ... to take Blanche away to an institution, and he is gentle enough to cause her to say, "I have always depended upon the kindness of strangers." So much for the assignment. There is no more to it than that.

When the actor playing this role arrived in Chicago, some long-unseen relatives called him to invite him to dinner. . . . At one point during the festive dinner, one breathlessly inquisitive niece said to her uncle, "We've heard so much about this 'Streetcar' play. Please would you tell us what the story is?" The old gentleman put down his soup spoon and smiled at the young lady (character actors are notoriously courtly) and said, "Of course I'll tell you what the story is, my dear. It's about a doctor who comes to New Orleans because he's received a telephone call from a young lady whose sister is having a nervous breakdown."

—WILLIAM REDFIELD
Letters from an Actor

Your directorial vision includes an attitude toward the people of the play; a concept about the meaning of their motivations, objectives, actions, and relationships with each other; and a perception of how their experiences relate to yourself specifically and humanity more generally. Your vision includes emotional response to the characters, perhaps a sympathetic response to one, delight in the foibles and eccentricities of another, fascination with the struggles of another, or respect for the integrity of yet another. This directorial concept is most frequently based on psychological insight into the characters and sensitivity to the unexpressed motivations for their speeches, silences, and actions. Part of a strong vision is a desire to work with actors to bring the characters to life so that audiences can experience your concept.

Detailed examination of characters is the foundation for accurate directorial vision, and many directors report that they come to know a play's characters as well as they know members of their families. As one of my directing graduates

Goldberg and McCann (standing) attack Stanley
(seated) in this scene from Harold Pinter's *The
Birthday Party* presented by the William and Mary
Theatre, directed by the author. — *Photograph courtesy
of the William and Mary Theatre*

now in professional theatre observed, "I know I'm ready to direct when I can see
all those people in my head, like they're in my own private doll house. But it isn't
enough for me just to see them in the plot, in the play's set. I have to watch them
going through their lives when they aren't in the play, in different settings, in
action when they are 'offstage,' so to speak."

Envisioning characters in their on- and off-stage worlds requires careful attention to their inner motivations. Modern directors, greatly influenced by Freud

and his followers, see drama as psychological actions and the stimulus-response cycles of characters. Directing is most enjoyable when you are working with fine performers, examining ways of understanding and presenting dimensional characters. The director's process of bringing the script's characters to life on stage is one of theatre's most fascinating and rewarding challenges.

Learning about Characters

A study of character relates to studies of the other elements of drama. For discussion purposes we separate plot, character, thought, music, diction, and spectacle, but we must remember that they are closely intertwined. Drama is characters responding to conflict, structured by plot. Those actions project an intellectual premise or meaning that we call thought. The characters have distinct speech patterns, or diction; and their speeches create music. On stage the characters move, according to the director's blocking, in visually pleasing and storytelling arrangements that we think of as spectacle. Throughout the process the central foundation for drama is character.

The richer your understanding of the characters, the easier your decisions about casting. Detailed knowledge of the characters will make your rehearsals more profitable and your work with performers more mutually satisfactory, and awareness of the characters' objectives will help you block the play organically. There are several steps to follow that will increase your knowledge, and thus your vision, of a play's characters. We will discuss some of these techniques briefly here.

OBJECTIVES

Finding characters' objectives is arguably the best single approach you can find in studying the play. As a director examining characters and performers' techniques, you can expect to encounter a complicated maze of terms — including objectives, superobjectives, intentions, spine, and through line of action — applicable to the study of character or acting. Unfortunately theatrical terminology is often rather vague, but perhaps we can derive comfort from knowing that others are also confused. In *Method or Madness* Robert Lewis writes that the driving force "has been called many things in many books and some people don't call it anything; but it is a process that is going on, if they are really acting. I myself don't care if you call it spinach, if you know what it is, and do it, because it is one of the most important elements. . . ."

Let us clarify some terms as we will use them here. We use the word *objective* to refer to our study of the playwright's character. In later discussions of performance techniques we will use *intention* to describe the actor's process of bringing character goals to life on stage.

By *objective* we mean the character's stated or implied compelling motivation to take action to achieve a goal. A master objective governs the character throughout the play; subobjectives refer to the character's goals in scenes. The objective

WM. H. CRANE

"STEWARD!!"

"ARREST ME! TAKE ME AWAY!"

THE PACIFIC MAIL BY PAUL M. POTTER

Turn-of-the-century melodramatic writing and then-
popular concepts of characterization combined to
create exaggerated performances of tragic events. Such
overblown acting would be comic today. Many
modern theatre practices evolved as direct rebellions
against such lack of truthful character depiction.
— *Photograph courtesy of the Library of Congress*

answers the question — Why? As a director, you ask — Why does Blanche come
to visit Stanley and Stella? — or — Why does Blanche try to drive a wedge between Stanley and Stella? Armed with the answer you see how the play is structured around the protagonist's objective. Your vision of the character is enhanced,
and so is your vision of the play's plot and theme.

As a director, you ask — What does the character want to *do*? You phrase the
answer with active verbs. For example, you can describe a superobjective this
way: Blanche wants to make a secure place for herself with her sister Stella; to do
that, she has to remove Stanley from Stella so there will be room for herself.
Therefore she takes the following actions. A subobjective for a scene might be
stated: Blanche wants to make her sister see Stanley's boorishness so Stella will
reject him. Therefore she takes the following actions.

You find specific information or given circumstances throughout the script. Character analysis profitably starts with these.

Stage directions. Because stage directions are clear and unambiguous, they provide a viable first step toward character analysis. You find two basic categories of stage directions: (1) those written by the playwright and (2) those based on the initial professional production of the play. The latter include set design drawings, costume and light plots, and property lists, and while they give you insight into one way of staging the play and may contribute to your vision, you can seldom use them directly because they are based on someone else's vision for theatrical situations unlike your own.

The playwright's stage directions describe age, relationships, behavioral patterns, and basic attitudes. Because these come from the play's creator you will find them useful in forming your interpretation.

Physicalization. As a director you will gain insight into characters by examining physical aspects, such as mannerisms, movement and speech patterns, age, height, and clothing, that give dramatic characters the unique qualities of real humans. Contrasting qualities aid significantly in defining characters: This character is formal in clothing and behavior, that one is casual; one character is seventeen years old and the other is forty-nine; one is messy and another is neat; one is tall and another is short; and so forth.

Names. Often the name of the character describes the person, giving an index of psychological traits and personal attributes. For example, in his *Ludlow Fair* Lanford Wilson names a character Agnes who asks in a despairing way, "What can you expect from an Agnes except a dull person with a large bust and a tendency to colds?" A young man named Mark or Duff, for example, may have different qualities from one named Billy or Jimmy. The former names represent dashing, brisk men; the latter, young men not yet mature. In these cases, the answer to — What's in a name? — is — a glimpse inside the psyche. For the director, names may be a key that helps unlock the essence of the characters.

Concrete qualities. Characters are constructed of concrete realities. Some of these specifics are:

- Age.
- Weight. Height. Physical structure: stocky? slim?
- Type of clothing: formal? informal? casual? neat? messy?
- Basic movement pattern: graceful? clumsy? athletic? quiet?
- Mannerisms: smoothing hair? playing imaginary billiards? always eating or drinking? smoking?
- Speech patterns: crude? polished?
- Environment: a neat apartment? messy? masculine items? feminine colors?

The basic social situation of *The Importance of Being Earnest* is clearly cheerful and elevated, as shown in this photograph of the Oscar Wilde comedy, directed by Garland Wright at the Guthrie Theater. Simultaneous movement and poses immediately convey the play's spirit. Left to right, Michele Farr as Gwendolen, J. Smith-Cameron as Cecily, Robert Burns as Jack, and Robert Curtis-Brown as Algernon.
— *Photograph by Joe Giannetti*

Economic, political, or social environment. Environment defines certain details of the characters. For example, we find a basic implication of class in such plays as Noel Coward's *Blithe Spirit* or Oscar Wilde's *The Importance of Being Earnest.* Characters in these plays are free of concerns about paying the rent, avoiding illness, or finding food and shelter; there is no urgency in their lives about mundane matters such as bathroom locations.

Characters in plays such as *Earnest* are markedly different from, say, those who live within Maxim Gorki's *The Lower Depths.* Gorki's characters are at the bottom of existence and perceive life as a series of deadly survival tests. Their environmental situation means they cannot be flip, comic, heroic, or energetic; nor can they be in love, innocent, or charitable.

Economic situations help define characters in such plays as Anton Chekhov's *The Cherry Orchard* or George Kaufman's *Dinner at Eight*. Both plays examine a vigorous and ambitious new financial class replacing the more static old monied class. Environment and socioeconomic conditions characterize many of Sam Shepard's plays, helping the director better understand characters in plays such as *Fool for Love* and *True West*.

EMOTION

Directorial vision responds to the characters' emotions. Drama is emotion in action; emotions are the spark plugs that keep characters alive throughout the play; they are the dramatic center of the action. For example, in *A Streetcar Named Desire* Blanche goes through a maze of emotions during the play, rising to ecstasy to breathe one of modern drama's most powerful poetic lines, "Sometimes . . . there's . . . God . . . so quickly!" and finally sinking to insanity bred of despair. In studying characters directors and actors must search out emotional ranges and complexities to bring the characters and the play to life on stage. Furthermore, because emotive and intellectual qualities are inextricably wedded, characters' emotions must be accurately portrayed to help audiences perceive the meaning of the action. Audiences are drawn into the play by experiencing characters' emotions through empathy; as they enter the universe of the play, they are led to think more about the play's basic intellectual precepts.

ACTIONS

Drama means to do, to show, to act; a play is built on the premise that actions speak louder than words. As a director you understand characters according to their actions by charting first their overall actions and then their actions at significant moments that illustrate the play's basic thought.

For example, a chart of Macbeth's actions from beginning to end is a definition of a man's fall. A once proud and noble warrior is reduced to a smaller person who is a murderer, hires assassins, and at the end can only snarl at servants. Armed with knowledge of Macbeth's overall action during the play you know that the character must first be shown as powerful and proud for his later frenzy and despair to be plausible and properly large.

INACTION

Inaction also defines character, and inaction can be remarkably active. For example, in Harold Pinter's *The Birthday Party* Meg and Petey take surprisingly little action when their boarder and surrogate child Stanley is persecuted by three strangers. They are defined by their lack of action. Obeying conventions, Mrs. Alving in *Ghosts* fails to take the self-protective action of leaving her husband. She is trapped by her lack of action. You and the performers will benefit from studying possible influences of inaction on characterization.

SPEECH

Dialogue is action; what a character says, and the way he or she says it, defines the character no less thoroughly than the character's actions and inactions. Your study of dialogue will often show you word choice and sentence structure that could be used only by a particular individual. To illustrate dialogue's ability to define character, note how each of the principals in *A Streetcar Named Desire* has a unique speech pattern that is a precise statement of character. For another il-lustration, look at Lady Macbeth's dialogue when her husband tells her that the king will visit. "How long will he stay?" she asks, in a few words showing that she is calculating, considering options, wondering if there will be time to kill Duncan. As a director analyzing characters you will need to keep in mind that what a character says, and the manner in which it is said, is often a clear self-definition, sometimes stated directly, but more often obliquely.

SILENCE

Just as a character's nonaction can be a definition, nonspeech can indicate personality. For example, consider the third scene of the first act of *Macbeth*. Macbeth and Banquo meet the three witches, who predict that Macbeth will have a wondrous series of promotions, ultimately to king. In the face of the witches' amazing predictions of ambition fulfilled, Macbeth is silent. Surprised at Mac-beth's silence, Banquo calls on him to respond, but Macbeth remains speechless. From that silence director and performer obtain a great deal of insight into the character. So important is that insight that the director must play the scene in a way that allows the audience to perceive that the witches have touched on a desire that Macbeth has kept hidden in the dark corners of his mind. As you work on production qualities, you will want to accent such silences so that they commu-nicate fully and correctly to the audience. A production that denies the silences by rushing through them will lose much of the play's subtle meaning.

REACTIONS

A character can be defined by the reactions of friends and foes. Because Iago has such a gigantic and unreasonable hatred, we know Othello's goodness. In *The Time of Your Life* Joe clearly must be a good person to be worthy of Tom's fond hero worship. In *The Crucible* John Proctor is more clearly an honest and moral man because of the pettiness of those who oppose him. The adage, "A man is known by his friends," is as clear in drama as in life.

Implied here is a definition of production demands. Suppose, for example, a director of *The Time of Your Life* cast as Tom a performer who lacked personable qualities and was instead easy to dislike, a young man with no heart, even some-thing of a bum. Or consider a director of *The Crucible* who made Proctor's ene-mies into stout-hearted, morally correct, grave judges. What would happen to these productions? If Tom were disliked, his hero worship of Joe would turn Joe into someone the audience would feel obliged to dislike, and Saroyan's concepts of gentleness and love would be corrupted. And if Proctor's enemies carried moral weight, Proctor would become wrong and the play's meaning would be lost. In seeking to understand characters you examine the attitudes of other characters, who often are present in the play to point out important characteristics of the principals, and in production you carefully ensure the proper performance of these personal attitudes.

OTHERS' DESCRIPTIONS

One character may define another by description. In the first scene of *Cyrano de Bergerac* there are over a dozen different statements about Cyrano, who has not yet made his entrance. The statements both build Cyrano's entrance and define him as a master swordsman, a brave fighter, and a man with a grotesque nose. Often the descriptions define both the target and the speaker: What Blanche says about Stanley as a greasy pig defines her as well as Stanley. Such descriptions must be viewed in light of the relationship between the character speaking and the character being defined.

PLACE IN THE PLAY

Analyze the character's place in the play. Some characters are representatives more than specific humans. For example, in Irwin Shaw's *Bury the Dead* the characters are representatives of "the war machine," not real people. In *Cyrano de Bergerac* there has to be a Valvert to receive Cyrano's wit and swordsmanship. And going back to the reference that begins this chapter about the character actor cast as the doctor in *Streetcar Named Desire,* remember that there must be someone to whom Blanche can say, "Whoever you are, I have always depended on the kindness of strangers."

Performers never think of themselves as playing representative characters, and only a clumsy or inexperienced director would ever tell an actor he is in the play simply to be the object of the leading female's final speech. Regardless of the size of the role, the performer needs your support in fleshing out what may be written as a skeletal outline. But if your analysis indicates that the character is primarily a representative personage, you will know not to let the performer overact the part and distort the script.

Types of Characters

Great errors are made because performers and directors think of characters as people rather than as *dramatis personae:* masks of dramatic action. A role conforms to the logic of theatre, not the logic of any other life system. To think of a role as a person is like picnicking on a landscape painting.

—RICHARD SCHECHNER
Environmental Theatre

Characters perform structural functions in the play, and each character is designed to fulfill specific needs imposed by the play's plot and thought. Basic characters are found in most plays. Armed with insight into such characters' contributions to the drama, you can more easily maintain the correct perspective and balance in analysis, casting, and production.

THE PROTAGONIST

The protagonist is the central character who strives to achieve a specific goal with a determination that generates the significant action of the play. Usually the plot's twists and turns affect the protagonist more than other characters. The protagonist commonly is present at all major plot actions from point of attack to climax. His or her goal (Macbeth, to become King; Blanche, to find a safe haven; Oedipus, to rid his town of the plague; and so on) is the play's central motif. The director who emphasizes a different motif will confuse the audience, who will conclude that the playwright wrote a muddy script.

Must the protagonist be "the good guy"? No, the protagonist does not necessarily wear a white hat. For example, Regina in Lillian Hellman's *The Little Foxes* is more villain than hero, but she is nonetheless the play's protagonist. More typically, however, the protagonist is neither villain nor hero, but a combination of emotional, moral, and ethical qualities, of which the audience will find some praiseworthy and some less acceptable.

Does the protagonist always achieve his or her goal? No.

Does the protagonist have a single goal? Yes. If you think the protagonist has several goals, ask yourself if they are not really subdivisions of one master plan.

Can a play have more than one protagonist? Yes, but rarely. In such cases the protagonists share a common goal, thus unifying the action. For example, in *Romeo and Juliet* the two protagonists have a single goal. Two-character one-act plays are often written so that first one character and then the other appears to be the protagonist.

Can a play have a group protagonist? Yes. The weavers in Hauptmann's *The Weavers* and the taxi drivers in *Waiting for Lefty* by Odets are group protagonists.

Can a play exist without a protagonist? Yes. Often plays about social issues do not have protagonists — *The Lower Depths,* for example, or *The Investigation.*

How should you cast the protagonist? As a director you build your cast around the protagonist. At auditions look for performers capable of projecting the qualities of your production's protagonist. Performers cast in other roles must be able to give stage to the actor playing the protagonist. This may mean that in casting a secondary role you have to bypass a fine performer in favor of a performer with less stage power who will not pull focus from the protagonist.

Find the protagonist's goal. Finding the protagonist's goal is not difficult if you examine the play solely from that character's perspective, getting into his or her skin, attempting to think as the character does, and seeing the protagonist as an active force consciously striving to achieve a goal. Helpful questions to ask yourself are — What does the character want? Why? What are the motivating forces that cause the character to select this goal? How does the character respond to obstacles?

Richard III is a fascinating protagonist, both sublime
and terrible, full of intellect and pride, yet loveless and
alone. Note how director Sidney Berger cleverly uses
levels, center stage placement, framing (Richard is
framed by the door upstage) lighting, contrast
(Richard is the only one not standing), and utilitarian
characters (all looking at the central character) to give
full stage focus to the protagonist (center, played by
Frank Barrie) in the Houston Shakespeare Festival
production of *Richard III*. — *Photograph © 1985 by Jim
Caldwell; used by permission of the Houston Shakespeare
Festival*

For example, in *Lysistrata* Aristophanes writes what may be the best solution
ever devised to stop war. Look at the protagonist's goal and see how this is responsible both for the marvelous comedy and the play's trenchant antiwar message. In *Oedipus* the title character wants to remove the plague that infects
Thebes. If he wanted that goal less, the play's action would fall apart.

As a director you will grasp the play's meaning by finding the protagonist,
verbalizing the protagonist's goal, and relating the plot to the protagonist's striving
for the goal. You will be confident of your play analysis if you are secure in your
understanding of these aspects of the protagonist.

Find the protagonist's statement of purpose. In some plays the protagonist verbalizes his or her goal. After the gauntlet has been thrown down at the point of attack, the protagonist picks up the challenge and directly or indirectly says what he or she will do in the protagonist's statement of purpose. As the play progresses, the protagonist may speak of steps he or she will take toward the goal, as Hamlet does when he says, "The play's the thing, wherein I'll catch the conscience of the king."

Block for the protagonist's statement of purpose. You will want to give stage focus to the protagonist when he or she is actively striving for the goal, applying appropriate vocal and visual emphasis to those moments. If the production muddies those moments, the play's meaning may be obscured. Of course this does not mean the director cannot be subtle; here, as elsewhere, art consists of hiding technique. As a director you seek to emphasize the goal statements without letting the audience sense your technique.

THE ANTAGONIST

The antagonist is the force that prevents the protagonist from reaching his or her goal. Without the antagonist, the play would begin with the protagonist being galvanized into action, setting up a plan, starting toward realization of that plan . . . and achieving it. Curtain down. The play's over in minutes. No excitement, no suspense, no opportunity to perceive the protagonist's personality as he or she responds to obstacles. For example, Eddie in *Fool for Love* is a strong protagonist because of May's strength as his antagonist. Othello is a strong protagonist because of Iago's strength as his antagonist.

The antagonist must be as strong as the protagonist. If one is markedly more powerful than the other, the conflict will end immediately. It is important that the battling forces be equal in weight. You cannot be sure you have correctly cast the part of the protagonist until you have considered carefully the casting of the antagonist. Don't cast the performer to play Othello until you judge him against the performer for Iago.

Can a play exist with no antagonist? Yes. For example, there is no antagonist in *The Investigation* by Peter Weiss.

Can a play have more than one antagonist? Yes. Consider, for example, *Cyrano de Bergerac.* The protagonist is so powerful that we would not expect the playwright to invent a matching antagonist. In such a case there is more than one antagonist (although usually, as in *Cyrano*, unified in a common opposition).

Will a play with a protagonist necessarily have an antagonist? Yes. Something must stand in the protagonist's path or else he or she will simply achieve the goal. That "something" is one or more antagonists.

Are there plays where the play's protagonist is his own antagonist? Yes, but you can expect to find an exterior antagonist even in plays where the protagonist goes through long self-doubt. For example, Hamlet's internal questions and doubts make him one of his own antagonists, but there are also visible exterior antagonists, primarily Claudius.

The struggle of the protagonist's will against the antagonist's obstacles provides strong conflict as exemplified in the above photograph from the outdoor drama, *Trumpet in the Land,* presented annually in New Philadelphia, Ohio. David Zeisberger (left, framed by ring of fire) sought to establish a Christian Indian State in Ohio in 1771–1781 against the objections of Simon Girty (top) and a band of menacing Indians. Director Kim T. Sharp uses that conflict to stage this intensely dramatic scene. — *Photograph by Bob Lauriha, courtesy of the Ohio Outdoor Historical Drama Association*

THE CONFIDANT(E)

The confidant(e) is the protagonist's friend, sometime advisor, and recipient of what otherwise would be the protagonist's soliloquies. Some playwrights give the confidant(e) little else to do, but better writers build that character with other dimensions. Phaedra has Oenone; Cyrano has Le Bret; Hedda Gabbler has Mrs. Elvstead.

How should you cast the confidant(e)? You need a *warm* person to be the protagonist's friend. The less dimensional the role, the more talented a performer you require to add flesh where the playwright wrote only naked bones.

THE FOIL

The foil is most often a minor character, designed to "feed" a major character by being a contrast. To make a major character appear smart, the foil will lack intelligence; to make a character appear happy, the foil will be sad; to make the leading man appear secure and popular with attractive females, the foil will be so unattractive that everyone tries to find him a date. We often find the foil in musical comedies: *My Sister Eileen, Brigadoon,* and *Guys and Dolls* use the foil character to develop major characters. But the foil character can also be written in a more subtle fashion. For example, Horatio is a fine foil for Hamlet, and Ben is a foil for Willy Loman.

How should you cast the foil? For the foil you need a strong character actor. The performer whose stage bearing projects personal warmth and a willingness to *give* is ideal. A performer who is guarded or closed may not be comfortable with the role's needs.

THE RAISONNEUR

The raisonneur is "the voice of reason" and the author's spokesperson. An example of the raisonneur as a "reasonable" person espousing virtues of moderation is Philinte in Molière's *The Misanthrope.* Examples of the raisonneur as "author's spokesman" include Tom in *The Glass Menagerie* by Tennessee Williams and the father in *Six Characters in Search of an Author* by Luigi Pirandello.

How do you play the raisonneur? The performer should be intensely sincere. You will want to guide the actor into creating a character who can speak message-bearing lines. If played simply as an announcer, the character will lack truth; if the character appears dishonest, the playwright's messages will seem shallow or, worse, comic overstatements.

THE UTILITARIAN CHARACTER

The utilitarian character delivers basic information. "Dinner is served, madam." "Somebody here call for a taxi?" "Who ordered the anchovy pizza?" Spear-carriers, ladies-in-waiting, butlers, maids, plumbers, newspaper boys, secretaries, and delivery people are all utilitarian characters. These are the characters so often grouped under the heading "also in the cast."

Stanislavski, we know, exhorts us to bear in mind that "there is no such thing as a small role, only small actors." I think that's nonsense. Stanislavski must never have played a utilitarian character. To an actor the utilitarian character can appear thankless, so as a director you should help performers respect their participation in the production. Give the actor playing a utilitarian character the same considerate, helpful comments you give to principals.

How should you cast the utilitarian character? Utilitarian roles provide performance opportunities for beginning actors seeking stage experience. Your guidance will help them improve their acting skills.

Character Evolution during the Play

Does a character remain static and unchanging during the play, or is the character dynamic and changing? Theorists have fashioned a debate over the stationary versus the moving personality in drama. One school holds that a character never changes from the beginning to the end of the play, and what appears to be a different posture is only a new view of the same person. Others argue that characters respond to stimuli by changing.

The question directly touches your work as a director. A study of various dramatic characters will help you reach your own conclusions. At the beginning of *Glass Menagerie* Laura is frightened and apprehensive. Does she remain fearful when she is with the Gentleman Caller at the end of the play, or is she emboldened by him, encouraged by his presence, and hopeful that a long-held dream might even come to pass? Is John Proctor the same person at the end of *The Crucible* as he is at the beginning? Does Blanche change from the beginning of *Streetcar* to the end? Does Macbeth evolve into a different person as he tastes power? Do Eddie and May change during *Fool for Love?*

Dramatic characters aside, do humans evolve as a result of stimuli? Does a young in-love-with-love romantic become different as years of despair accumulate and a marriage turns sour? Are we the same people today we were a year ago, or have we changed in response to experience?

On stage dynamic growth is dramatic, which leads us to conclude that it is poor theatre to assume characters do not change. Directors and performers must seek change and growth to give dramatic impact to a production. To assume that characters have static qualities is to lose the power contributed by dynamic change.

Dramatic characters must evolve. You and the performer must carefully unmask the true character, a little at a time, in a dynamic movement. Too much at once will make the subsequent disclosures tedious or comic.

An essential quality of any work of art is its homogeneity. For a staged play, then, to make good its claim to be one it would seem to follow that the actors must continue what the dramatist has begun by methods as nearly related to his in understanding and intention as the circumstances allow. And it is probably true that the staged play is a satisfying work of art to the very degree that this homogeneity exists.

—HARLEY GRANVILLE-BARKER
The Exemplary Theatre

In *The Glass Menagerie* a series of emotional stimuli cause Laura to evolve. In the beginning of the play Laura is a lonely self-reflective girl, hiding in her private world of a glass menagerie, so powerfully symbolized in the photograph above. Later Laura becomes animated, optimistic, delighted by the "Gentleman Caller," as shown in the picture opposite. Notice the many visible changes that show Laura's evolution, and note, too, how directorial vision was responsible for bringing the characters to life. This production was directed by Alan Schneider for the Guthrie Theater with Ellen Geer as Laura, Ruth Wilson as Amanda, and Ed Flanders as Jim. — *Photographs by Dan Nordstrom*

Exercises

INDIVIDUAL CHARACTERS

Apply these questions to principal characters in the play you will direct.

1. What is the character's name?
2. How is the character defined in stage directions? Quote from the appropriate stage directions.
3. What is the character's age? How does that help define the character?
4. Does the character have a distinguishable vocal range?

5. What is the character's height? Weight? Physical size?
6. What are the character's habits and mannerisms?
7. How does the character dress? Formally? Informally? Neatly?
8. Are there other physical aspects of the character? Describe them.
9. How is the character defined by the socioeconomic environment of the play?
10. What are the character's major emotions? What sparks them? When does the character show different emotions?
11. What actions define the character's personality?
12. How is the character defined by his or her nonactions?
13. How is the character defined by speech patterns and word choice?
14. Is the character silent in a situation where speech is expected? What does this say about the character?
15. How do other characters react to this character? How do others describe this character?
16. What are the character's relationships with each other character?
17. Why did the playwright put this character in the play?

SPECIFIC CHARACTERS

Answer the following questions in detail.

1. What is the name of the play? The playwright?
2. Who is the play's protagonist?

3. What is the protagonist's goal? What does he or she want?
4. What motivates the protagonist to work to achieve his or her goal? How strong is the protagonist's motivation?
5. How does the play's inciting incident relate to the protagonist's goal?
6. How does the play's point of attack influence the protagonist's goal?
7. Who is the play's antagonist? Are there more than one?
8. What motivates the antagonist to oppose the protagonist?
9. What actions of the antagonist oppose the protagonist? List them in order.
10. Is there a confidant(e)? Identify him or her by name and list the scenes where the character behaves as a confidant(e).
11. Is there a foil? Identify him or her by name and describe how the foil contributes to other characterizations.
12. Is there a raisonneur? Identify him or her by name. What is the position taken by the raisonneur? Does that position appear to reflect the playwright's theme? Quote the speeches that make the character the author's spokesperson.
13. Are there utilitarian characters? If so, list them by name.

... the Art of the Theatre is neither acting nor the play, it is not scene nor dance, but it consists of all the elements of which these things are composed: action, which is the very spirit of acting; words, which are the body of the play; line and color, which are the very heart of the scene; rhythm, which is the very essence of dance. . . .

The reason why you are not given a work of art on the stage is not because the public does not want it, not because there are not excellent craftsmen in the theatre who could prepare it for you, but because the theatre lacks the artist — the artist of the theatre, mind you, not the painter, poet, musician. . . . I speak of the stage director.

—GORDON CRAIG
The Art of the Theatre

CHAPTER SIX

Thought: The Meaning of the Play

What is the basic action of the play? What is the play about from the standpoint of the characters' principal conflict? What is the play's core? For Gordon Craig, *Hamlet* is the story of man's search for truth. Saroyan's *My Heart's in the Highlands,* to its New York director, was the story of people eager to give things to one another — lovers all, in a sense. For me, Odets' *Night Music* had to do with the search for a home.

Whether these formulations are correct or not, the point is that the director's most important task is to find the basic line of the play. I call it the *spine* of the play because my first teacher in this field, Richard Boleslavsky, used the word.

—HAROLD CLURMAN
"The Principles of Interpretation," cited in
Producing the Play, edited by John Gassner

Thought, the intellectual focus of the play, is a crucial component of effective play analysis leading to your directorial vision. Thought is the play's meaning; the play-wright's observations about life that motivate writing the play; and the writer's philosophical, moral, or ethical assessment of the world. Thought is the play's subject matter; it is the play's action and the significance of that action; and it is the consequences of characters' goals, successes, and failures. Thought is, in the classic sense of the word, the *argument* of the play; it is, in contemporary terms, the play's *message*.

Your directorial vision is constructed first on a careful investigation that leads to a precise understanding of the play's thought, and secondly on your attitude toward the play's thought. The former ensures that the latter will be an accurate directorial point of view.

Thought is often called "spine." In this sense the play's spine, like the body's, is a central core that unites and controls all parts of the unit into a cohesive whole. As a director charged with the responsibility of artistic unification of the whole, you must determine the play's spine. You ask questions such as — What conclu-sion do I draw from the play's basic conflict? What do these people want, and what am I to conclude is the meaning of their goal? What is the common linkage

Paul Hildebrand as Hamlet (center) confronts the
Ghost in this production of *Hamlet* directed by
Howard Scammon at the College of William and Mary.
— *Photograph courtesy of the William and Mary Theatre*

of all the play's actions, and what meaning is implied by the totality of those actions? What is the play's protagonist-antagonist structure, and how does that lead me to see the play's basic conflict? What does this struggle mean? What is the relationship between the play's inciting incident, point of attack, climax, and resolution? What does this relationship mean?

Your selection of a play to direct will often be based on your perception of the relevance of the play's thought to your own beliefs. Many directors prefer to direct plays that focus on concepts they find important, explaining that the thought of a given play "speaks to me, hits me where I live," because this leads to a strong vision of the production. For example, my advanced directing students often select plays more for thought than for character or plot, so they prefer plays such as *Bent* and *Extremities*. In my own case, concern about one aspect of injustice has led me to direct such works as *The Diary of Anne Frank, The Investigation, Fiddler on the Roof, Incident at Vichy,* and *Cabaret.* Despite obvious differences in form, these plays are similar in thought and focus on a particular issue I find important. As you gain directorial opportunities you will experience rich personal satisfaction in selecting plays dealing with issues that are significant to you.

I have discovered that the director's function is not so much to explain the author's "meaning" to his actors — whose need to express that meaning clearly to the audience is not necessarily assisted by their understanding it intellectually — but rather to lead the actors, by some theatrical and dramatic means, to *do* those things which will *result* in transmitting the author's meaning. No actor can act out the *meaning* of . . . any play.

—ALAN SCHNEIDER
Entrances

Techniques for Understanding Thought

A number of techniques will help you unlock the mysteries of a play's thought. Logically you start with the script, examining all internal evidence such as the play's action, the protagonist's goal, and the major dramatic question. In this discussion of thought, we look first at internal evidence. Later we will discuss research techniques. You can shape your own logical methodology based on the approaches described below. The list cannot apply to every script, but it gives you a basis from which you can work to increase your sensitivity to the play.

Internal Evidence: Seeking the Play's Thought

SUBJECT AND THEME

In analyzing a play's thought, your logical first step is to subdivide the play's meaning into subject and theme. Knowledge of the play's subject and theme will lead you to a secure grasp of its basic thought. As you work with this process, you will discover that understanding a play's thought becomes easier and more precise.

Subject. Subject is the core of the play, the answer to the question — What is the play about? Typically the answer is an abstract concept: justice, revenge, compassion, truth, destiny, right versus wrong. To understand the play in carefully precise terms you will learn to express the play's subject in a single word or two, a discipline that will sharpen your ability to perceive a play's thought. Do not expect to find one word that is accepted by everyone; each of us responds differently to plays, and we all have subtly different concepts of significant words. On the other hand, be prepared to reconsider your conclusion if your one-word statement of subject sharply contradicts that of other knowledgeable theatre directors.

Annie Sullivan (standing) is a strong protagonist, and
Helen Keller is an equally strong antagonist in *The
Miracle Worker.* From their conflicts throughout the
play the meaning becomes clear: Discipline is essential
for education. In this emotional scene at the pump,
Annie finally succeeds in teaching young Helen Keller
that there are words for things. George Black directed
this production at the University of Virginia.
— *Photograph courtesy of the Heritage Repertory Theatre
at the University of Virginia*

Theme. A play's theme is the playwright's attitude, expressed in this particular
play, toward its subject. The theme is the play's point of view about the subject.
Usually, then, your statement of the theme will contain the word that defines the
play's subject. Express the theme with a phrase or sentence.

For illustration, assume we agree that the subject of *Macbeth* is power. The play's theme might be stated as, "A driving greed for absolute power is absolutely destructive." If the subject of *You Can't Take It with You* is family, the play's theme might be stated as, "Family love is warm, strong, and enduring no matter what the trials or how many strange eccentrics come along." With practice you will become more comfortable with the subject-theme approach to thought.

THE DRAMATIC TRIAD

To ensure an accurate understanding of the play's thought look for a link between thought, the protagonist's objective, and the point of attack. This connection can be called "the dramatic triad," and it is as important to the theatrical director learning how a play is constructed as the sonata allegro form is to the musical conductor learning how a symphony is put together. Not every play has a tight bond, and even those with close connections may be so artistically written as to disguise the technique. Nonetheless the dramatic triad linkage exists in enough plays to warrant searching for it in each play you study.

The point of attack. As we discussed in Chapter Four, the point of attack is the play's first shift in existing equilibrium. Typically it is a continuation of the inciting incident. Because it is the first active part of the plot, and because all subsequent plot growth necessarily arises from it, the point of attack helps you perceive the play's overall action and thus discloses answers to questions such as — What happens in the play? What is the play's story and plot?

The protagonist's goal. The protagonist is the play's central character and, as we discussed in Chapter Five, both cause and recipient of the major action. Therefore the protagonist's goal or objective begins with the point of attack and continues until the climax. Finding the goal illuminates plot points and answers such questions as — What does the protagonist want? What is the point of attack? How is the play structured around complications? What is the climax? What are the character relationships?

Thought. Thought, the spine of the play, is shown by the play's action and the protagonist's goal. To find thought you determine action, which starts at the point of attack, and the protagonist's objective, which conventionally is directly or indirectly stated as a response to the stimulus of the point of attack. When you comprehend the play's thought, you necessarily recognize both the plot and the protagonist's goal.

In most plays the dramatic triad gives you three ways to check your analysis. The value of the triad is that it tends to be self-completing: If you can identify two of the three parts of the triad, the third should become clear. Find the point of attack and the thought, and you find the protagonist; find the protagonist and the thought, and you find the point of attack; find the protagonist and the point of attack, and you find the thought.

THE MAJOR DRAMATIC QUESTION

As a director you want to be certain you have a correct analysis of the play's thought because a mistake here can lead to a muddied production. Therefore you add to the dramatic triad an investigation of the major dramatic question (MDQ), which was defined in Chapter Four. For each play, you need to ask — What is the play's major dramatic question? Typically the MDQ is thrust into the audience's minds by the point of attack when the protagonist faces a dilemma and must set goals to solve it. To be certain your analysis of thought is correct, specify the play's major dramatic question. Once you have that information, compare it to your understanding of the play's subject, theme, and protagonist's goal. No basic differences should exist. If these qualities conflict with one another, rethink your conclusions.

THE PLAY'S TITLE

A play's title often expresses a great deal of the subject. You can gain insight into the play's thought by examining the title. Think, for example, of *Ghosts, Fiddler on the Roof, After the Fall, The Crucible, The Miracle Worker,* or *Streamers.* The astute director examines the play's title to see if it contains clues to the play's basic meaning.

PRACTICE SESSION

Of the plays listed below, select those you know well and for each list subject, theme, point of attack, protagonist's goal, and major dramatic question.

Medea *by Euripides*
    Subject:
    Theme:
    Point of Attack:
    Protagonist's Goal:
    Major Dramatic Question:

Lysistrata *by Aristophanes*
    Subject:
    Theme:
    Point of Attack:
    Protagonist's Goal:
    Major Dramatic Question:

King Lear *by Shakespeare*
    Subject:
    Theme:
    Point of Attack:
    Protagonist's Goal:
    Major Dramatic Question:

Hamlet *by Shakespeare*
    Subject:
    Theme:
    Point of Attack:
    Protagonist's Goal:
    Major Dramatic Question:

The Misanthrope *by Molière*
    Subject:
    Theme:
    Point of Attack:
    Protagonist's Goal:
    Major Dramatic Question:

Death of a Salesman *by Arthur Miller*
    Subject:
    Theme:
    Point of Attack:
    Protagonist's Goal:
    Major Dramatic Question:

A Streetcar Named Desire *by Tennessee Williams*
    Subject:
    Theme:
    Point of Attack:
    Protagonist's Goal:
    Major Dramatic Question:

Fool for Love *by Sam Shepard*
    Subject:
    Theme:
    Point of Attack:
    Protagonist's Goal:
    Major Dramatic Question:

I have only one obligation, and it is to the playwright. If I have chosen to do the play it means that I like the play or find something interesting or challenging in it (or both) and by discharging my obligation to the playwright I will take care of the audience at the same time.

You see, the very act of choosing the play contains the assumption that it is something the audience will want to see. Then it's up to you, as the director, to try to achieve the play for the playwright in the way that the playwright has suggested both openly, in his words, and in the more subtle and mysterious things contained in the play. The playwright has the right to expect you to find and explore those elements that aren't simply and clearly indicated. And when you achieve — as it were — all of the potentialities and possibilities of what the playwright has done, then you've done the job.

—MIKE NICHOLS
quoted in *Showcase* by Roy Newquist

The poker scene from *A Streetcar Named Desire* as presented by the Virginia Players, University of Virginia, directed by Chris Hunter. The scene is another illustration of Stanley's masculine personality. Left to right are Mitch (Skip Sudduth), Steve (Mark Scharf), Stanley (Steve Tharp), and Pablo (Allen Stone). — *Photograph courtesy of the Virginia Players*

External Evidence: Research to Find the Play's Thought

You will not want to base your directorial vision solely on a personal examination of the play. All directors research other sources to guarantee accurate perception of the play's thought. Some research areas are indicated here.

THE PLAYWRIGHT'S "FIVE-FOOT SHELF"

"The Harvard Classic Five-Foot Shelf" was based on the concept that all the great books of the world could be collected to fit on a five-foot library shelf. Here

A study of choices — to take one's own life or to continue living — makes Marsha Norman's drama, *'Night, Mother,* an engrossing drama of two people struggling to understand their lives and their love for each other. Richly complicated *thought,* as well as engrossing characters and a strong plot, combine to make the play appealing to audiences as well as theatre workers. In this Guthrie Theater production directed by Christopher Markle, Veronica Castang (left) is Jessie, the daughter who calmly announces, "I'm going to kill myself." Georgine Hall is her mother. — *Photograph by Joe Giannetti*

Thought dominates character and plot in docudramas, an abbreviation of *documentary dramas,* which are based on actual events, often court records. Knowledge of the historical events influencing the playwright helps the director interpret the script correctly. In *The Investigation* (above), which is drawn from Nazi war crime trials, the playwright's clear intent is to make audiences aware of the chilling facts of the Holocaust to prevent such occurrences in the future. *The Trial of the Catonsville Nine* (opposite), also drawn from records of a court trial, is an unmistakable protest against the Vietnam War. The photographs are from William and Mary Theatre productions directed by the author. — *Photographs courtesy of the William and Mary Theatre*

the phrase refers to the belief that every writer consciously or subconsciously seeks to create a personal five-foot shelf to express a total view of the world. Each play is merely one portion of a whole, and it is difficult to comprehend a solitary piece without using the others to illuminate the way.

Study of the playwright's other works helps you perceive the writer's overall concept of humanity and the world, and thereby helps you understand the given play you direct. For example, the director preparing a production of *Summer and Smoke* by Tennessee Williams will gain insight into that play's Alma by studying other Williams females, such as Amanda in *The Glass Menagerie* and Blanche in *A Streetcar Named Desire.* If you are preparing to direct Arthur Miller's *The Price,* your understanding of the play will be enhanced by a study of his novel *Focus*

and his plays *All My Sons, Incident at Vichy,* and especially *Death of a Salesman* because *Price* can be seen as a continuation of that work.

THE PLAYWRIGHT'S PERSONAL OBSERVATIONS

Not all playwrights comment about their plays; writers usually do not want to explain the full play in a neat sentence or two. When they are available, however, playwrights' statements can be valuable. Playwrights such as Ibsen, Shaw, O'Neill, Eliot, Williams, Albee, and Miller have commented about their plays in essays, interviews, personal notes, and journals. These observations give you a more secure vision of the play.

STUDIES OF THE WRITER

Some books about playwrights are unfortunately marred by a gossipy atmosphere, amateur psychological connections of childhood events with events in plays, and focus on the writer's social life instead of his or her work. There are superior studies, however, such as Arthur and Barbara Gelb's book about Eugene O'Neill, and you will benefit greatly from such excellent works.

THE PLAYWRIGHT'S TIMES

Understanding a play's thought often requires a knowledge of its time. For example, ancient Greek playwrights such as Sophocles and Aristophanes wrote in a time when the world was the center of the universe and free humans had conscious control over their actions. Modern playwrights have learned that the sun and stars do not circle around the world and that layers of subconsciousness control humans. Along with humanity's changing view of itself has come a change in art's reflection of humanity: As a director you need be sensitive to the prevailing views influencing the playwright. For another example, society's changing views of war influenced this country's plays, from the highly jingoistic *Andre* (1798) about the Revolutionary War, the sentimental *Shenandoah* (1888) that treated the Civil War as a noble adventure, and George M. Cohan's glorification of World War I, to World War II's realistic *Command Decision* (1947) and the "Hell, no, we won't go" Vietnam War bitterness seen in *Viet Rock* (1964) and, after the war, in *Streamers* (1976) and *Strange Snow* (1982). Clearly, as you seek to understand the play, you should look to the author's times.

THE PLAYWRIGHT'S THEATRE

Playwrights designing works for modern Broadway theatre approach playwriting differently from those writing for off-off-Broadway. The former use a more traditional approach — Neil Simon's *The Odd Couple* is an illustration — and the latter often write works more intended to shock, such as Megan Terry's *Viet Rock*. Your insight into the play is improved by knowledge of the theatrical conventions that influenced its author.

INFLUENCES ON THE PLAYWRIGHT

Eugene O'Neill wrote in his journal of his fascination with the Greek sense of fate. Tennessee Williams said he was influenced by the works of D. H. Lawrence. Arthur Miller's concept of *The Crucible* had its roots in McCarthyism's persecution. The playwright's works become easier to understand when viewed through the perspective of various forces that affect the writer and, therefore, the work. You discover details about such influences with research and reading.

CONTEMPORARY THEATRE PRACTICE

Arthur Miller's *Death of a Salesman* was influenced by Jo Mielziner's set design, and his *After the Fall,* which premiered at the Lincoln Center, was influenced by the thrust stage concept of that theatre, as well as by director Elia Kazan. You can gain added insight into the writer's work from a study of the theatrical life of the playwright's time.

VIEWS OF OTHER THEATRE PEOPLE

One excellent insight into the plays of Tennessee Williams, and particularly *A Streetcar Named Desire,* is found in director Elia Kazan's sensitive notes on *Streetcar.* Research will reveal other directorial views, such as those of Tyrone Guthrie, John Gielgud, and Peter Brook on Shakespeare, Mike Nichols on Edward Albee, and Alan Schneider on Samuel Beckett. Such excellent directors have superior insight into plays they have directed successfully.

Many directors confess themselves disenchanted with critical or scholarly articles that magnify the minute and reveal little understanding of the creative process. Unfortunately such pieces can be "full of sound and fury, signifying nothing." Nonetheless you should accumulate your own experience with scholars and critics. Start by reading theatre magazines and journals for scholarly articles, and *The New York Times* and the *New York Theatre Critics' Reviews* for newspaper criticism.

"Drama is action, sir, action and not confounded philosophy."

—LUIGI PIRANDELLO
Six Characters in Search of an Author

Pitfalls to Avoid

As you seek to discover a play's thought, there are some danger areas that are best avoided. We discuss a few briefly here.

LOOKING FOR ONE SPEECH THAT EXPRESSES THE PLAY'S MEANING

Beginning directors sometimes believe they should search a play to find one speech that contains the playwright's expression of thought. But no playwright with production experience risks a two-and-a-half-hour play on one sentence. What if the actor muffs the line? What if someone in the audience has a coughing fit at that key moment? You do a disservice to the play and yourself if you believe the play's meaning can be reduced to one neat summation speech. If the playwright could say what the play means in one sentence, he or she would not have needed to write 120 pages!

Given speeches can illuminate aspects of the play, however. "He had the wrong dreams. All, all wrong. He never knew who he was." Although this speech from the requiem scene of *Death of a Salesman* does not speak the play's thought, it does cast light on an issue of the play. The director looks for these clues in the play. It is possible to find various speeches, drawn from various portions of the play, that add up to an expression of the play's thought.

PLAYING UNIVERSALITY

Universality is the quality that enables a play to live for audiences of later times or other lands. That *Oedipus* or *King Lear* are vitally alive theatrical pieces today is a tribute to their universality; that *Death of a Salesman* moved successfully from America to China indicates that universality is not limited to plays of the past. But the values of universality should not be exaggerated. Because many teachers stress universality in defining "good" theatre, student directors can easily fall victim to a belief that their productions must express the play's universal qualities.

To illustrate the dangers of exaggerating universality, I draw from my own error when I directed John Steinbeck's *The Moon Is Down,* a quietly intense drama about the Nazi invasion of Norway. I wanted to stress the play's universal qualities. Directing this play at a time when I was critical of America's foreign policy, I saw it as the story of any superpower's arrogant takeover of any secondary power. I changed the few references to *Germany* into *the enemy,* substituted *us* for *Norway,* and had wardrobe design abstract tunics representing any time or place instead of the usual storm trooper uniforms. Universal? Oh yes, certainly. Meaningful? No. It was a directorial error bred of careless thinking and forgotten priorities. By ignoring the specific, I turned a clear play into a fuzzy piece that failed to communicate the power of Steinbeck's thought to the audience. Sadly they blamed Steinbeck not me.

Drama must be specific in both script and production. The specific communicates from stage to audience, and as a result the audience perceives the universal. Shakespeare's *King Lear* is not a universal tale of "Everyman and his daughters"; it is a specific story about a unique father and three particular daughters. Arthur Miller's Willy Loman is not a universal salesman, or a universal lost man with all the wrong dreams; he is a highly individualized human with a particular mixture of strength and weakness. A director who sought to stage *Lear* as "all families" or to turn Willy Loman into "all traveling salesmen" would make either work considerably less significant.

Universality must exist in the mind of the beholder. It is pretentious, self-important, and sophomoric for a production to tell the audience that they are participating in a universal experience. If there are universalities present, the audience can discover them quite nicely, thank you, without pompous emphasis by the director.

DIRECTING IN THE "FOOTNOTE" STYLE

Research can improve your play analysis by enhancing your insight into the playwright's works, but good theatrical sense keeps that research in perspective. A colleague of mine describes another director's work as "full of footnotes," unfortunately nontheatrical and pompous, a manner of directing the play with a bow to all opinions as if writing a doctoral dissertation. One finds such productions all too frequently in university theatre. They are earmarked by a dull earnestness and the visible inclusion of "important" (and all too often contradictory) essays on the play. This approach lacks directorial conviction; instead of presenting the playwright's thought, it presents a mishmash of critical "interpretations" of the play's content. A lively sense of theatre will guide you away from the footnoted production.

It is not difficult to discover, with the help of scholars and commentaries, what the actual words [in Shakespeare] mean, where cuts may be sanctioned, how the act waits may best be placed. But one cannot digest too many outside opinions, and it is always dangerous

The thematic universality of Arthur Miller's *The Crucible* is achieved by emphasizing the specific, as shown in this photograph of the trial scene from the Guthrie Theater production directed by Len Cariou. Although Miller's play has clear resonances with modern-day "witch hunts," successful productions avoid attempts to stage the universal qualities and thus encourage audience members to use imagination and intelligence to apply the play to today's world.
— *Photograph courtesy of the Guthrie Theater*

in the theatre to substitute scholarship and critical opinion, however brilliant, for contemporary instinct and fresh, vital imagination.

—JOHN GIELGUD
Stage Directions

Exercises

The following questions on the play you are to direct will help you examine the play's various elements. The last six questions in particular will help you see if you have found a link between plot, character, and thought.

1. What is the name of the play? The playwright?
2. What is the significance of the play's title?
3. What is the play's major dramatic question?
4. What speeches illuminate the play's meaning? Use direct quotations from the play.
5. What is the play's subject? Express it in one word.
6. What is the play's theme? Express it in a sentence.
7. Describe the playwright's "five-foot shelf." What are the author's other works? What common denominators link the plays?
8. What are the playwright's personal observations about the play?
9. Are there studies of the playwright? What do you learn from them about the playwright in general and this play in particular?
10. What do you learn about the play from a knowledge of its time? Describe the time.
11. For what theatre did the author write the play (children's theatre, commercial or amateur, off-off Broadway, Broadway, etc.)? What do you learn about the play from a knowledge of its intended theatre?
12. What influences (novelists, poets, other playwrights, directors, etc.) affected the playwright?
13. What were the comments of directors who produced the playwright?
14. What were the critical reviews of this play?
15. What scholarly comments on this play help you perceive its thought?
16. Does the play have significant universality? If so, explain. Discuss, too, how the play uses specifics to communicate the universals.
17. Who is the protagonist?
18. What is the protagonist's goal?
19. What is the play's inciting incident?
20. What is the play's point of attack?
21. What is the play's climax?
22. Do you find connections between subject-theme and the protagonist's goal? Does the point of attack link with the inciting incident? Does the protagonist's goal logically connect with the point of attack? Does the protagonist's drive to the goal stop at the play's climax?

The style of acting in a production is an interpretive problem which the director alone can solve. The problem is not simply a matter of taste but of meaning. What does the play say? Is *The Dybbuk*, for example, a play of quaint folk customs regarded with sentimental affection, or a play about a ritualistic world seen as a frightening phantasmagoria of the past? It may be either. The director decides which.

—HAROLD CLURMAN
Lies Like Truth

CHAPTER SEVEN

Diction: The Language of the Play

POLONIUS:

What do you read, my lord?

HAMLET:

Words, words, words.

> — Shakespeare
> *Hamlet,* Act Two, Scene 2

Words, like Nature, half reveal
And half conceal the Soul within.

> — ALFRED, LORD TENNYSON
> *In Memoriam A. H. H.*

As you shape your directorial vision, you find that diction, the language of the play, subtly half reveals and half conceals the play's heart and soul while communicating the play's unique style and characters. On your imagination's stage you "hear" the words of the play as they ebb and flow, weaving a compelling spell that seizes your attention. Diction ranges from the elevated poetic diction that makes Shakespeare's plays at once so powerful and so difficult to the modern, poetically terse understatement found in the plays of Harold Pinter, for example, and the prosaic expressions of realistic drama, which often contains lyric moments, as in plays of Lanford Wilson and Sam Shepard. For director, performers, and audience, diction enriches the understanding of the play's character and thought, creates imagery and beauty, and establishes the play's rhythmic beat. Written by a master playwright and spoken by a sensitive performer, diction is a significant aesthetic pleasure of theatre. As a director, you find that bringing diction to life on stage is an exciting challenge.

Novelist Ernest Hemingway said that every novelist engages in a perpetual battle to write the perfect sentence. For the novelist, as for the essayist and poet, much of the joy of writing comes with winning that battle. However, directors know that the playwright distrusts the "perfect sentence" because it draws atten-

The Duke of Cornwall (standing, back to camera) prepares to blind the Duke of Gloucester (lying on the floor) in this Guthrie Theater production of Shakespeare's poetic tragedy, *King Lear,* directed by Michael Langham. — *Photograph courtesy of the Guthrie Theater*

tion to itself; the dramatist freely violates rules of grammar because dialogue consists of characters speaking. Incomplete sentences, elliptical phrases, searchings for words are typical of "real life" people; the playwright uses them because they are the way people really speak. Therefore, as you study a play's diction, read it less with the eye and more with the ear.

Emotion

Your vision of the play's primary emotional tenor is derived in large part from the pattern of diction, which shows you the play's heart and soul. For example, your vision would perceive a sense of tragedy as measured as the tolling of a funeral bell in John Millington Synge's one-act play, *Riders to the Sea.* If you were to direct *Riders,* its diction would help you envision a somber atmosphere that would encourage you to visualize production design, tempo, and character intensity. Diction sparks your imagination to see and feel the characters. The following sequence from *Riders to the Sea* is introduced by the two girls, Nora and Cathleen, who speak of possible hope. But Maurya, the mother, counts her men lost at sea. (Envision "keening" as a multitoned, wordless wail of despair intoned by someone who is rocking back and forth as if in a trance.)

CATHLEEN
(Begins to keen.)
It's destroyed we are from this day. It's destroyed, surely.

NORA
Didn't the young priest say the Almighty God wouldn't leave her destitute with no son living?

MAURYA
(In a low voice, but clearly.)
It's little the like of him knows of the sea . . . Bartley will be lost now, and let you call in Eamon and make me a good coffin out of the white boards, for I won't live after them. I've had a husband, and a husband's father, and six sons in this house — six fine men, though it was a hard birth I had with every one of them and they coming to the world — and some of them were found and some of them were not found, but they're gone now, the lot of them. . . . There were Stephen, and Shawn, were lost in the great wind, and found in the Bay of Gregory of the Golden Mouth, and carried up the two of them on the one plank, and in by that door.
(She pauses for a moment. The girls start as if they heard something through the door that is half open behind them.)

NORA
(In a whisper.)
Did you hear that, Cathleen? Did you hear a noise in the northeast?

CATHLEEN
(In a whisper.)
There's someone after crying out by the seashore.

MAURYA

(Continues without hearing anything.)

There was Sheamus and his father, and his own father again, were lost in a dark night, and not a stick of sign was seen of them when the sun went up. There was Patch after was drowned out of a curagh that turned over. I was sitting here with Bartley, and he a baby, lying on my two knees, and I see two women, and three women, and four women coming in, and they crossing themselves, and not saying a word. I looked out then, and there were men coming after them, and they holding a thing in the half of a red sail, and water dripping out of it — it was a dry day, Nora — and leaving a track to the door.

Synge's diction gives you an awareness of the emotional mood and the tragedy of these people who wrestle a living from the unforgiving sea. Significantly, as we discuss in a later chapter, diction dictates the play's basic rhythm. For illustration, reread the passage aloud several times, swaying your body to and fro with the speeches or tapping your finger against a desk to capture the rhythm.

Repetition

In performance how should the performer handle repetitive lines? In *Riders to the Sea* you find significant repetitions. Among them are: "It's destroyed we are. . . . It's destroyed, surely." "I've had a husband, and a husband's father, and six sons in this house — six fine men, . . . and some of them were found and some of them were not found, . . ." "Did you hear that . . . ? Did you hear a noise . . . ?"

The standard directorial rule to performers facing repetitive lines is simple — Speak each repetition differently; find in the character a different attitude for the repeated line. Repetitive readings lack imagination and quickly grow tedious. As the director you help the performer avoid the trap of reading a repeated line exactly the same as the first line. You direct the performer to use one set of tonal inflections, volume level, timbre sounds, rate, and pitch on the line the first time; and for the repeated line you ask the performer to change most, perhaps all, of those vocal qualities. Stagewise directors enforce this rule as a valid guide for performers.

In *Riders to the Sea,* however, the standard rule is less valid. Repetition in the hands of a master poet-dramatist like Synge has a carefully gauged effect; he uses repetitions as a symphony composer would use the tolling of a bell. Furthermore, character objectives are not changing in those repetitions. Vocal pyrotechnics for the sake of variations in readings of repetitions are wrong here; readings of the repetitive lines should vary only subtly.

Pronunciations and Definitions

As a director you use available resources to check meanings and pronunciation of all words in the play during the preparation period before auditions. Even a short passage like the above selection from *Riders to the Sea* can raise many questions — What's a curagh? How is it pronounced? How is Shawn pronounced? Sheamus? Is there really a Bay of Gregory of the Golden Mouth? If so, where is it? Why does Maurya mistake her verbs, as in "There were Stephen, and Shawn...."? How would daughters of a seafaring family pronounce *northeast*? Why does she ask for white boards for her coffin? Is there a symbol in "half of a red sail"? You will need answers to such questions.

Resources for pronunciation and meaning abound. Of course you know to look first in the dictionary, but which pronunciation do you select if several are given? Common advice has it that one should pronounce the word as it is given in the first entry in the dictionary, but that's erroneous: The correct pronunciation is the one used by the learned members of your community. After the dictionary look to recordings of the play; for plays such as *Riders to the Sea,* so-called spoken-word recordings can help you better understand the musical lilt and overall sound of the play. Ethnic dictionaries can also be helpful. And don't ignore resident experts in your area — a rabbi, priest, historian, language teacher, or native of the land of the play — who can contribute additional insight into the diction of the play you will direct.

Character

What a character says can be a key to the workings of his or her mind. Therefore each character, or at least each major character, has a distinctive speech pattern. Diction, then, is a way of delineating character. As a director you look for those distinguishing qualities, and work with the performers to present the differences to the audience.

In *Fiddler on the Roof,* for example, diction shows that Tevye the father and dairyman has a highly individualized way of working out problems, examining both sides of a question as a rabbi would. In the following illustration Tevye responds to Motel the tailor who has just asked to marry Tevye's daughter Tzeitel. Moments earlier in a pep talk that encouraged him to ask her father for her hand, Tzeitel had told Motel that even a poor tailor has a right to happiness.

TEVYE
Stop talking nonsense. You're just a poor tailor.

MOTEL
(*Bravely.*)
That's true, Reb Tevye, but even a poor tailor is entitled to some happiness.
(*Looks at TZEITEL triumphantly.*)
I promise you, Reb Tevye, your daughter will not starve.

TEVYE
(*Impressed, turns to the audience.*)
He's beginning to talk like a man. On the other hand, what kind of match would that be, with a poor tailor? On the other hand, he's an honest, hard worker. On the other

hand, he has absolutely nothing. On the other hand, things could never get worse for him, they could only get better.

Diction also shows Tevye's comfortable relationship with his God as evidenced by his frequent talks with Him during the play. At times Tevye talks to God as he would to a neighbor. Sometimes he asks for guidance. He also feels free to ask for material things, as here in the short speech just before the song, "If I Were A Rich Man."

> TEVYE
> As the Good Book says, "Heal us, O Lord, and we shall be healed." In other words, send us the cure, we've got the sickness already.
> *(Gestures to the door.)*
> I'm not really complaining — after all, with Your help, I'm starving to death. You made many, many poor people. I realize, of course, that it's no shame to be poor, but it's no great honor either. So what would have been so terrible if I had a small fortune?

Diction teaches you a great deal about Tevye. He is a reverent man, earnestly seeking to follow a moral path. His one-on-one friendship with God shows a charming piety; that much of his humor is shown while he is talking with the Lord also shows a warm-hearted strength. His simple and direct diction — plain words and short sentences — displays Tevye as a common man, and the audience should identify with him easily. These diction techniques help you make vital decisions about casting and performance.

Silence

Just as a character's speeches are a clue to the mind and soul, silences also illustrate the character. The speech unspoken is a loud communication. If you are alert to the playwright's techniques, those silences take on added meaning. You will find yourself looking at a crucial moment in a character's existence and wondering — Why is this character silent now?

Not all silences are significant, however. When you ask why a character is not speaking, the answer may well be that the playwright simply was not thinking of the character at that time. You should not build conclusions about the character based on the fact the writer happened to blink for a moment.

How can you decide if a silence is accidental or important? If the play contains only one silence that lasts but a moment, you can conclude the writer meant little by it. In contrast, a meaningful silence will be emphasized. The following dialogues illustrate the difference between unnoticed and meaningful silences. This is Act One, Scene 3, of *Macbeth*. Banquo and Macbeth are entering the blasted heath where the three witches wait.

> *(Enter MACBETH and BANQUO.)*
>
> MACBETH
> So foul and fair a day I have not seen.

Harold Pinter's plays are filled with meaningful silences. The so-called "Pinter pauses" are communications without dialogue — character reactions, thoughts, emotions. Actors in such scenes are expected to "fill the silence" to communicate the unspoken dialogue. In this tensely "silent scene" from the William and Mary Theatre production of *The Dumb Waiter*, directed by the author, James Graves (left) and Richard Merriman (right) played Ben and Gus. — *Photograph courtesy of the William and Mary Theatre*

BANQUO

How far is't call'd to Forres? What are these,
So wither'd, and so wild in their attire,
That look not like th' inhabitants o' th' earth,
And yet are on't? Live you? or are you aught
That man may question? You seem to understand me,
By each at once her choppy finger laying
Upon her skinny lips. You should be women,
And yet your beards forbid me to interpret
That you are so.

Banquo (played by John Woodson, left) and Macbeth
(Michael LaGue, right) encounter the witches in Act
One, Scene 3 of *Macbeth*. This important scene is the
play's point of attack; it establishes Macbeth's
motivations for subsequent actions through the play; it
asks the Major Dramatic Question; and it contains the
meaningful silence discussed in the text. Note how
director Louis Rackoff uses levels, focus by the
witches, and full front body position to emphasize the
reactions of Banquo and Macbeth in this 1988
production at the North Carolina Shakespeare Festival,
High Point, N.C. — *Photograph by Bill Savage, courtesy
of the North Carolina Shakespeare Festival*

MACBETH
Speak, if you can. What are you?

FIRST WITCH
All hail, Macbeth! Hail to thee, Thane of Glamis!

SECOND WITCH
All hail, Macbeth! Hail to thee, Thane of Cawdor!

THIRD WITCH

All hail, Macbeth, that shalt be king hereafter!

BANQUO

I' th' name of truth,
Are ye fantastical, or that indeed
Which outwardly ye show?
If we can look into the seeds of time
And say which grain will grow and which will not,
Speak then to me, who neither beg nor fear
Your favors nor your hate.

Is there a meaningful silence in the above sequence? No. Perhaps you notice that Macbeth does not speak, but you think little of it because the playwright does not emphasize the point. It therefore seems to be merely accidental silence.

But the above dialogue is not the way Shakespeare wrote the scene. Here is the scene as Shakespeare wrote it, emphasizing Macbeth's silence:

MACBETH

Speak, if you can. What are you?

FIRST WITCH

All hail, Macbeth! Hail to thee, Thane of Glamis!

SECOND WITCH

All hail, Macbeth! Hail to thee, Thane of Cawdor!

THIRD WITCH

All hail, Macbeth, that shalt be king hereafter!

BANQUO

Good sir, why do you start and seem to fear
Things that do sound so fair? I' th' name of truth,
Are ye fantastical, or that indeed
Which outwardly ye show? My noble partner
You greet with present grace and great prediction
Of noble having and of royal hope,
That he seems rapt withal. To me you speak not.
If you can look into the seeds of time,
And say which grain will grow and which will not,
Speak then to me, who neither beg nor fear
Your favors nor your hate.

Is the silence emphasized now? Indeed yes. We have insights into Macbeth's nonverbal reactions — he starts, he seems afraid of what he hears, he is "rapt withal" — to help us see inside his character. Here you want the performer to play the scene's *subtext,* the character's inner feelings and intentions not expressed by dialogue. Note that Banquo uses the word *speak* twice and a synonym *(you greet)* as if Shakespeare wished to draw further attention to Macbeth's silence. Clearly communication with silence can be significant.

Beats and Thought Units

The simple word *beat* has two complex and different meanings. For the director the word often refers to what we earlier called the action unit. In this usage the director thinks of the play as one major movement that is subdivided into many smaller cohesive units, or beats; often the director perceives the beat as the interval from the beginning of one complication to the next.

More commonly, as we shall examine in detail in a later chapter, a *beat* is an actor's measurement of a single unit of purpose or intention. This usage follows Stanislavski's description of the play's smallest action that has its own complete shape and deals with one given subject. A beat begins with a character's *intention,* or subobjective, and ends when that intention is completed.

In the latter sense a character has many beats, each an *action-reaction,* or *stimulus-response,* cycle. The character has an intention and therefore takes an action that causes a reaction, which in turn is a stimulus for another reaction. For both director and performers discovering character beats lends insight into characters' thoughts and actions; the frequency of the beats also helps the director perceive the play's basic rhythmic structure.

The character beat may or may not be explicitly stated in dialogue. If it is found in dialogue, we can call it a *thought unit* within a speech. Regardless of length, a given speech may have one thought unit or several. Typically the longer the speech, the more units there are, each representing different intentions or goals and usually accompanied by changes in action and emotion.

It is important to realize that these changes necessarily demand different readings. To illustrate this concept, let us examine Banquo's speeches in the scene from *Macbeth* discussed earlier.

BANQUO

How far is't call'd to Forres? What are these,
So wither'd, and so wild in their attire,
That look not like th' inhabitants o' th' earth,
And yet are on't? Live you? or are you aught
That man may question? You seem to understand me,
By each at once her choppy finger laying
Upon her skinny lips. You should be women,
And yet your beards forbid me to interpret
That you are so.

The first thought unit is easy to see. If Banquo reads his first two sentences with the same thought pattern and emotional mood, the scene becomes farcical: It is comic to use the same inflections when asking "How far away is Forres?" and "Who are these frightening and strange-looking creatures?" Inserted stage directions clarify the change from one thought unit to the next.

BANQUO
(Idly, speaking to Macbeth; disinterested.)
How far is't call'd to Forres?

(Suddenly the witches appear in front of him; he leaps backwards in self-protection, half-drawing his sword and crouching as for battle; he peers through the haze to try to see them better, and he speaks in a half-whisper, half-growl.)

What are these,
So wither'd, and so wild in their attire,
That look not like th' inhabitants o' th' earth,
And yet are on't?

Stage directions for Banquo's next speech further illustrate shifts of intentions.

BANQUO
(Watching Macbeth closely, speaking in a low voice for Macbeth only.)
Good Sir, why do you start and seem to fear
Things that do sound so fair?
(Pause, waiting for Macbeth to reply; wondering why he doesn't; then a physical turn to face the witches, stepping several steps from Macbeth to the witches. He now speaks in a loud and very clear voice as if to deaf people.)
I' th' name of truth,
Are ye fantastical, or that indeed
Which outwardly ye show?
(He looks back at Macbeth who still is entranced, and speaks to the Witches in a voice that indicates he is concerned about Macbeth, looking more at Macbeth than at them.)
My noble partner
You greet with present grace and great prediction
Of noble having and of royal hope,
That he seems rapt withal.
(Pause; Banquo is thinking of Macbeth more than of himself or the witches. Then he quite visibly throws off those concerns. He turns fully to the witches.)
To me you speak not.
(Now Banquo is the bold warrior, afraid of nothing, chin up, he steps toward them confidently.)
If you can look into the seeds of time,
And say which grain will grow and which will not,
Speak then to me, who neither beg nor fear
Your favors nor your hate.

Action in dialogue is communicated by identifying and playing the thought units; the scene's rhythm is dictated by the frequency and duration of the units. One prime contribution to any boring production is likely to be the performers' inability to play the shifts. On the other hand, electrifying performances are at least in part a result of well-played thought units.

As the director you can use two approaches to achieve necessary dynamics in thought units. In the first approach the performer plays the character's intentions and therefore changes with the intention. Banquo, for example, is dynamic because of his goals and reactions. The second approach uses vocal technique: You instruct the performer to use variations in rate, pitch, volume, and timbre to achieve vocal dynamics. Each approach, or a combination of both, will achieve the desired results if done artistically, not mechanically, and without letting the audience perceive the technique.

Thought shifts involve both vocal and physical changes because the two belong together: Physical action helps vocal change. The process helps the performer get into the character's soul and brain, creating an enriched projection of a dimensional human to the audience.

Subtext

"Spectators come to the theatre to hear the subtext," Stanislavski says. "They can read the text at home." *Subtext* refers to the implied message *under the text,* or *between the lines* — the character's emotions, attitudes, and desires that are not spoken. It is related to significant silences in that both communicate without specific dialogue, but here we look at the meanings that hide inside the spoken lines.

As a director you help the actor discover these messages by finding the character's goal in the speech. Subtext often results from the character's need to conceal information from other characters and thus indicates relationships between the characters.

Directors define good performers by their ability to project subtext: The good actor can enter with an innocuous line like "Good morning, and how are you today?" and convey layers of additional meaning, such as "I had a perfectly rotten night," "I'm delighted you are here," or "I know I'll hate everything you're going to tell me." The premise is that a given line of dialogue is not dramatically significant until the actor projects the implied meaning below the apparent surface of the line. The audience never notices how the performer accomplishes the communication — as always, art consists of hiding technique — but the messages are clear because the performer has found the subtext, often with the director's guidance, and played it.

Directorial guidance includes being certain the actor perceives the character's basic *motivating drive,* or reason for the line and subtext; you also ensure that the actor sees a basic *through line of action,* a consistent and logical series of actions related to the character's *spine* or *superobjective* throughout the play.

Let us return to the *Macbeth* scene and look at subtext.

FIRST WITCH

Banquo and Macbeth, all hail!

MACBETH

Stay, you imperfect speakers, tell me more!
By Sinel's death I know I am Thane of Glamis;
But how of Cawdor? The Thane of Cawdor lives,
A prosperous gentleman; and to be King
Stands not within the prospect of belief,
No more than to be Cawdor. Say from whence
You owe this strange intelligence, or why

Upon this blasted heath you stop our way
With such prophetic greeting. Speak, I charge you.
(*The witches vanish.*)

You know that Macbeth has been "rapt" by the predictions. Therefore you safely conclude there are layers of meaning in "Stay you imperfect speakers, tell me more!" Why does he say that? What is the emotion behind that line? What else might he say, if he could? Is he excited? Does he want to hide his emotions? Is he so involved that he loses dignity? Answers to such questions allow you to perceive the subtext.

Macbeth's next lines are more complicated to analyze because they include necessary plot information. The playwright must let the audience know first that Macbeth's father, Sinel, is dead, and that Macbeth has inherited the title of Thane of Glamis. Shakespeare also wants to communicate Macbeth's belief that Cawdor is alive and well because information will soon come to confirm that Macbeth has become Thane of Cawdor, thereby fulfilling the witches' prediction.

This necessary plot information must be communicated if the play is to succeed, but the character is not merely a spokesperson. Macbeth still has motivations for his speech. What would cause him to explain to strangers details about Sinel? What feelings would motivate him to say that Cawdor not only lives but also is prosperous? Macbeth may be eager to find out what the witches know or can predict, but would he let them or Banquo see that eagerness? The answers to these questions reveal more subtext. Ignore a twentieth century person's responses to the weird sisters; put yourself in the seventeenth century and ask yourself what superstitions are part of Macbeth's core. Finally, look at Macbeth's last two sentences.

Say from whence
You owe this strange intelligence, or why
Upon this blasted heath you stop our way
With such prophetic greeting.

What if you have the witches begin to exit during the last few words? With what intensity would Macbeth then read his final line, "Speak, I charge you"? Desperate? Frenzied? Despairing? Does he think of an evil force when he demands to know the source of their information? Is he concerned that others may see in him what the witches perceive? What conclusions might Macbeth reach about the reason the weird sisters appeared to him? Is he attempting to peer at them more closely, to see them through their ragged veils and the ground fog? As subtext becomes clear, you discover staging ideas, thus enhancing your directorial vision.

Problems with Diction

Dr. Spooner has had his shair fare of thespian disciples. "Stand back, my lord, and let the coffin pass," became in the mouth of one unfortunate actor in Leicester, "Stand back, my

Shakespeare's poetic diction often is as strong a factor as characters or plot and requires special attention from director and performers to achieve the necessary communication of verbal beauty to the audience. Above, *A Midsummer Night's Dream,* directed by George Black for the Virginia Players of the University of Virginia. — *Photograph courtesy of the Virginia Players, University of Virginia*

lord, and let the parson cough." Early in her career, the great Maude Adams once rendered the line from *A Midsummer Night's Dream,* "You spotted snake with double tongue," as "You potted snake with ham and tongue." Even Charles Kemble was able to transform the line, "Shall I lay perjury upon my soul?" to "Shall I lay surgery upon my Poll?" And in a Broadway thriller in 1980 the line, "This is the chair Schmidt sat in when he was shot" had to be cut after an unfortunate transposition on the first night.

—GYLES BRANDRETH
Great Theatrical Disasters

Not all lines are written with an ear for performers' possible problems. For example, on opening night of *Waiting for Godot* the performers fell victim to the play's repetition of lines and cues and skipped back and forth over a number of pages before they settled down again into the script. Playwrights often forget performers' difficulties in memorizing repetitive lines, or the problems of a per-

Modern playwrights such as Sam Shepard often write in a blend of poetry and realism that gives their plays a special style, elevating the subject matter and the characters while keeping the plays firmly rooted in today's world. Above, Shepard's *The Curse of the Starving Class* at the University of Wisconsin, Madison, as directed by Robert Skloot. Note the attention to minute realistic details of the kitchen environment and the characters' clothing, a visual depiction of the play's realism. — *Photograph courtesy of the University of Wisconsin, Madison*

former inclined to whistle on ess sounds who must speak swift speeches of hissing sibilants. Tongue-twisters can be an especially arduous task.

What can you do, faced with script problems? Unfortunately you have few alternatives. One admittedly unhappy solution is to slow the pace for awkward lines. Another solution is to avoid the problem: Either do not direct the play or find performers who can overcome the problems. If the playwright is present,

101

Playwrights who tend to be "talky," such as George Bernard Shaw, require special directorial attention to the performers' vocal skills. Vocal dynamics can help keep talky plays alive and interesting. Above, Shaw's tongue-in-cheek statement about the American Revolutionary War, *The Devil's Disciple,* directed by George Black for the Heritage Repertory Theatre, University of Virginia. — *Photograph courtesy of the Heritage Repertory Theatre, University of Virginia*

ask for rewrites; if the playwright is absent, you might reluctantly change a few words yourself.

If the playscript contains repetitive lines, like those in *Godot,* you should anticipate memorization difficulties. In the early stages of rehearsals you can help performers memorize lines securely. Frequent nonstop run-throughs of scenes are useful, and memorization drill can become part of the rehearsal process. Here, as in so many other instances, it is your responsibility to plan carefully, avoiding problems before they arise.

Faithfulness to the Playwright's Words

How carefully should you work to be sure performers are faithful to the playwright's words? In a word, *very.* Personal experience with new playwrights nervously watching premiere productions of their plays has made me aware that when performers depart from the playwright's script they injure not only the playwright but also the play. Playwrights spend days working to get a speech right. Performers can destroy the effect with a casual change. A playwright may carefully place exposition in the middle of a speech where it is less noticeable; a performer's inversion of lines can make that exposition obvious and distracting. Your concern for diction includes sympathy for the playwright's efforts.

Exercises

Answer the following questions about diction in the play you will direct. Be as specific and detailed as possible.

1. What is the name of the play? The playwright?
2. What is the play's diction style (poetic, prose, modern, colorful, terse, ornate, etc.)? What do you find most distinctive about the playwright's diction?
3. What words or terms will be troublesome for performers because of pronunciation or definition? List all such words, and indicate proper pronunciation and definition.
4. What reference books, dictionaries, recordings, films, and local experts do you plan to consult? Indicate the record's title, manufacturer, and performance company; and title, studio, distributor, director, and leading performers in a movie.
5. What is each character's distinctive diction? Give examples. How does diction differentiate between characters?
6. Does the playwright use silence to communicate? List such silences and describe the communication.
7. Do you anticipate that performers will experience unusual difficulties with diction, such as memorization and handling sibilants? Specify possible problems and indicate what you plan to do to help performers overcome the difficulties.

Delivering the words mechanically with set, intellectualized intonations, projecting them beyond the object they are trying to reach and into the audience in the old-fashioned manner, or mumbling without verbal intention or action in the "modern" manner — all come from a misunderstanding of true verbal action. The errors can arise even before rehearsals have begun. The misinformed, diligent actor, if he has time, will sometimes memorize the words and mechanize the inflections before he comes to the first reading of the play. That can be fatal to his final performance. During rehearsals he can hunt for and find intentions for his character, he can attempt to genuinely receive from his partners and his surroundings, and still he will fall back into the identical pattern of the mechanical and rigid "line readings" he had begun with. He can no more change it than he could change arbitrary and unjustified stage blocking which had been arrived at and set for quick convenience. We must learn what our character wants, from whom and under what circumstances, if we are to be propelled into genuine verbal action.

—UTA HAGEN

with Haskel Frankel, *Respect for Acting*

CHAPTER EIGHT

Music: The Sounds of a Play

Why does the "Blues" music fit [*A Streetcar Named Desire*]? The Blues is an expression of the loneliness and rejection, the exclusion and isolation of the Negro and their (opposite) longing for love and connection. Blanche too is "looking for a home," abandoned, friendless. "I don't know where I'm going, but I'm going." Thus the Blues piano catches the soul of Blanche, the miserable unusual human side of the girl which is beneath her frenetic duplicity, her trickery, lies, etc. It tells, it continually reminds you what all the fireworks are caused by.

—ELIA KAZAN
Notebook for "A Streetcar Named Desire"

Music refers to all the sounds of the play, not merely those created by instruments. Music is the complete aural nature of the play: performers' voices, the sounds of the words, sound effects, and integral or incidental musical accompaniment. It may be a major or minor force in the play, called for by the playwright or created and added by the director to fulfill directorial vision. A production's music is to the ear as spectacle (discussed in Chapter Nine) is to the eye.

Music is a major ingredient of your directorial vision because it is a total communication to the audience's emotions and imagination, light fingers touching the soul or stirring the inner corners of the mind. Depending on the requirements of your vision, the music in your production may be subtle — a gentle whisper, the mutter of distant thunder — or striking — a Sousa march with fireworks. For your production it can include the harmony or dissonances of performers' voices; the rolling sounds of words in prose or poetry; the preshow, entr'acte, chaser, and incidental or integral music taken from stock recordings or written especially for your production; and sound effects ranging from the flushing of a toilet to the sound of a breaking harp string.

A generation trained on motion picture and television production values already knows the effect of sound. Certainly those with training and experience in musical theatre know the many positive attributes of such strong total sound communication. But years of directing straight drama had not made me sensitive to

The original production of *Oklahoma!* (first titled
Away We Go during its out-of-town tryouts before it
opened on Broadway in 1943) was directed by
Rouben Mamoulian and featured Joan Roberts as
Laurey. — *Photograph courtesy of the Library of Congress*

all the values of music in this large sense. While directing full-scale musical productions and observing their richness of communication, however, I grew aware of music's potential contributions to all theatre from classical tragedy to modern satire.

Performers' Voices

The director, not the playwright, decides the qualities of performers' voices. Playwrights may indicate something about certain characters' vocal qualities, but they do so infrequently. As director you make final decisions about vocal qualities during auditions, based on your directorial vision of the musical qualities you seek to achieve in production. Your vision tells you each character's vocal attribute — this one has a southern accent, that one tends to whine, another booms

Music adds to the excitement of Chekhov's *Three Sisters* in this production at the Guthrie Theater directed by artistic director Liviu Ciulei. Paul Goldstaub was musical consultant. Note the two instruments and the percussive effect of clapping hands and stamping feet. A director's creative vision can enhance production values by including music.
— *Photograph by Joe Giannetti*

out, and here is a whiskey tenor — and one portion of your casting process is based on that vision.

CAST FOR VOCAL QUALITIES

In the best of all worlds you would have the luxury of choice at auditions. Basic acting abilities must take priority of course, but given those you would like to cast for ensemble vocal qualities: You cast this performer because she *sounds* good next to another performer, that performer because he sounds different from others; you don't cast another performer because his or her voice is displeasing or too similar to another's. In the ideal situation you could use voices to fine-tune the production's music, selecting the cast according to their overall musical sound, as well as their acting abilities, cooperativeness, and physical-emotional attributes. In the real world, however, you are not likely to have such luxurious choice.

You do not seek to cast "golden voices" — the era of oratorical acting is long gone, happily — but vocal tonality remains important. And although you do not cast for vocal ranges as a choir leader would, the production's overall sound is significant, and you may consider casting an ensemble that includes a bass, a baritone, a tenor, an alto, and a soprano.

USE VOCAL QUALITIES TO CONTROL FOCUS

One of your never-ending directorial concerns is controlling *focus,* that is, where the audience looks on the stage. Because audiences hear with their eyes as well as their ears, if they are confused about who is speaking they may lose vital parts of the speech. If the audience cannot *see* who is speaking, they have difficulty *hearing* the speech. The busier the stage and the larger the cast, the more difficulty the audience will have.

Many devices help you control focus — elevated levels, movement, stage area, lighting, a triangle arrangement of performers pointing at the speaking performer, and so on — but one of the more subtle is audience identification of voice. A particular distinctive voice causes the audience to look at performer A; another unusual voice shifts audience attention to performer B. If all your performers sound alike, the audience will not be able to locate the speaker as easily. Thus casting for ensemble sound permits aesthetic plus technical advantages: smooth control of focus as well as effective music.

Does this mean that in casting your first priority is sounds of voices? No. You must cast the play with well-trained and talented performers who are capable of playing the assigned roles and who will be dedicated and cooperative during rehearsals and production. But the more you can include sounds of voices in your selection criteria, the stronger the final production will be.

Sound Effects

Sound effects are communications. They may be everyday sounds that enhance the mechanical details of the stage action or motivate performers' actions — such as a ringing telephone, the doorbell, thunder, or a toilet flushing — or abstract sounds that stimulate the emotions — such as a "fiddle in the wings," the "sound of a breaking harp string," or a blues piano. Sound effects are usually recorded to be played over the theatre's amplification system, but they can also be live. Sound effects can be realistic and from a motivated source — that is, from a radio or a dance hall across the street — or stylized and from no particular location except the mind.

Sound effects reached new heights during the golden age of radio. They set locale, described environment, and gave emotional cues. Sound effects awoke the audience's imagination. Sound technicians were remarkably inventive. They cut coconuts in half and struck them against a table to create the sound of horses walking or running, crumpled cellophane close to the microphone to sound like a fire (curiously, it also sounded like audience applause), and opened and shut tiny doors to let the listeners know of entrances or exits.

One classic sound effect sequence was the trip to Jack Benny's vault: from the house through the cellar door; down creaky steps; through a hollow stone chamber; under a waterfall; past all sorts of traps that sprang noisily shut; over a wooden bridge; and past an angry dog, a teeth-snapping alligator, and a guard who asked about a long-dead president. Then came the ticking of a bomb that had to be defused in three seconds, the clicking of the combination lock outside the vault, and so on. In radio soap operas there were the "stingers" — rolling organ chords during foreshadowing, sharp chords at the crisis — that continue to be heavily used in today's television soaps.

Led by a director with a musical vision and blessed with dedicated technicians and a decent sound system, there is nothing to limit theatre's use of music. Ours is an aural as well as visual art, and surely we can employ music's effects just as tellingly as radio did.

MECHANICAL SOUND EFFECTS

Mechanical sound effects are those needed principally to motivate action. Such effects as the ringing of a doorbell or telephone supply motivation to the characters or make action logical. For Saroyan's *The Time of Your Life* there must be remarkable noises of a pinball machine paying off. In Pinter's *The Dumb Waiter* an offstage toilet flushes repeatedly. In some plays from the 1930s through the 1950s a radio or television set is turned on at a remarkably convenient time to catch a news flash that is, in an unfortunate stretch of plausibility, highly significant to the ongoing stage action.

Mechanical sound effects may be live or recorded. Doorbells and telephones are poorly represented by recordings, and therefore you may use live, battery-powered outfits from the hardware store. Usually these are activated by an offstage technician, but in the amateur theatre directors usually prefer to have a cast member, who knows the show's tempo and demands from many rehearsals, operate these effects.

ENVIRONMENTAL SOUND EFFECTS

Sound effects can suggest the onstage environment or the universe beyond the stage proper. Those familiar with radio programs remember cricket sounds that suggested an exterior at night, horns and racing motors that invoked street scenes, or sea gull cries that indicated a beach scene. The stage director may use sound effects such as rain, thunder, traffic noises, forest sounds, and the like. These may be in the script or invented by the creative director. For example, a mournful foghorn might be a significant directorial addition to O'Neill's *Anna*

Christie or Pinter's *The Birthday Party*. Construction noise may be a wise addition to Saroyan's *The Cave Dwellers* or Wilson's *The Hot L Baltimore*.

Sound effects are sometimes found in stage directions at selected moments of the play. As an illustration, in *A Streetcar Named Desire* Williams calls for a symphonic harmony of sound including a tinny "blue piano," an offstage tamale vendor calling "red-hot!," rhumba music from a radio Blanche turns on, the song "Paper Doll" in the bar around the corner, dissonant brass and piano sounds that have no realistic source, "confusion of street cries like a choral chant," thunder, expressionistic minor and major key varsouviana music and a revolver shot from Blanche's memory, a Mexican street vendor calling "flores para los muertos," and cathedral chimes. A dedicated and talented sound crew is essential if such a production is to have the richness envisioned by the playwright.

MOOD-ENHANCING SOUND EFFECTS

Sound effects are at their most magical when they go beyond the mechanical into higher levels of communication. One of theatre's most remarkable uses of sound effects occurs at the end of Chekhov's rich play, *The Cherry Orchard*. The production is full of sound effects in the last moments before the curtain. There is a flurry of exit noises, then finally everyone has left the house. The stage is empty.

First sound effect: carriages driving away.

Silence.

Second sound effect: an ax chopping at a tree.

Old Firs enters, ill and tired. He finds they've forgotten him and left him alone. He lies on the sofa and then is motionless.

Silence.

Third sound effect: "A sound . . . that seems to come from the sky, like a breaking harp string, dying away mournfully."

Silence.

Fourth sound effect: the ax chopping in the orchard.

Curtain.

Few illustrations better demonstrate the power of music — sound effects in this case — to communicate concrete information (the destruction of the cherry orchard) and abstract emotion (grief suggested by the mournful breaking harp string). Chekhov's fondness for sound is also seen in other plays. For example, to the sad farewell scene of *The Three Sisters* he adds a cheerful army band playing in the distance, increasing the poignancy of the moment. Such effects are not limited to the nonmusical production: In the musical-play *Sweeney Todd: The Demon Barber of Fleet Street,* Stephen Sondheim uses an ear-splitting factory whistle as a symbol of the industrial revolution and, by extension, man's inhumanity to man.

Difficulties with sound effects prove the truth of Murphy's Law. Radio broadcasts generally had effective sound, but there were frequent problems. Microphones were sometimes not turned off when expected, and on one show a kindly old uncle figure finished his readings of kiddie stories, assumed his mike was dead, and growled over the airwaves, "That'll hold the little bastards." Often cues were missed. In one tense drama the endangered protagonist told the villain, "All right, you forced me to this: I'm going to shoot you! Take that!" Silence. Desperate, the performer recued the sound technician, "I'm going to shoot you! Take that!" Silence. "I said I'll shoot you. There!" Silence. "All right, my gun doesn't work so I'll throw it away. Luckily I have this knife and I'll stab you to death!" The sound technician finally awoke. "Bang!"

Difficulties with sound effects also plague stage productions: Doorbells stubbornly refuse to ring on cue, telephones do not ring at all so that performers ad lib desperately about hearing the phone and pick up the receiver to talk only to have the phone ring loudly and incessantly; and sound technicians leave the speakers live while cuing in the next band on a record or tape, projecting loud wows to the audience. These technical errors are almost guaranteed to ruin a scene and can be avoided only by careful rehearsal.

Volume levels are difficult to establish correctly. We know movie techniques so well that we ignore the essential difference between film and stage. Of course sound levels are correct in the motion pictures: Sound and voices are both blended electronically, and corrections are made in postproduction editing processes. On the stage, however, natural projection of the voice is always preferred over distracting, intrusive electronic amplification, and there can be no electronic mixing of natural voices and recorded music. The "background music" device so popular in cinema and television must be carefully rehearsed if it is to work for the stage.

Technical problems can happen even in the best-run sound shops with talented operators who love the theatre and faithfully attend rehearsals to become sensitive to the feel of the production so their sound will integrate smoothly with the whole. A careful educational program to train sound booth personnel, attention to detail, and frequent checks of equipment are essential.

One unexpected difficulty with sound effects is that if the effect is not identified by action or dialogue, the audience may not be able to identify it. For example, Pinter's *The Dumb Waiter* calls for a prosaic sound effect: many offstage toilet flushings. Interestingly that particular sound effect is remarkably difficult to achieve, as I learned during rehearsals of the play. Rather confidently we recorded the flushing of toilets in the theatre rest rooms. But when I had the sound played to people unfamiliar with the play, they were unable to identify what they were hearing. We recorded toilets in homes, in restaurants, in apartments, even in a train station. Each time we tested the sound, the listeners did not recognize it. Compounding the problem the play calls for the toilet to flush *after* the character has used it, pulled the chain, and returned to the stage. The belated sound is symptomatic of a failed piece of plumbing and of the way everything is going wrong for the characters. There is no specific dialogue to identify the sound.

Finally I added a piece of business: The man returned, fastening his belt and starting to zip up his pants — cue sound— he heard the belated flush, reacted, and then finished zipping. We tested that on an audience, and they immediately identified the sound correctly.

Sound effects can be remarkably effective if thoroughly tested and carefully worked into the production. Action and words will help the audience identify sound effects, but before opening you should test the effect on an audience unfamiliar with the show and sound. You must be prepared to spend rehearsal time working to find the correct effect, sometimes testing dozens of effects; more time will be necessary to ensure that everything works, including cues, timing, speaker location, duration of sound, and volume.

Instrumental Accompaniment

Instrumental accompaniment for stage drama has a distinguished history. The Greek theatre used instruments to emphasize special moments in both tragedy and comedy. The Elizabethans, too, had an orchestra for plays; Shakespeare's Globe had a special balcony constructed for musicians, and Shakespeare's plays are rich in song and dance. The seventeenth-century French dramatists used instrumental selections before, during, and after productions. Colonial theatre in America also depended heavily on the talents of instrumentalists.

Modern playwrights frequently use music to enhance the play's mood and environment. For example, Lanford Wilson has a radio playing in the opening of *The Hot L Baltimore,* William Saroyan uses a jukebox in *The Time of Your Life,* and Arthur Miller uses a phonograph in *A View from the Bridge.* In *The Glass Menagerie* Tennessee Williams has Tom become a narrator to say that this is "a memory play" and "that explains the fiddle in the wings," and throughout the play there is both realistic music (from a nearby dance hall) and nonrealistic music (the threatening tones from the dance hall and waltzes without source).

Musicals make rich use of music to tell the story and enhance emotion. Music is to the drama as poetry is to prose: Sometimes mere words cannot fully express an emotion; only music is large enough to express the feeling. Words cannot handle the need for faith as well as the song "You'll Never Walk Alone" from *Carousel.* Bleak dark humor is given special musical emphasis in "A Little Priest" from *Sweeney Todd: The Demon Barber of Fleet Street.* Emotions are stirred repeatedly in *Fiddler on the Roof* with "Sabbath Prayer," "Tradition," and "Sunrise, Sunset." In *My Fair Lady* "I've Grown Accustomed to Her Face" tells the audience that Professor Higgins misses Eliza; its nonmusical forebear *Pygmalion* relies on well-played subtext to make the point.

PRESHOW, ENTR'ACTE, AND CHASER MUSIC

Your vision may suggest music to open the show, to be played during intermissions, or to close the show. The music can be recorded or live, composed especially for this production, or drawn from stock. Music should be instrumental

A successful production of *The Time of Your Life*
requires careful attention to musical effects. Notice the
pianist up left center, playing for the dancer center
stage (Gene Kelly, in this photograph from the original
Broadway production codirected by Eddie Dowling
and William Saroyan). During the play there will be
music from the juke box down left. And the young
man down right plays the pinball machine during the
entire play, which means there must be subtle sound
effects that will not distract from the action; in the last
act he finally wins the game, calling for a number of
special, varied sound effects to accompany his victory.
— *Photograph courtesy of the Library of Congress*

not vocal. If timing problems make it necessary, the sound crew can fade out
instrumentals without causing much pain to music lovers, but fading out vocals
calls attention to technique and suggests poor timing.

Preshow music, playing when the audience arrives, can stimulate emotional
sensitivities and help the audience prepare for the production just as an overture
prepares the soul for a musical. In a clean-running show the music will be back-
timed so it ends precisely as the house lights are fading into show lights.

Entr'acte music is played between the acts. It usually begins in the spirit that
concludes the preceding act, and then makes a transition to the mood that opens
the following act. Entr'acte music should be carefully back-timed to end just as
the next act is ready to begin.

Chaser music (the term used in musical theatre) is played as the audience
leaves the theatre. Chaser music may reflect the mood of the play's conclusion or,
in a tragedy, it may create a more positive atmosphere. Such music does not need
to be timed because it can play until the entire audience has left the auditorium.

BRIGHTON BEACH MEMOIRS
SOUND DESIGN FINAL PLOT

PRESHOW

	NBC Chimes	.05
1932	Say It Isn't So	2.57
1917/1938	Oh Johnny	4.05
1939	Oh! You Crazy Moon	3.22
	It's A Sin To Tell A Lie	2.44
	In The Still Of The Night	3.08
	Brother Can You Spare A Dime	3.08
1929	Until The Real Thing Comes Along	3.13
1936	The Glory Of Love	2.50
1927	Stardust	3.19
	The Clouds Will Soon Roll By	3.13
1929	This Joint Is Jumpin	2.39
1937	You Made Me Love You	3.53
1938	Moonlight Serenade	3.19
1928	Let's Misbehave	2.04
	It's The Girl	3.12
1935	Summertime	4.26
1931	I Surrender Dear	3.30
1931	Life Is Just A Bowl Of Cherries	1.21
	I Want To Be Bad	3.03
1933	Did You Ever See A Dream Walking	3.17
1929	Ain't Misbehavin	2.10
		TOTAL TIME 62.38

ENTR'ACT

1936	Pennies From Heaven	3.48
1933	Temptation	3.01
1929	Your Feet's Too Big	2.54
	Pepsi Cola	
	Halo Shampoo	.51
1939	Little Brown Jug	2.46
1933	We're In The Money (The Gold Digger's Song of 1933)	3.06
1939	Pavanne	3.10
		TOTAL TIME 19.36

CHASER

1939	In The Mood	3.17
1929	Broadway Melody	1.04
1935	Rug Cutter's Swing	2.59
1930	Peanut Vendor	4.24
1939	Glen Island Special	2.57
	Let's Put Out The Lights And Go To Sleep	3.36
		TOTAL TIME 18.17

EMERGENCY MUSIC		
	Swing Low	2.20
1924	Lady Be Good	3.00
1923	Linger Awhile	2.46
1927	Me And My Shadow	2.58
	Don't Get Around Much Anymore	3.16
		TOTAL TIME 14.20

A sound design by Tyler Lincks for a William and Mary Theatre production of Neil Simon's *Brighton Beach Memoirs,* directed by the author. Because Simon's comedy takes place in 1937, selection of music was designed to evoke the period (the left column indicates the year of the recording). To help audiences enter the spirit of the 1930s, all preshow, entr'acte, and chaser music was piped not only into the auditorium but also into the lobby where the music apparently emanated from an antique wooden radio. Numbers on the right indicate each piece's playing time, to help ensure accurate timing of all effects to coordinate with the beginning and ending of each act.

INTEGRAL OR INCIDENTAL INSTRUMENTAL MUSIC

Instrumental music may be integral or incidental. *Integral* music is built into the script by the writer or the director; dialogue stops for integral music. *Incidental music* is "background music" usually added by the director. It plays at a significantly lower volume than the dialogue, which normally continues over the music.

Instrumental accompaniment may be recorded or live. You can often purchase or rent recordings of instrumental music from the play's professional production. The play publisher–leasing agent's catalog describes the availability of the recordings, or you may find reference to them in the playscript. Experience suggests you order such records early and test the effect to be sure you want to use it. Quite candidly many are pretty awful.

Even if the recorded music is good, the effect is inflexible; performers must cope with the recording's timing, which may not fit the dramatic values of your production.

If your music is live, you must plan well in advance to deal with the physical presence of the musical group: music stands, orchestra lights, a place for the musical director to lead the group while at the same time seeing and hearing the performers, and the visual distractions musicians may create when playing or waiting for the next cue. Despite the many seemingly insurmountable difficulties, given a choice, most directors would prefer live musicians to a static recording.

Music may be original for the production or drawn from stock. If drawn from stock, you will be sure that the music exists and is ready for use when rehearsals begin. You will know its quality from the beginning. On the other hand, stock music will have been written for a different purpose from your production and at best can only be wedged into the show.

Original music has the potential of being much more effective than stock music. Original music is particularly exciting if the composer is sensitive not only to musical values and the playscript but also to the developing qualities of the performers and the director's goals. Such composers, admittedly rare, may live within your area and may accept the challenge of composing original music for your production.

Musical Effects and the Director

Regardless of what effect is used — from mechanical sound effects to original music with a live orchestra — it must be brought into rehearsals early and made part of the whole production. It is a disservice to the production to postpone sound rehearsals until the week the show is to open. As an effective director you should ensure that performers can work with sound, just as they work with props, costumes, and sets, to exploit the music's contributions to the production. Careful rehearsals with the effects are essential.

Often the playwright calls for a particular effect. However, you should not hesitate to use music and sound effects even if they are not written into stage directions. You should feel free to use music just as you use costumes, makeup, scenery, or lighting to enhance your production.

Exercises

Analyze music's contributions to the play you are to direct. Discuss each of the following items in appropriate detail.

1. What is the name of the play? The playwright?
2. What are the musical effects of the play's diction? Use quotations to illustrate your conclusions.
3. What is each character's ideal vocal quality? Assuming you will have the luxury of choice at auditions, what vocal qualities will you seek?
4. What effects does the playwright call for? What is the purpose of the effect? What would be the sound source? Will the sound be live or broadcast over the speaker system? Where should speakers be located?
5. What instrumental music is called for by the playwright? Why does the author call for it? What type of music is it? What would be the sound source?
6. What instrumental music do you want to add? What would you seek to accomplish? Would the music attempt to be of its period (e.g., Elizabethan for a Shakespeare play) or to contrast against it (e.g., jazz for a Shakespeare play, Bach for a modern drama)? Explain your choice. Will the music amplify the script's emotion or deliberately be its opposite? For each effect, specify cue, timing, and duration.

7. What preshow music do you want? Name the album, the name of the record company, and the band number(s).
8. What entr'acte music will you use? Be as detailed as in your answer to question 6.
9. What music will be appropriate for the chaser? Be as detailed as in your answer to question 6.
10. If the music is live, what is the desired effect? What should be played? When? For what duration? Describe the physical arrangement of musicians, their location on- or offstage, lighting, music stands, etc.

I have rarely had so strong a sense of the physical presence of words as I did while watching Moses Gunn overmaster *Othello* at Stratford, Connecticut. Words are intellectual constructs, they come dry from the mind and we try to keep them dry, like powder. Tools to be bandied about swiftly, used for our bland busy projects, little efficiency experts to be sent trotting down hallways on trimly shod feet. . . .

Mr. Gunn, patently and justly and joyously in love with Shakespeare, treated them otherwise — as sound formed by lips, with the lips lingering over the birth rite, as pulsations from a larynx that was soft and giving to begin with, as reverberations from cords that might have a twanging toughness of their own but that made their first impact on flesh. . . .

Thus Mr. Gunn, thus the singing *Othello*. . . .

We knew, in this moment, that we were listening to an aria. We also realized, at the moment, that *Othello* is in very large part composed of arias. That is an easy thing to forget when we busy ourselves with character motivations and all the paraphernalia of textbook criticism.

—WALTER KERR
God on the Gymnasium Floor

CHAPTER NINE

Spectacle: The Visual Aspects of Production

If one believes that "theatre" merely means the drama of the word, it is difficult to grant it can have an autonomous language of its own: it can then only be the servant of other forms of thought expressed in words, of philosophy and morals. Whereas, if one looks on the word as only *one* member of the shock-troops the theatre can marshall, everything is changed.

But the theatre is more than words: drama is a story that is lived and relived with each performance, and we can watch it live. The theatre appeals as much to the eye as to the ear.

—EUGENE IONESCO
Notes and Counter-Notes

Theatre, an intensely visual art, derives a significant amount of its aesthetic appeal from spectacle. *Spectacle* is to the eye as *music* is to the ear. It refers to all the visual aspects of theatre, such as scenery, lighting, costumes, and makeup; the performers' physical appearance and placement on stage; dance, movement, and gesture; and the auditorium and stage themselves. When you direct, you use the stage's visual attributes to touch the audience, seeking to stimulate imagination; project a sense of beauty; and communicate the play's meaning, plot, and character to the audience.

Spectacle has been a significant force in Western theatre from the art's origin centuries ago in Greece. Available evidence indicates that the Greeks were canny showmen who used spectacle to create exciting theatre. They built fine bowl-shaped amphitheatres with excellent views of the stage, and appealed to the audience's eyes with such devices as costumes and masks that enriched and heightened the performer, and dance movement in the entrances and exits of the chorus. Even though we cannot actually experience that production style today, there are modern outdoor dramas that share distinct similarities to the visual elements that characterized the Greek theatre. Because we cannot travel in a time machine to see those productions, to help explain Greek theatricality many theatre experts conjecture that today's grand operas are roughly comparable, in content and staging, to the Greek tragedies, and our musical comedies approximate the Greeks' comedies. In our opera and musical comedies, as in Greek theatre, spectacle is a major element.

The old adage that says "one picture is worth a thousand words" helps one understand why spectacle has been and is important in theatrical productions. Our audiences speak of going to *see*, not *hear*, a play. Theatre's appeal to the eye can be exciting, a source of satisfying beauty, a remarkable contributor of variety, and a communication of abstract and concrete details of the play's story, characters, and thought. Spectacle provides stimulating opportunities for the creative expressions of production personnel, and they expect your directorial vision to indicate guidelines that will help them make meaningful contributions to visual aspects of the production.

Spectacle is more than mere visual adornment. It is a vital communication from the director through the stage to the audience. In an art that depends on showing rather than telling, we can perceive spectacle's significant contributions to theatrical production:

1. Spectacle establishes environment. It shows when and where the play takes place; it shows the relative importance of the environment on the play's action.
2. Spectacle enriches characterization. Costumes and makeup show significant aspects of the characters; scenic environment shows important qualities concerning income or social class; visual elements such as set, furniture, and set dressing add details about characters' hobbies or other personal interests. Directorial movement and placement of the characters show their individual qualities and relationships with each other.
3. Spectacle indicates mood or style. Colors, lighting intensities, shapes, and characters' movement patterns can show whether the play is tragic or comic, realistic or nonrealistic.
4. Spectacle enhances the play's meaning. Sensitive use of spectacle can communicate a sense of balance or imbalance, an atmosphere of happiness or gloom, a feeling of struggle or peace. The director can use such visual communications to impart the thought of the play.
5. Spectacle helps capture and hold the audience's attention. The director's vision may use a great deal of spectacle's effects — as is so often typical in productions of musical comedies such as *My Fair Lady* and *42nd Street* — or may sharply limit spectacle to a few economical devices — as might be appropriate for certain intense dramas such as *Agnes of God*, where too many visuals could distract from the psychological action.
6. Spectacle contributes to the audience's aesthetic pleasure in the theatrical experience. In many productions spectacle contributes a distinct sensory pleasure similar to that of dance, sculpture, painting, or architecture.

Framing your directorial vision of the production, you imagine its visual life in the theatre; on your mind's stage you picture colors, textures, shapes, elevations, and movements combined in a rich panoply for the eye. Your production may have elaborate spectacle — think of *Sunday in the Park with George*, the

At the turn of the century audiences demanded extravagant spectacle, such as Imre Kiralfy's *Venice, the Bride of the Sea.* The artist's versions of two of the many scenes from the 1891 production indicate the remarkably proficient stagecraft techniques of the time. Although much of today's theatre has moved away from this kind of "superb spectacular creation," directors of plays and musicals often search for production techniques that enhance meaning, characterization, and plot while fulfilling audiences' hunger for visual stimulation. — *Photographs courtesy of the Library of Congress*

"Ascot Gavotte" from *My Fair Lady,* or the swirl of the colorful beginning of *Cyrano de Bergerac* — or you may decide the production is best served by limiting visual elements to performers and eliminating all scenery, lighting, and costuming, as described in Jerzy Grotowski's book, *Towards a Poor Theatre.* The sources for spectacle are many: the playwright; designers of makeup, scenery, costumes, and lighting; choreographers; theatre architects' designs of stages and auditoriums; and inventive directors. In the final analysis, spectacle realizes the director's image of the production, derived from careful study of the script.

THEATRE ARCHITECTURE AND SPECTACLE

Modern theatre buildings typically lack the grandeur of Greek amphitheatres or the easy flow of movement of the Elizabethan Globe. Today's theatre is often

kept within the confines of the proscenium arch, which has its roots in the Teatro Farnese at Parma (1618). The proscenium design is with us yet, even though the Teatro Farnese was a haven not for theatre but for scene painters and operatic productions, the former because the picture frame concept encourages drawing with forced perspective, and the latter because opera benefits from the aesthetic distance the proscenium provides.

There are notable exceptions to the proscenium design in buildings designed for dramatic productions instead of old scenic design techniques. The Stratford, Ontario, Festival Theatre is one such exception, as is a revised version of that building, the Guthrie Theater in Minneapolis. Both theatres use the thrust stage design, sometimes called a cloud stage, which makes the stage a peninsula bound on three sides by the audience. Another modern design concept is theatre in the round, also called arena staging, exemplified by the Arena Stage in Washington, D.C. Arena staging, with its central playing area completely surrounded by audience, provides excellent intimate relationships between audience and performer.

Production Styles

Style has things to say. In art, stylistic position is a moral position, an intellectual position, and carries the real content, the real meaning.

—RICHARD FOREMAN
cited in *American Theatre,* July/August, 1987

Today's outdoor dramas have many production devices similar to those in ancient Greece, as illustrated in this picture of The Old Mill Theatre, home of the outdoor drama, *The Shepherd of the Hills*, in Branson, Missouri. Note the bowl-shaped amphitheatre, large audience capacity (seating for 3000 people), and excellent views of the playing area. The structure on center stage is reminiscent of the Greek *skene* or stage house; the stage design permits a number of entrances and exits including several from the audience area. Outdoor dramas such as *The Shepherd of the Hills* are popular with a widely divergent audience, another resemblance to Greek theatre.

Style is a characteristic way of expressing a vision. When a number of artists share the same basic qualities of that expressive statement, we perceive a *genre* or class. For example, in pop culture we know there is a heavy metal rock musical genre, a television sitcom genre, and a gothic romance novel genre. In theatre we speak of a playwriting genre we call realism and a directorial staging genre we call presentational. Style, then, applies to individuals or groups.

Style is the province of all artists, but in our specialized study of play direction we are concerned with style as it pertains to playwright, director, and performer. By style in the playscript we mean the way the playwright has consciously, even subconsciously, decided to put together the various elements of the play to achieve a unified artistic whole. Of course the process is necessarily affected by his or her era and contemporaneous events, as well as by existing theatrical prac-

Well-planned visual excitement combines a theatrical
replica of the tramp freighter "S. S. Glencairn" with
fine compositional placement of performers to create
spectacle in this production of Eugene O'Neill's *The
Moon of the Caribbees* by the Minnesota Theatre
Company, codirected by Douglas Campbell and
Edward Payson Call and designed by Lewis Brown. The
designer's use of levels allows freedom in composition;
and despite an apparently complex arrangement, the
director can easily focus the viewer's eye on significant
action at any place on the stage.

Outdoor drama uses many forms of spectacle, as
exemplified by this production of Paul Green's
musical-drama *Texas* presented in Palo Duro Canyon
State Park near Amarillo, Texas, directed by Neil Hess.
The rich natural setting, clever directorial composition
and use of the stage areas, and large casts (over 80
actors, singers, and dancers) contribute to this outdoor
drama's popularity: *Texas* has played to some 1.8
million spectators in 21 summers. Note the stage
architect's contribution of a tripartite stage — a large
center playing area with two smaller stages on each
side — which allows increased spectacle while
bringing the action closer to the audience.
— *Photograph by Bill Rhew*

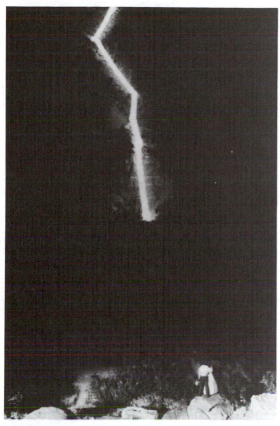

Vivid lighting effects add to the spectacle of *Texas* and enhance this outdoor production. A flash of lightning crackles down a 600-foot cliff, and fireworks are part of a sound and light show finale. L. Lynn Hart is lighting designer and technical consultant for *Texas.*
— *Photographs by Bill Rhew*

tices. As directors we respond to the style present in the script to develop the requisite staging style that brings the script to life. Style in production refers to conscious and subconscious directorial choices of staging techniques — such as representational or presentational, realism, or other approaches — and concrete theatrical techniques, including acting and design elements.

Influenced by Freud, Jung, and others who taught that heredity and environment shape humankind today and direct tomorrow's destinies, modern theatre frequently uses physical surroundings as a mirror that reflects the character and his or her environment, telling the observer a great deal about the hidden personality of the occupant. Using a myriad of details or simple implied sketches of area, spectacle communicates important details to enhance the play's plot, character, and thought. Thus you may stage a play in a naturalistic down-and-out bar

Musical theatre excels in spectacle, using scenery, costumes, lighting, and performers. Here director-choreographer Gower Champion perfectly uses performers and set to create an exuberant scene in *42nd Street*. The well-planned symmetrical placement of performers frames the dancer's jump, and the director cleverly lowers the head line of the performers up center to make that jump appear even higher. — *Photograph copyright 1984 by Martha Swope*

with murky corners that do not threaten the drunk *(The Iceman Cometh),* in a realistic room with exaggerated mammoth masculine furniture and animal heads on the wall *(Happy Birthday Wanda June),* or on a nonrealistic set consisting of platforms surrounded by black curtains with performers dressed in brown shirts and pants and wearing white wire skeletal outlines of horses' heads *(Equus).*

To develop spectacle in your directorial vision of the play you will direct,

American theatre buildings at the beginning of the
nineteenth century were based on a "bigger is better"
concept, as seen here in an artist's rendering of The
Bowery Theatre in New York. Imagine what it would
have been like to sit in the back row straining to hear
and see the action! Performers attempting to project
character and words to the 3000-seat house would
have to rely on the largest gestures and the loudest
tones. Modern theatrical practice avoids such
exaggeration and seeks subtler qualities in pursuit of
truth. This requires architectural designs that offer
more intimacy by placing audiences closer to the
action. — *Illustration courtesy of the Library of Congress*

think of scenery, lighting, and costuming, which use shape, texture, color, and
movement to impart to the audience a sense of the play's emotional qualities, its
time and place, and an expression of its subject and theme. A vital part of your
vision is selection of the production *style,* its approach or image.

Depending on your vision and play interpretation you have a number of
styles from which to choose. Your first choice is between two basic styles: *representational,* or *realism,* and *presentational,* or *nonrealism.* To illustrate the visual

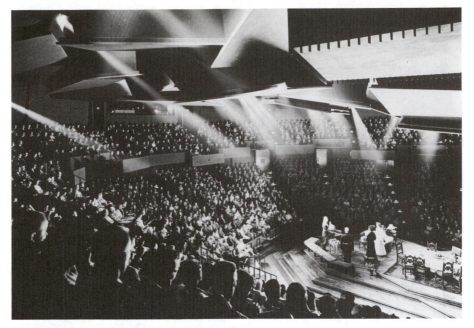

Thrust stages, such as the Guthrie Theater in Minneapolis (above), and theatres in the round, such as the Arena Stage in Washington, D.C. (opposite), are designed specifically for theatrical productions and allow each audience member to sit relatively close to the stage. The Guthrie also features *vomitoria*, or ramps under the audience, downstage left and right, to facilitate entrances and exits. Both of these organizations are known nationally for their fine productions, which are aided by their excellent architectural designs. — *Photographs courtesy of the Guthrie Theater and Arena Stage*

aspects of these two styles, let us assume you are planning to direct *Agnes of God*. A representational scenic approach would depict a psychiatrist's crowded office and the sparsely furnished rooms in a convent, changing scenery elements to show movement from the office to the convent, and using motivated light sources (lamps, windows). A presentational scenic approach to the same play might use black curtains for walls, no changes of scenery, a few selected pieces of furniture to suggest the doctor's office, and pools or shafts of lights that ignored motivational sources. Both styles are truthful; a nonrealistic approach simply uses symbols to achieve its goal. Representational theatre suggests a photographic reality; presentational theatre implies use of suggestive images. Most theatrical productions of *Agnes of God* employ the presentational approach; the movie version, however, clearly used the representational concept.

A popular design style today is *realism,* or its adaptive form called *selective* or *modified realism,* but among the many other options are naturalism, expres-

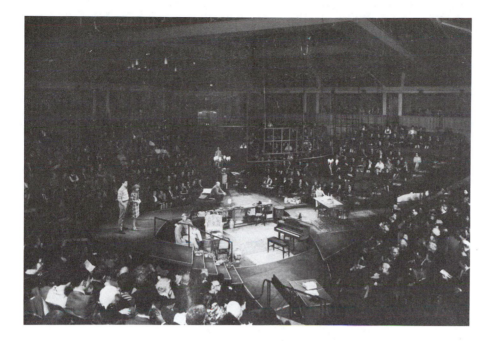

sionism, constructivism, and theatricalism. These styles are often interwoven, and combinations, such as expressionism-realism, are frequently employed.

It is beyond the scope of this book to examine all design styles, but the following discussion covers concepts that are important to you as a director. You will want to study the large number of production values that contribute to spectacle. Practical backstage experience plus lighting, scene, and costume design texts will be valuable aids to your education. Most importantly you will want to attend many productions to discover how spectacle communicates to the audience.

REALISM

Realism is a concept applicable to script, design, and performance. In this context it means a selective representation of the objective world, faithfully depicted without exaggeration. Realism is immediate and contemporary, in contrast to romanticism's focus on exotic places or long-past times. Typical action examines a social situation, as we see in such plays as Ibsen's *Ghosts* and *Hedda Gabler;* the thought usually carries an implied criticism of the situation the play portrays; the characters are like "those who may live next door," not aristocrats; and the diction is an artistic reproduction of "the way people usually speak" without soliloquies or asides. Performers seek to reproduce lifelike characters.

The visual aspects of realism depict the environment one would expect to find within the world that the particular characters inhabit, one the audience can recognize as true or even like their own. Realistic scenery, often married to the box set, stresses dimensionality and practical doors and windows, not flats

Realism's fidelity to detail is shown in this photograph of *Hedda Gabler*. Note the furnishings, carpet, chandelier, door and window treatments, wall decorations, properties, and costumes, which all combine to give the production a sense of its time and place. Barbara Clayton directed the production at the University of Wisconsin, Madison. — *Photograph courtesy of the University of Wisconsin, Madison*

painted to suggest doors and windows; its scenery is also designed according to accepted architectural concepts about placement of stairs, interior and exterior doors, and room location. Costumes, furniture, and properties are carefully selected to fit the time and place.

MODIFIED OR SELECTIVE REALISM

Theatre now is less enslaved by realism than it was in Ibsen's time, and scripts and production design freely marry a number of forms into an eclectic style that

Modern theatrical realism presents details of the play's
universe. In this production of Marsha Norman's
'Night, Mother note environmental details such as the
wallpaper, carpet, furniture, books, photographs, and
other specific items the characters would realistically
have in their home. The visual aspects of the stage
echo the play's concern with love and communication
between mother and daughter, played by Georgine
Hall (left) and Veronica Castang (standing), in the
production at the Guthrie Theater directed by
Christopher Markle; set and costumes by Jack Edwards.
— *Photograph by Joe Giannetti*

uses parts of many styles. Modified realism, popular today, is more suggestive than
"pure" realism's attention to a detailed representation. Carefully selected portions, not the fully detailed set, are put on stage, giving theatre an exciting freedom. Modified realism appeals to the audience's imagination, stimulating them
to participate actively in envisioning the set and, in a sense, fill in the missing
pieces.

EXPRESSIONISM

Expressionism is a term applied to script, production techniques, and performance. While realism is an objective representation of the world perceived
through the five senses, expressionism is an intensely subjective and nonobjective
view of the world seen through the mental eyes of one individual, typically the
play's protagonist.

A realistic set frames the action of the comedy *Arsenic and Old Lace* as presented by the Heritage Repertory Theatre at the University of Virginia, directed by George Black and designed by Charles Caldwell. Note the dimensionality shown in the door, walls, and stairs. Furnishings, too, are realistic: The antique phone (center) and the twist doorbell (to the right of the door handle) show realism's attention to theatrical detail. — *Photograph courtesy of the Heritage Repertory Theatre, University of Virginia*

Expressionism has two basic origins. One, which we might call the Strindberg variation, attempts to reflect the workings of the inner mind, inevitably warped and distorted. The world of the play is seen through the mind of a central character, usually the protagonist, who goes through trials that further disturb the mind. This form of expressionism was influenced by the studies of Freud and others into dreams, nightmares, and the layers of the subconscious mind. Two examples of the Strindberg variation are his play, *The Ghost Sonata,* and the old German silent film, *The Cabinet of Dr. Caligari.*

The second variation of expressionism is the German school, initiated after that country's defeat in World War II by what was seen as victory of machine over

Selective or modified realism often features incomplete or cutaway walls, as used here for a production of Harold Pinter's *The Dumb Waiter*. Included are the essential stage pieces such as the dumb waiter (center), furnishings, and doors; nonessentials are eliminated, and the whole is placed in front of black curtains that mask backstage areas. Such selectivity encourages the audience to imagine the rest of the environment. Pragmatic as well as artistic considerations may suggest the use of selective scenic concepts: This Pinter play was one of six one-acts presented three a night on alternating nights at the College of William and Mary, and six full-scale sets were not feasible. All six productions had design by Larry Miller, technical direction by Al Haak, and direction by the author. — *Photograph courtesy of the William and Mary Theatre*

humankind. In this variation the individual is seen as a victim of machinery. Two examples of this variation are Elmer Rice's play about a vast mechanism, *The Adding Machine,* and the Chaplin movie, *Modern Times.*

Naturally enough distinctions between the two variations blur with time and experimentation, and a combined expressionistic style is seen in plays such as O'Neill's *The Hairy Ape* with its exaggerated machinery — the furnaces — and distorted view through the central character's eyes — the people who completely ignore Yank as if he were not present.

In its origin expressionism demanded of the performers a highly stylized approach, vocally oratorical and physically stiff and stilted. Many characters were designed to be played mechanically rather than humanly. Performers were to reflect the characters' nonreal nightmare existence, and therefore the acting style had to be deliberately nonrealistic, declamatory, and erratic. Today that acting approach has mostly disappeared on the premise that audiences do not accept what appear to be merely poor performance techniques; today's directors are likely to use realistic acting within expressionistic productions.

Expressionism does not necessarily demand a full stage set: An expressionistic approach may focus on significant portions of the whole. Expressionistic scenery usually shows tilted walls or jagged unfinished lines, with details enlarged to express the play's basic concept. For example, in *The Hairy Ape* expressionistic scenery for the stokehole might double or triple the size or number of furnaces, making the humans small slaves in comparison. The furnaces might be warped, perhaps shaped vaguely like a monster's maw. Brilliant white-red lights from the fires inside would create grotesque shadows of the stokers when the doors were open and contrasting gloom when closed. The furnaces could be less dimensional than a realistic approach might demand. With emphasis on the furnace openings, the rest of the set might be nondescript.

Expressionism as a "pure" form is seldom seen in today's theatre. The modern director is not likely to have many opportunities to direct a totally expressionistic production. But if pure expressionism is no longer alive, portions of the form are found in otherwise realistic productions. For example, the appearance of Ben in Arthur Miller's *Death of a Salesman* is expressionistic — Ben exists only in Willy's memory, not in the objective world — and all of Tennessee Williams's *The Glass Menagerie* has a certain expressionistic diffused quality because, as Tom says, it is a "memory play." Both plays *use* expressionism, but are not expressionistic. Musicals, too, make effective use of expressionistic moments: The crap shooters' scene in *Guys and Dolls* is enhanced by expressionistic distortion, and the various deaths in *Sweeney Todd: The Demon Barber of Fleet Street* have expressionistic overtones.

THEATRICALISM

Theatricalism is an innovative style that shows the audience the artifices of the theatre. Instead of realism's illusion, which claims the stage has been transformed into someone's bar or living room, theatricalism shows all the trappings of the stage. One common aspect of theatricalism is visible light sources, with the instruments and towers seen on the stage instead of hidden away as would be required for realism Theatricalism marks typical productions of *Jesus Christ, Superstar; Indians;* and such nontraditional techniques as multimedia, epic theatre, or environmental theatre productions.

Brecht works, such as his epic theatre play, *The Private Lives of the Master Race,* and musicals such as *Sweeney Todd: The Demon Barber of Fleet Street* can make effective use of theatricalism. Theatricalism is typically an inherent quality

The Glass Menagerie, basically a realistic play, has expressionistic overtones as shown in this picture of the Virginia Players (University of Virginia) production directed by Paul Stenard. The scrim, or theatrical gauze, diffuses this dinner table scene to give it the mystic aura of memory — as Tom says in the play, "This is a memory play" — that is a characteristic device in expressionism. — *Photograph courtesy of the Virginia Players*

of arena stage productions because there are no backstage areas for concealment of theatrical devices.

SYMBOLIC VALUES

Spectacle can also be a symbolic statement. Federico Garcia-Lorca's *Blood Wedding* takes place in a white room in which women dressed in blue are winding red yarn. The symbols are important to the play: white for the body, blue for veins, and red for blood. The stokehole is an operational symbol for *The Hairy*

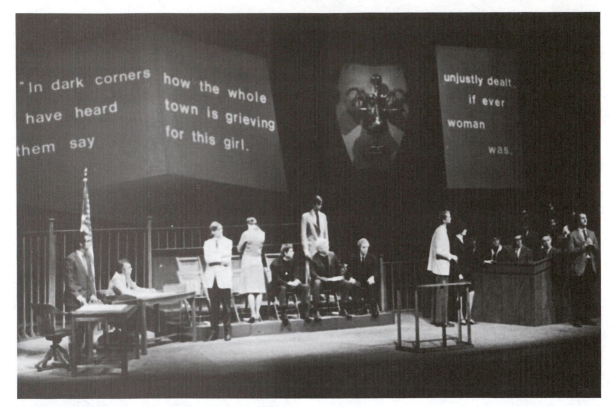

Theatricalism adds impact to Daniel Berrigan's *The Trial of the Catonsville Nine*, a controversial docudrama that dramatizes the trial of protestors to America's involvement in the Vietnam war. The projection screens (the production used two more screens not visible in this photograph) were used for photographs, abstract images, and words, as seen here in this picture of the William and Mary Theatre production designed by Jerry H. Bledsoe and directed by the author. A mask composed of the scales of justice loomed heavily over the action. — *Photograph courtesy of the William and Mary Theatre*

Ape; it furthers the action of men laboring like animals to carry the spoiled upper-class passengers.

Spectacle often shows various cosmic, social, and personal influences on the universe of the play. For example, in Sam Shepard's *Fool for Love* the walls imprison the characters; the "feminine" flowers illustrate thematic questions in Harold Pinter's *A Slight Ache;* and the open stage, without scenery, allows Thornton Wilder freedom to explore universal concepts in *Our Town*.

As you analyze the play to develop a conceptual interpretation, clearly you must consider the many contributions of spectacle. Start by searching for the author's vision of the play (often explicitly stated in stage directions). When you are confident you understand the playwright's reasons for calling for this or that visual aspect of production, you will be ready to move to your interpretation of those visual qualities and shape your directorial vision of the production's spectacle.

Exercises

Analyze the elements of spectacle in the play you will direct. The following questions will help you explore visual aspects of the play.

1. What is the name of the play? The playwright?
2. How many different scenes are in the play? Describe the spectacle in each. What are the playwright's specifications?
3. How is spectacle an environmental influence to the characters and the action?
4. Is spectacle a symbolic statement of the play's actions, thought, or characters? Describe.
5. Can the play take place in an environment other than that specified by the playwright, or is that particular environment essential? What other environment is possible or why is the specified environment essential?
6. Should the production use realistic design? Expressionist? Theatrical? Constructivist? Modified realist? Explain your conclusions.
7. What is the prime source of spectacle? Performers? Costumes? Scenery? Lighting? Choreography?
8. What are the pertinent elements of spectacle — costumes, properties, furnishings, makeup, lighting? Explain how each connects with the play's subject and theme.

. . . in the Broadway version of the rock opera, *Jesus Christ, Superstar,* the visual effects almost overshadowed everything else. The entire stage was on hydraulic lifts and rose like a ramp to a height of 20 feet. Amidst clouds of smoke and incense, trapezes holding singers, sinners, and saints were lowered and raised from 40 feet above the stage, while huge sculptured figures moved in and out from the sides. At one point a large shell opened revealing Christ standing on a small platform. Invisibly, the platform rose and Christ ascended in the air as his white robe billowed out below him, blown by a wind machine. At the very end Christ hangs on a cross in a triangle at the back of the stage, which slowly moves toward the audience, suspended in space. Clearly, the interest in spectacle is still with us.

—EDWIN WILSON
The Theater Experience

PART THREE

Preparing for Production

CHAPTER TEN

The Prompt Book

Every element in a staged play is part of its direction. The director writes the "score" or "notes" of the theatrical production; the others play them. One might say that the director is the author of the theatrical production, except for the fact that in the collaborative art of the theatre no one can be more than a crucial collaborator. In the playing of the director's "notes," each of the collaborators — actors, designer, costumer, and so on — brings something of his own individuality or talent to bear.

. . . .

In sound theatrical practice the director should be held responsible for the overall interpretation of a play and its parts. The director should not only set the outline of the actor's interpretation but help him find the method for its concrete embodiment.

—HAROLD CLURMAN
Lies Like Truth

The prompt book contains every detail of the director's plans to construct the production, a concrete design to help you achieve your all-important but often necessarily intangible vision. More than simply "a book from which one prompts the actors," the effective prompt book is a complete record of the director's vision — what Clurman calls the director's "score" or "notes" — encapsulating every aspect of your research, preparation, interpretation, production values, rehearsals, journal or log of the steps along the way, and review of the final production. It will contain all the analysis exercises you completed in Chapters Four through Nine. The prompt book is often called "the production bible" because it is the reference source not only for director and performers but also for the stage manager, property crew, costume workers, lighting personnel, sound effects designer, and all others involved in rehearsals and production.

Aware of the necessity to complete all possible steps of preplanning before any production work begins, experienced directors complete most details of the prompt book before they feel they are ready to conduct auditions. Such directors know that the more planning they do before production work begins, the easier and more profitable rehearsals will be. Countless materials and notes are added during rehearsals and production, so a reader, even one who did not see your

Well in advance of casting and auditions the director carefully plans the staging of special scenes, recording blocking and interpretation notes in the directorial prompt book. Such preplanning allows the director to place focus on dominant characters, as shown here in this scene from *Eccentricities of a Nightingale*, directed by George Black at the Heritage Repertory Theatre, University of Virginia. — *Photograph courtesy of the Heritage Repertory Theatre*

show, would have a richly detailed sense of your work as "the author of the theatrical production."

Think of your prompt book as a toolbox. Like a master carpenter's meticulously cared for equipment, your prompt book should reflect a craftsman's pride in craft and working habits, a sense of pleasure in doing things right. Take pains to be sure your prompt book is rich in details, organized in a logical fashion with all information filed in appropriate divisions that are well marked so that you or an assistant can find necessary data quickly and easily. Even though it is a working document, the prompt book should be reasonably neat; certainly all entries should be legible.

You generally give an assistant the responsibility for much of the mechanical processes of preparing the prompt book and maintaining it during rehearsals. Experienced directors know that during rehearsals they cannot sit with their noses in the prompt book but must concentrate on the performers; as you work with the actors, the assistant writes in the prompt book all new information regarding line interpretation and readings, characterization, blocking, properties, and so forth.

Preparing the Prompt Book

THE PLAYSCRIPT

The core of the prompt book is the playscript. Assuming you are using a standard acting edition obtained from a play publisher–leasing agent such as Samuel French or Dramatists, there are two popular cut-and-paste systems for insert-

Figure 10-1. Tools for constructing the directorial prompt book include (1) a large, sturdy, three-ring notebook; (2) an ample quantity of three-hole-punched, unlined paper for the script plus lined paper for notes in other sections of the prompt book; (3) a sharp knife or scissors; (4) rubber cement (preferred to glue or tape because excess rubber cement can be rubbed off when dry); (5) pencils; (6) colored highlight pens; (7) tab dividers; and (8) the playscript.

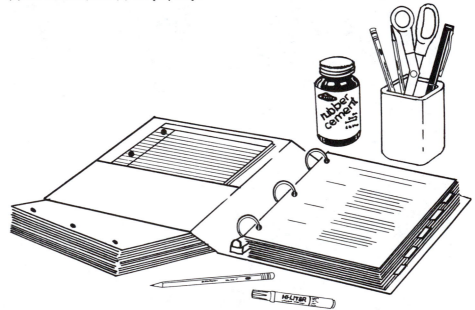

ing the playscript into the prompt book, a sturdy three-ring notebook large enough to contain the script and all other details. Directors often assign this cutting and pasting job to the directorial assistant.

The first method of getting the play into the prompt book requires taking apart two copies of the script. Remove individual pages from the stapled scripts, cut each page into a neat block, and glue the page to three-hole-punched paper. Include all pages from the script, including property lists, sound effects, costume notes, and the like. You now have one script page centered on each sheet of paper, allowing ample room to write notes on the margins and on the opposite, blank page.

The second technique requires taking apart one copy of the script. Remove the script pages but do not trim the margins. Measure the size of the printed area and cut "windows" the dimensions of that area in three-hole-punched sheets of paper. When you glue each script page onto the paper, you will be able to read both sides of the script page. You have, in effect, glued a large margin to each of the script's pages. Both of these prompt book construction processes satisfy the same goals:

1. The director must have a handy copy of the script. It is possible to direct from the playscript instead of the prompt book, but the large prompt book is a constant reference for many production personnel, so it is more efficient to have all materials in one convenient location.

The "Cut-Out Windows" Approach

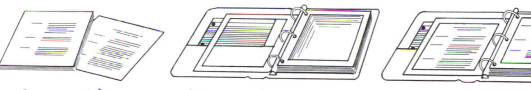

Pages are cut from one copy of the script.

Windows are cut a quarter inch smaller than the pages, and the pages are pasted at each window...

resulting in a prompt book that allows you to see both sides of each script page.

Figure 10-2. The illustration above indicates the use of cutout "windows" to hold the playscript. Note that both sides of the script pages are visible through the window.

The illustration below shows the system of cementing one script page on one page. This provides a blank left page, allowing more room for directorial notes.

The "Non-Window" Paste-Up

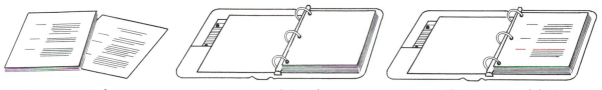

Pages are cut from two copies of the script.

Pages are pasted on the paper...

resulting in a prompt book that leaves the left side blank for directorial notes.

2. Most acting editions are fragile; before production your copy may have fallen apart, but the sturdy prompt book will survive.
3. There must be written notes about line interpretation, lighting cues, blocking, properties, and a host of other information that simply cannot be squeezed onto the tiny margins of the acting edition. The 8½-by-11-inch pages of the prompt book are essential for making these directorial notes.

LINE INTERPRETATIONS, TEMPO GUIDES, AND BLOCKING

On the playscript pages in the prompt book you will write all the decisions and ideas you work out with performers regarding such matters as line interpretations, tempo guides, and blocking. You will write many of these even before meeting with performers and will add others during the rehearsal process. Devise a consistent method of making such notes on the margins — for example, blocking along the right margin, line interpretation and tempo notes in the left margin.

TECHNICAL PRODUCTION DATA

You or your assistant should carefully mark properties, sound effects, lighting changes, curtain cues, and other aspects of production in the margin of the script in the prompt book. You can also list props and other technical materials in a special section of the book. As the director you will create technical cues pertinent to this particular production and will carefully mark them in the prompt book.

HIGHLIGHTING THE SCRIPT

You can use colored highlight pens to mark significant information, lines, or stage directions in the script with eye-catching transparent colors that do not obscure the printed words. You can use the variety of colors in a special code — perhaps orange for lighting, sound, and curtain cues; blue for properties; and yellow for characters' entrances and exits.

[*Scene eight*]

The same. Alarums. Re-enter Antony in a march; Scarus, with others.

IN DARKNESS: shouts of joy; victory off R.
MUSIC: distant military flourishes.

LIGHTS: (delay) fade-in D.R. cove.
ENTER R-1: ANTONY, armed X DRC
SCARUS, wounded
EROS, 3 SOLDIERS
EROS exit L-L

ANTONY is invigorated, magnificent, HERCULES; his troops are chopped to bits. He does not see.

SCARUS' R. arm in bloody sling. He will fail to follow-through, to pursue the escapees — he gets drunk instead.

He is addressing 300 or more, not just the 3 soldiers we see. Use audience as encamped "host."

ANTONY

We have beat him to his camp. Run one before,
And let the Queen know of our gests. To-morrow
Before the sun shall see's, we'll spill the blood
That has to-day escaped. I thank you all,
For doughty-handed are you, and have fought
Not as you served the cause, but as't had been
Each man's like mine. You have shown all Hectors.
Enter the city, clip your wives, your friends,
Tell them your feats, whilst they with joyful tears
Wash the congealment from your wounds, and kiss
The honoured gashes whole.

X base R. steps
SCARUS: shift R. of steps.

ENTER L-3 above, to R. platform:
CLEOPATRA
CHARMIAN, IRAS
EROS

Audience & troops realize that a celebration is premature.

LIGHTS: fade-in R. platform.

Left margin notes (interpretation):

Seen running in silhouette over elevated steps & landings, the women should look like fancy moths or birds alighting in the safety of Anthony's company.

SCARUS in great pain, ANTONY oblivious. SCARUS is propped up by his comrades. Shakespeare's art is verbal! Did any soldier say it half as well?

The great physical joy and the passion of their reconciliation is almost embarrassing to the company.

His nightingale, his girl ...
Here they are at their very best together—young Lovers.
Recalls III-xiii "That head, my lord?" The Lion's head.

This violates decorum. SCARUS is aware of ANT's notorious jealousy. Is this a trick?

Recalls III-xiii, when Thidias is beaten for kissing CLEO's hand.

Again this action causes much pain for SCARUS. ANT. does not see.
ANTONY addresses a huge army, a "host."

Image: Colossus of Rhodes, the demi-Atlas, Dido and Aeneas.

Center (play text):

Enter Cleopatra, attended.

[*To Scarus.*] Give me thy hand,
To this great fairy I'll commend thy acts,
Make her thanks bless thee. O thou day o' th' world,
Chain mine armed neck, leap thou, attire and all,
Through proof of harness to my heart, and there
Ride on the pants triumphing.

CLEOPATRA

Lord of lords.
O infinite virtue, com'st thou smiling from
The world's great snare uncaught?

ANTONY

My nightingale,
We have beat them to their beds. What girl, though grey
Do something mingle with our younger brown, yet ha' we
A brain that nourishes our nerves, and can
Get goal for goal of youth. Behold this man,
Commend unto his lips thy favouring hand.
Kiss it, my warrior. He hath fought to-day
As if a god in hate of mankind had
Destroyed in such a shape.

CLEOPATRA

I'll give thee friend,
An armour all of gold; it was a king's.

ANTONY

He has deserved it, were it carbuncled
Like holy Phoebus' car. Give me thy hand,
Through Alexandria make a jolly march,
Bear our hacked targets like the men that owe them.
Had our great palace the capacity
To camp this host, we all would sup together,
And drink carouses to the next day's fate,
Which promises royal peril. Trumpeters,
With brazen din blast you the city's ear;
Make mingle with our rattling tabourines,
That heaven and earth may strike their sounds together,
Applauding our approach.

[*Exeunt.*

Right margin notes (technical/blocking):

CLEO. et al arrive R. platform, above.
CLEO. X d. steps to ANT.
take SCARUS' hand.

CLEO. tap ANT's L. shoulder
ANT. turn, drop S's hand, give shield to EROS.

ANT. & CLEO. passionate embrace, reverse positions R. to L. on steps, kiss.

General positive vocal reaction.

again reverse positions & Kiss.

Removes helmet.
CLEO's hands in his hair.

Indicate SCARUS, R.
CLEO X R., gives hand.

SCARUS nervously kiss her hand.
3 SOLDIERS disapprove, give R.

3 SOLDIERS advance (reward).

Take her hand from SCARUS, kiss it.
Lead her up steps to R. platform, put on helmet, turn front.
3 SOLDIERS X below steps.
LIGHTS: fade-out D.R. COVE & R. steps.

step forward, grand gesture.

Exeunt L-3 (above), laughter, noise: ANTONY CLEOPATRA

Figure 10-3. For his production of *Antony and Cleopatra* at the College of William and Mary, director Jerry H. Bledsoe prepared the prompt book carefully to ensure a quality production. In these pages from Act Four, Scene Eight, we see the results of that preparation, completed well before his auditions.

Directors create personalized approaches to constructing the prompt book. Bledsoe used the left margin for notes on interpretation and the right side of the page for technical effects such as lighting and music (note the use of all capital letters and underlining), entrances and exits (in all capital letters), and traffic patterns and blocking. Standard abbreviations save space in the crowded margins: Note this director's codes, such as L-1, which refers to the exit-entrance Stage Left 1, and D.R. COVE for the Down Right Cove exit-entrance (downstage of the proscenium opening).

Such meticulous work is necessary for all productions; the work in advance is even more essential when dealing with a complex play such as *Antony and Cleopatra*. The large number of entrances and exits requires charting to maintain a dramatic logic in the physical space and prevent hectic crossovers backstage.

Antony's last speech in Act Four, Scene Eight shows
the results of director Jerry H. Bledsoe's careful
preparation of the prompt book for this production of
Antony and Cleopatra at the College of William and
Mary. Pictured here is the last moment of the scene
detailed earlier in the illustration of sample pages from
a prompt book. Harvey Credle is Antony; Glenn Close,
then an undergraduate student at William and Mary, is
Cleopatra. The director's vision of the script, recorded
in the prompt book in advance of rehearsals, leads to
an exciting theatrical production. — *Photograph
courtesy of the William and Mary Theatre*

TAB DIVIDERS

You can improve your prompt book's organization with tab dividers indicating acts, scenes, French scenes, and action units. In addition, use tab dividers for the information discussed in the following sections of this chapter.

INFORMATION ABOUT THE PLAYWRIGHT

Each playwright is a unique individual with a particular voice and a distinctly personal view of the world and its people. To develop your understanding of the playwright's work you should research the author. Your prompt book should include a section covering such topics as these concerning the playwright:

- Chronological data: birthdate, marriage, and the like.
- Other works: plays, novels, other writing, occupation.
- Playwright's own statements regarding influences. For example, it is helpful for the director to know that Arthur Miller was influenced by Henrik Ibsen, that Tennessee Williams was influenced by D. H. Lawrence, or that Harold Pinter was influenced by American gangster films.
- Education.
- Critical comments and evaluations of the author's work.
- Personal correspondence with the playwright. Many writers will reply to interesting letters from directors.

The playwright's times and theatre. A playwright of the 1980s will necessarily differ from one of the 1960s, who in turn will write differently from a playwright of the 1930s. Equally, a playwright working for today's Broadway theatre will write differently from one writing for off-off-Broadway. Your prompt book should have notes regarding the author's times and theatre.

- For what theatre did the playwright write in particular? For example, we obtain additional insight into *After the Fall* by knowing that Arthur Miller wrote it for Lincoln Center. We can better understand Lanford Wilson's *The Madness of Lady Bright* when we see it in light of his work with Ellen Stewart and her remarkable off-off-Broadway Cafe LaMama.
- What historic events influenced the playwright? Those who wrote in the 1930s — such as Irwin Shaw in *Bury the Dead* and Clifford Odets in *Waiting for Lefty* — were influenced by America's depression. The director who is sensitive to the turmoil around the writer will be able to perceive that writer's plays more accurately.
- Who were the theatre people influencing the playwright? Think of director Elia Kazan's well-documented influence on Tennessee Williams, for example.

The playwright's other works. Playwrights create a rich tapestry of work, individual pieces that combine to create a meaningful whole. If you study only one thread and ignore the others, you miss the richness of that whole. A study of one work enhances your awareness of the others, and a study of all the playwright's works enhances your insight into each particular play.

Include in your prompt book a study of the playwright's other plays or writings as they relate to the play you are directing. If you are directing Arthur Miller's *The Crucible,* for example, you should include comparisons with his novel *Focus* and such plays as *Incident at Vichy* and *The Price.*

INFORMATION ABOUT THE PLAY

Genre and type. Is your play a comedy, tragedy, or drama? Is it realistic, naturalistic, or absurdist? As a director you must take a definitive stand regarding the play. Too many directors, especially those who lack experience, will attempt a Polonius-type answer like, "This is a somber-neoclassic-comedy-tragedy-in-the-modern-absurdist-light-hearted-farcical-vein-with-serious-intent." Such definitions define nothing. A director who defines the play with quibbles is ill-equipped to start rehearsals. Write down your definition, supporting it with specific references to the play, and put it into the prompt book.

The thought. Thought is the intellectual cohesiveness that ties together all the parts of the play. It is, if you will, the play's message. All plays contain thought. You will want to state the play's subject in one word (i.e., "the subject of *Macbeth* is power"). Identify the play's theme — the author's attitude toward the subject as expressed in this play — in a simple sentence (i.e., "the theme of *Macbeth* is that a hunger for absolute power will become absolutely destructive"). When you can identify subject and theme cleanly without equivocation, you have a clear vision that will allow you to communicate precisely with actors, designers, and technicians to create a unified production. Your conclusions regarding subject and theme belong in the prompt book.

Use of the six elements. A given play will stress two or perhaps three of the six elements of drama, may have relatively average use of perhaps four of those elements, and may ignore one or two of them. Your prompt book will contain notes on the play's use of the elements. A simple checklist, such as the following, will help you begin this entry in your prompt book:

The Six Elements	*Playwright's Use* (1 = most; 6 = least.)
Plot	_____
Character	_____
Thought	_____
Diction	_____
Music	_____
Spectacle	_____

The people of the play provide fascinating study. Your prompt book will record significant information about the characters. Among the questions you will need to answer for each character are the following:

- What is the character's superobjective?
- What is the character's spine?
- What are the character's emotional ranges?
- Should the audience like this character?
- Why does the playwright put this character in the play?
- What is the character's "type" (protagonist, antagonist, confidant, utilitarian character, etc.)?
- What is the character's effect on the plot? Does the character cause plot events? Is the character present simply to provide exposition?
- What is the character's importance? For example, is the character essential because he or she is the protagonist, the playwright's spokesperson at the end of the play, or a representative victim to show the negative aspects of a major character?

Include in your prompt book descriptions of characters' specific qualities, including goal or objective; ways in which the character is different from the others, including age, social status, educational background, occupation, mannerisms, and speech patterns; emotional tonality; relationships with other characters and changes in attitudes and relationships as the action progresses; motivational core; reasons for the character to oppose or support other characters; and physical characteristics such as height, weight, and coloring.

AUDITION DATA

Your prompt book should contain materials you need to make auditions effective. What do you need to know at auditions to decide who should be cast? What are you looking for at auditions? What is your ideal cast? Here you want all necessary information to keep a clear concept of your needs during auditions.

Your prompt book should also contain the specific passages from the play that you will use to audition for the protagonist, the antagonist, the confidant, and so on. Include passages to test for a marriage between characters A and B and other pieces to assess characters in groups. The prompt book should contain copies of audition forms you will ask performers to complete.

THE GROUND PLAN

The prompt book should contain copies of the ground plan (also known as the floor plan), which is a scale drawing of the stage floor as seen from overhead. The ground plan shows levels, steps, doors, windows, fireplaces, furniture pieces, and the like. Your scene designer should be able to provide you with the necessary copies of the ground plan, and your assistant will use the plan to place rehearsal furniture correctly on the makeshift stage you use during rehearsals. The ground plan will be essential for blocking.

Some directors photocopy a miniature ground plan onto each page in the prompt book so an assistant can record blocking for each page of dialogue. This system is especially helpful when working with a large cast or a complex set with many levels and the like.

LISTS OF CHARACTERS BY SCENES

The prompt book should contain a checklist showing what characters are in each scene. You will already have divided the script into acts, scenes, French scenes, and action units. Now you will make a "characters by scene chart," as shown here in simplified form.

	ACT ONE				ACT TWO			ACT THREE			
	1-1	1-2	1-3	1-4	2-1	2-2	2-3	3-1	3-2	3-3	3-4
JB	X	X		X	X				X	X	X
TR	X	X			X						
MS			X			X	X	X			
OS			X	X		X	X	X	X	X	X
LT									X	X	X

For a complex production like a musical comedy there will be additional entries for songs, dance numbers, and perhaps ten times as many characters.

The chart helps the director in many ways. For example, if you wish to use actors' rehearsal time efficiently, the chart shows you what scenes you can rehearse in one evening with the same performers. The above chart suggests that rehearsing scenes 1-1, 1-2, and 2-1 together would use the time of JB and TR efficiently; rehearsing scenes 1-1, 1-2, 1-3, 1-4, and 2-1 would be an inefficient use of TR. Of course this is but one technique of scheduling rehearsals. You will often need to schedule continuity rehearsals that ignore efficiency concerns.

The "characters by scenes" chart also gives you insight into the playwright's organizational approach to the play. For instance, in the above example the playwright does not introduce the character of LT until the last scenes of the play, which indicates that the character is brought in to help with plot resolution. That insight may help you cast the role of LT and structure the scenes for production.

REHEARSAL SCHEDULE

Your production's detailed rehearsal schedule, drafted well before auditions, is kept in the prompt book. Changes in the schedule may be necessary when you discover actors' commitments following auditions and casting; but you must have a complete schedule from which to operate. The latest version is kept in the prompt book.

Your rehearsal schedule should be specific. There are no benefits to a schedule that vaguely says, "Monday–Friday, rehearsals 7:00–11:30." You want a more detailed schedule along these lines:

Monday   6:30, company call

6:30–7:00, physical and vocal warmups

7:00–7:15, general announcements

7:15–8:30, work 1-1 for characterization, motivations, goals

8:30–9:15, work 1-2 for characterization, motivations, goals

9:15–10:00, run 1-1 and 1-2 for continuity

10:00–10:30, work with LT and JR for character

BUSINESS MATTERS

The prompt book should contain records of all business dealings. Here you keep copies of your correspondence with the copyright holder; the publisher–leasing agent's statement giving you permission to present the play; and financial records, including copies of checks.

A DAILY JOURNAL

The day-by-day journal in the prompt book is a record of what happened at each rehearsal. You should conscientiously make notes in the journal following each rehearsal. What problems did you encounter? What solutions were attempted? Were they effective? What were your experiments; which seemed beneficial and which counterproductive? What mistakes did you make, and how can you avoid such errors in the future? What went right, and how can you ensure repeating the correct process in the future? Did your schedule call for completion of more than was reasonable?

The journal has a number of advantages for the director's professional growth. If you are faithful about recording the details of each rehearsal's work, the summing up process will be highly educational. If you take time to rethink each rehearsal, you will learn how to handle comparable problems in the future. And you will benefit from thinking over the constant "victories" and "defeats" that fill every director's rehearsals. The ideal journal will be so complete that it will echo the step-by-step creation of the production. It will not achieve its purpose, however, if you miss days and attempt to fill it in a week later.

GOALS FOR THE NEXT REHEARSAL

As you work on the journal you will be thinking of goals you want to pursue at the next rehearsal. Record the goals in your prompt book. Refer to those written goals at the beginning and conclusion of each night's rehearsals. This will help you keep track of your progress as you and the performers work toward opening night.

Exercises

These exercises give you practical steps toward the construction of your prompt book.

1. Purchase a three-ring notebook, several packages of both lined and unlined 8½-by-11-inch paper, and a number of packages of tab dividers.

2. Using the unlined paper, do the cut-and-paste process described earlier to prepare the prompt copy of the script, and insert it in the prompt book.

3. Go through the script with colored highlight pens to mark light, sound, and curtain cues in one color; properties in another color; and characters' entrances and exits in still another.

4. At the top right-hand corner of each script page write the headings: Lights, Sound, Curtain Cues, Properties. Then go through the script and fill in information about each category at the top of each page.

5. Use tab dividers to separate the script into acts and action units.

6. Put the lined 8½-by-11-inch paper and remaining tab dividers into the notebook following the script pages.

7. Label one divider The Playwright. In this section of the prompt book include information about the playwright:
   a. Date and place of birth
   b. Chronological development
   c. Education
   d. Employment
   e. Family life
   f. A chronological list of plays (novels, poems, etc.) written
   g. Statements by the playwright regarding influences on his or her work
   h. Critical reviews of the playwright's work overall and especially of the play you are directing
   i. Scholarly evaluations of the playwright's work, especially of the play you are directing
   j. The theatre for which the playwright worked
   k. The times and historic events influencing the playwright
   l. Theatre people who influenced the playwright
   m. Comparisons and contrasts of other plays

8. Label one tab Genre and Type. In this section define the genre and type of the play you will direct. Is it comedy, tragedy, drama? Is it realistic, poetic, absurdist? Supply specific references from the play to support your definitions.

9. Label one tab Thought. Include in this section:
   a. The play's subject, expressed in one word
   b. The play's theme, expressed in a simple sentence
   c. Specific quotations from the play that indicate something of the play's thought
   d. The relevance of the play's title to the thought

10. Label one tab Plot Analysis. Include in this section:
    a. The inciting incident

     b. The play's point of attack

     c. Foreshadowing, specifying how each instance helps you understand the plot and characters

     d. Complications, giving each a descriptive title

     e. The play's climax

11. Label one tab Characters. Include in this section a list of all the characters. Describe each according to the questions and qualities discussed in this chapter under the heading "Characters: Identification and Relationships" (also see Chapter Five). Include a list of characters by scenes. In particular be sure to identify the protagonist and antagonist, as well as other character types; specify each character's objectives, motivations for those objectives, and obstacles in the path of the objectives.

12. Label one tab Audition Materials. Include audition passages you will use, the form or questionnaire you will ask performers to complete at auditions, and copies of informational materials to be given to performers.

13. Label one tab Ground Plan. Include a copy of the ground plan.

14. Label one tab Production. Include lists and descriptions of scenery, lighting, costumes, sound, properties, makeup, and furniture.

15. Label one tab Rehearsal Schedule. Include a detailed rehearsal schedule.

16. Label one tab Business. In this section place records of expenses and copies of correspondence regarding copyright and production permission.

17. Label one tab Daily Journal. This section will contain your personal record of each rehearsal.

18. Label one tab Goals. Here you will record your goals for each rehearsal.

19. Label tabs for all aspects of play analysis you completed for exercises in earlier chapters, and include your information under appropriate headings.

Before rehearsals begin the director should start planning what has to be created in the background for his concept of the production. He relays this concept and overall style of production to those in charge of music, costumes, props, lighting and scenery, so they too can work to evoke a consistent style. Directors can visit museums and study paintings for composition ideas. Planning sessions with heads of crews . . . help to ensure communication and common goals.

    . . . the director subjects his play to literary, historical, artistic and theatrical analysis. Long before casting and rehearsals begin, the director researches pertinent historic and geographic factors, even visits the locale or a similar location if he thinks it useful. Plays concerned with historical events or periods require careful research. The director's goal is a creative production that accurately reflects the customs and practices of the time frame and stimulates the actors' and audiences' belief.

                                 —LORRIE HULL
                                   Strasberg's Method

CHAPTER ELEVEN

Auditions

John Gielgud greets auditioning actors in a manner which other directors could well emulate. The house lights are half lit, thereby eliminating one of the actor's pet peeves: seeing merely a vast black void out front from which parental voices instruct him. An audience should be a void, no doubt, but a director never should.... Most actors have learned to "perform" at auditions in order to reassure producers, directors, and authors who are normally more terrified than the actor himself, if the actor could only so realize. But such "performances" are parodies, and the director who does not invite them will be given a great deal more. Gielgud is looking for that great deal more. He stands alone, just below the footlights....

And so I read. Some five lines later, Gielgud turned his back and strolled up the center aisle. Momentarily disconcerted, I continued reading. Three lines later, he turned around and returned to the footlights with a smile. He stopped my reading and offered me the part. I realize now that his seeming discourtesy was nothing of the kind. He wanted to hear me for a moment without watching me and also from a distance.

—WILLIAM REDFIELD
Letters from an Actor

Auditions are theatre's mass employment hall, bringing performers and director together under carefully designed conditions that allow performers to show their abilities and the director to evaluate whether their artistic and personal qualities will contribute to the planned production. For performers auditions are uncertain times at best, and the necessary ego involvement creates complex psychological reactions that require you to exercise great sensitivity; your friendly and sincerely supportive attitude helps performers demonstrate their true abilities. Charged with the responsibility of conducting auditions in a manner that is both artistically effective for the production and visibly fair from the performer's view, you may find auditions even more difficult than performers do, and your vision of the production will often seem at risk until auditions have produced a satisfactory cast.

Casting, which is based on directorial insights obtained during unfortunately brief and often regrettably harried auditions, determines much of the produc-

Properly conducted auditions permit the director to
select the best performers for the roles, resulting in a
cast that will bring the director's vision to theatrical
life. One important goal is to achieve an ensemble
with actors who will work closely together in a
dynamic production, as was the case when Richard
Merriman (left) and James Graves performed in the
William and Mary Theatre production of *The Dumb
Waiter*, directed by the author. — *Photograph courtesy
of the William and Mary Theatre*

tion's ultimate quality. Auditions have long-range impact on the tone of rehearsals, the attitudes of performers toward you and the playscript, the interpretation of the script and production, and your ability to weave all portions of production into a single and cohesive whole.

Performers who are cast will have a number of conscious and subconscious conclusions about your professional abilities and interest in the cast, based on how they feel you conducted auditions. Your management of auditions may even affect their responses to one another; poorly conducted auditions may create images of favoritism, special favors, or disregard of talent that can be burrs in actors' minds during rehearsals.

Auditions may also lead performers who were not cast to speak of the director or production in a way that positively or negatively influences public perception of the play. Those comments can affect ticket sales, audience expectations, and other performers' willingness to participate in future auditions conducted by that director or theatrical organization.

Because of the importance of auditions, all members of the theatrical staff — designers, technicians, assistants, and secretarial and office staff — must help the director make the process run as smoothly as possible. Your staff should minimize distractions; nothing should be permitted to interfere with smooth-running auditions, because you must be free to concentrate fully on the performers, searching for those who will bring the desired personal and artistic qualities to the roles.

In well-rounded amateur theatres, auditions encourage those interested in technical theatre to meet with appropriate backstage personnel. This practice helps the theatre find badly needed recruits for properties, carpentry, scene painting, lighting, costumes, box office, and publicity. Educational and community theatres interested in building a core of support workers will encourage this aspect of auditions by having the technical staff present to answer questions and to show, by their presence and attitude, interest in volunteer workers. The theatre with too few volunteer workers is generally one that fails to recruit people at auditions and conveys an attitude that inexperienced volunteers are not worthy of attention.

A Preaudition Checklist

A checklist will help ensure that all necessary preparations are satisfactorily completed before auditions begin. Such a list will vary from organization to organization, but certain basic concepts are always applicable. The sample list below is suggestive, not inclusive; you will think of other steps that are appropriate for your particular situation.

1. Create an effective promotion and advertising campaign well in advance of auditions to inform all potential performers of details such as date, time, and place of auditions; script availability; audition systems; roles available; performance dates; and the like. Promotion avenues you can use include newspaper releases, radio and television announcements, paid advertisements, posters, a telephone campaign, and direct mailing

of postcards or letters.

2. Order scripts four to five weeks before auditions and make them available for performers' preparation.

3. Prepare an informational packet for performers to pick up at the theatre. Include details of rehearsal and production schedule, character descriptions, information about play and playwright, and the story line. Indicate special talents sought, such as dancing, singing, fencing, and tumbling.

4. Select audition passages that will help you judge performers. You will need pieces that challenge performers and show their abilities for major or minor roles.

5. Select audition passages by numbers: one male and one female, two males, two females, three males, and comparable combinations.

6. Arrange for two or three assistants to staff the lobby audition desk, greet performers as they arrive, have them fill out necessary forms, answer questions, and escort them into the audition hall.

7. Prepare audition forms.

8. Reserve the audition hall. Your assistant should be sure the room is ready, with a desk and chairs for the production staff as well as facilities for performers. If you are auditioning for a musical, you'll need a piano and a wooden rather than concrete or tile floor for dance auditions.

9. If you anticipate a large turnout, which will make it difficult to remember every performer, have an audition assistant use an instant camera to take photographs of performers, individually or in groups of five or so. The assistant should write names on the back of the picture, ready to jog your memory later.

10. Prepare to take notes during auditions. Detailed comments are necessary to help you recall each performer's strengths and weaknesses. (Save the notes even on performers you do not cast; you may need to contact a performer later to fill in for an actor who must leave the cast for some reason.) Make a list of the play's characters on the left side of a sheet of paper, with room to write in the name of each performer who is a viable candidate for the role.

Nothing so betrays the leader as reluctance to stand behind, defend and pay the price of the course of action he has chosen to follow. He must be willing squarely to shoulder the responsibility; and it is at this point that many people reveal deficiencies which debar them from real strength as leaders.

—ORDWAY TEAD
The Art of Leadership

Priority Considerations

The first priority of auditions allows no exceptions: Auditions must be conducted in a manner that best permits the director to evaluate performers and make decisions about casting. Allow no activity that conflicts with that prime directive;

allow nothing to divert you from that work. Within a nicely organized and cooperative theatre organization, the rest of the production staff will give you logistic and moral support during auditions.

Your second priority is to help performers audition well. The effective director works with performers to bring out their best efforts. In order to evaluate performers accurately, the director must help them overcome temporary problems with nervousness, unfamiliarity with script and character, or uncertainty about what is wanted from them.

A third priority has to do with a spirit of fairness. It is your responsibility to be as fair and impartial as possible, allowing all performers an equal opportunity to exhibit their abilities. No less important is a clear communication to performers that you are taking pains to treat them justly. Because performers experience stress during auditions, they may perceive a slight where none is intended, and often they interpret a director's innocent remark as evidence of favoritism. You should carefully avoid any word or act that can be interpreted negatively. The point is not that you should *be* impartial — important as that is — but that you should be *seen* to be impartial. Experienced directors know that all too many actors will seek to salvage their egos by accusing the director of evaluating them on grounds other than talent and dedication; to forestall this the wise director carefully follows standard practices to be fair.

GUIDELINES FOR FAIRNESS

The following guidelines will help you demonstrate your concern about equal treatment of all who audition for you:

1. Be equally and unfailingly polite to all who audition.
2. Avoid giving special attention to those with whom you've worked in the past.
3. However, if you have seen a given performer audition several times and he or she shows special growth this time, your praise will encourage that performer and let others in the audition hall know you care about individual improvements.
4. If a performer auditions poorly, remember it is the audition, not the person, you find unacceptable.
5. Show you are concentrating on the performer's audition: Do not talk with others. If you must talk with an assistant, apologize to the performer and ask him or her to wait until you finish the conversation.
6. Praise every performer equally. Do not allow a performer to think you enjoyed his or her work less than others.
7. Self-conscious performers may hear you laugh at something other than their auditions and conclude that you are joking about their ineptness. Carefully avoid jokes at the production desk.
8. Let performers know you are carefully giving each equal time to audition; do not give one performer more time to audition than others. If you want a given performer to do more for you, ask him or her to return later for callbacks.

9. If you fall behind schedule, as can often happen, do not shortchange a performer's audition to get back on schedule.
10. It is tiresome to hear the same passages repeatedly, but the performers are not at fault and do not deserve censure. Avoid commenting about having to hear overly popular selections.
11. If you are auditioning groups of performers, and one appears to be an excellent candidate for your production, control your enthusiasm. Do not ignore the others in order to work with the outstanding actor.
12. Provide all performers equal details about your audition process. As actors arrive, a directorial assistant outside the audition hall should carefully explain what you will do in auditions.
13. Auditions can tire the director. Schedule free time to relax and stretch your mental and physical self. Be aware that your fatigue might lead you to cursory treatment of individuals who, after all, are not responsible for your exhaustion.
14. Make a point of inviting all performers to continue auditioning for future productions.

If you have done your best to treat all performers fairly, you will be able to weather the inevitable complaints from those who disagree with your casting. We who direct can only do our best at auditions, knowing that many actors will criticize our conclusions.

A *regisseur* is a triple-faced creature:
  1. the *regisseur*-interpreter; he instructs *how* to play; so that it is possible to call him the *regisseur*-actor or the *regisseur-pedagogue*;
  2. the *regisseur*-mirror, reflecting the individual qualities of the actor;
  3. the *regisseur*-organizer of the entire production.

> —VLADIMIR NEMIROVICH-DANCHENKO
> "The Three Faces of the Director"
> quoted in Cole and Chinoy, *Directors on Directing*

Audition Systems

Not surprisingly there are several different audition systems. No one procedure is best for all needs. You should select the variation that most suits your situation. As you gain experience you will create new methods by combining pieces from these standard systems.

GENERAL, OPEN

The general, open audition accepts all interested performers without restriction (hence "general") and takes place in an auditorium or comparably large room where all performers listen to others while waiting their turn (hence "open"). There are no reservations. The performers are called to read at least once and often repeatedly. This particular technique is popular in educational and community theatres.

Advantages. The system allows detailed communication, director to performers: If all are present at the beginning of the audition period, the director can make announcements to the assembled group, clarifying what will happen during auditions and describing essential elements of the play and characters. Open auditions allow performers to observe auditions of others, which may lead them to understand your final selection of a cast as well as allowing them insight into acting techniques. Good readings often inspire other performers to higher achievements. The open audition helps build a new stock of performers for the college or community theatre because it encourages inexperienced actors, bolstered by friends and the presence of so many others, to try out spontaneously.

Disadvantages. The general, open system is inefficient if many performers show up, and long delays can be enervating. The presence of a crowd can be distracting, and often this system creates an impersonal "cattle call" atmosphere. Good readings may produce either carbon copies or deliberate efforts to avoid imitation; neither alternative is especially desirable.

GENERAL, CLOSED

The general, closed audition system accepts all who are interested, but instead of having all performers in the room listening to others audition, the closed audition brings small groups of performers into the audition room while others wait outside in the lobby. Usually you limit the groups to two to five actors at a time.

Advantages. The general, closed procedure has fewer distractions because you deal with only a few performers at a time. The cattle call atmosphere is lessened, at least in the audition room itself. Further, performers' auditions are their own, not influenced by others who auditioned earlier.

Disadvantages. The general, closed audition technique is inefficient because of the time it takes each group of performers to leave and the next group to enter. Further, because you do not see the size of the waiting crowd, you may tend to work with each group to the point that those waiting outside grow impatient and simply leave without auditioning. The closed audition does not allow performers to hear and see each other, lessening its educational value for actors. Finally the closed audition may convey a star-chamber image, which bothers some performers.

BY APPOINTMENT

Auditions by appointment require performers to make reservations. This system is usually worked in conjunction with one or more other audition techniques. For example, to use the appointment concept with the open and closed audition methods you might set up appointments for ten or twelve actors per hour.

Advantages. Appointments are an efficient use of both the performers' and your time. You control the amount of time you wish to work with performers. Because all will be in the audition hall, you can make announcements that all will hear. The method encourages performers to plan ahead and to prepare audition pieces carefully.

Disadvantages. With back-to-back appointments, it is easy for you to get off schedule; once off, the effect accumulates unless you have anticipated the problem and allowed several "cushion" periods with no appointments. The appointment system also discourages the spontaneous, spur-of-the-moment audition. Most seriously, if the appointment system is for individuals instead of groups, the performer's solo reading does not allow you to evaluate how well the actor responds to others.

INTERVIEW

The interview audition consists of a private meeting, often in the director's office, between performer and director. This system gives you and the actor an opportunity to get to know each other and to pursue questions about the play, production, character interpretation, and working conditions.

Advantages. The interview system is favored by directors and performers who believe that the large cattle call audition techniques do not encourage individualism. Interviews permit actors and director to exchange ideas. A basic premise underlying this system is that the performer is a known quantity — the interview system is seldom found in the amateur theatre — and that the director already has an idea of the performer's ability.

Disadvantages. Interviews can be wearing for the director. Only a few performers can be seen per day. The interview provides few opportunities for the performer to show acting abilities.

SEASONAL

The seasonal audition seeks to cast a full season's shows, not just one production. Performers audition for the theatre's annual or summer season, often a matter of four or more productions involving a like number of different directors.

Advantages. The seasonal audition system is convenient for organizations drawing from a fixed company to produce a limited number of shows in a set period of time, such as a summer or an academic year. It is useful in repertory theatres. Because the system allows carefully planned assignment of performers for their artistic growth and for the theatre's advantage in selecting plays, it is used in some universities with specialized acting programs, such as those that lead to MFA performance degrees, and in summer theatre programs, such as Shakespeare festivals.

Disadvantages. The seasonal audition system is not popular in many educational or community theatres because if a given performer is cast in, say, three of the four shows of the season — hypothetically numbers 1, 3, and 4 — the later productions may distract the actor from full concentration on the earlier show, especially if the director of show 4 begins work while the performer is still rehearsing show 1 or 3. More significantly, if an entire season is cast, performers who move into town or enroll in classes after seasonal auditions will have no chance to participate, thereby making the theatre appear to be a closed shop. Finally, if the full season is cast but several performers must leave a production for some reason, will the director wish to reopen auditions for all roles in order to rebalance the production? If so, morale problems loom on the horizon.

READINGS FROM SCRIPT AND IMPROVISATIONS

Readings from the script to be produced allow you to hear the performer read from the play to be cast; improvisational auditions without script give you insight into performer abilities not likely to be visible from merely reading the script. The former method shows the actors' interpretive ability for characters they may play; the latter eliminates an overlay of interpretation that may be incorrect.

Drawbacks. Readings from the script can become monotonous, especially if a large number of people are auditioning and you have selected only a few passages from the script. The improvisational approach is often time-consuming, especially if the performers involved are relatively inexperienced and need instructions and situational setups; improvisations also require you to know how to create plausible situations.

PREPARED PIECES OR COLD READINGS

The director can choose between asking performers to bring prepared pieces to auditions or to read "cold," or unprepared. Each has advantages and disadvantages.

Prepared pieces may be from the play you are casting or from other plays. The former is preferred because the latter gives you little to use in judging the performer. The prepared piece from another play is typically a scene the actor has already performed, full of interpretations and blocking perhaps correct for the circumstances of that production but awkward without all of those trappings. At best a prepared piece from another production shows you only what the performer did in collaboration with another director and other performers. In musical auditions, however, a selection from a previous production is acceptable because it shows the performer's technique, dancing or singing range, and polished best efforts.

Prepared pieces from the play you are casting gives you insight into a performer's ability to create the particular roles you are considering. Here you must exercise a great deal of insight to see past the performer's interpretations of the play; the actor's vision of the character is less significant than his or her ability to bring the character to life. The prepared piece has the advantage of letting you see the performer with the rough edges sanded down a bit.

The "cold" piece shows you the performer's ability to sight-read the play and interpret lines out of context. The cold reading has two advantages: It opens auditions to a number of performers who have not been able to find the script to prepare; and it serves as a preliminary screen to put performers into the "acceptable" or "not acceptable" category, with further decisions to be made at a subsequent audition.

THE CALLBACK

The callback is an essential ingredient of all audition systems. After you have worked through all performers, you put together a list of the top contenders and ask them to return for callbacks, which will determine final casting. For both you and the performer, callbacks are the final audition. It is in the production's interest for each performer to do the best audition possible, and therefore you should be as supportive and helpful as possible during callbacks.

Callbacks allow you to consider the ensemble. You seek to cast the group, not solo performers, and you need to look at combinations (directors often refer to these as "marriages") of the top candidates. For example, if you have three candidates for Juliet and two for Romeo, your decision-making process involves not only which is the "best" Juliet and which the "best" Romeo but also which pair will work together most effectively. When casting *Cyrano de Bergerac* your choice for the actor to play Le Bret need not be the "best" Le Bret, but he must be the one who best supports the performer playing Cyrano.

Logistics of callbacks. Often you will call six performers for two roles. To prevent misunderstandings and distress, you must be sure that performers understand that four will not be in the production at all. A callback list is best when it tells performers what you wish them to do at callbacks. You might say, for example, "Actor James Smith is called back to read the role of Proctor, the final scene, pages xx through xxx, showing the character's emotional state." All performers who are called back should be given ample opportunity to prepare the selections.

The theater isn't its successes, though of course they help give it a certain position in polite circles. The theater is its continuum, a living muddle of good and bad that takes its vitality from the equally muddled world about it. It's a hand held out to meandering man as he makes his way through swamps and over cloverleafs, now mired, now soaring, always in motion. It's the motion that's recorded, both by design and by accident, and the speedometer never, never reads the same.

—WALTER KERR
God on the Gymnasium Floor

Judging Performers' Abilities

The experienced director learns to work with performers to uncover abilities not shown during the audition or to overcome apparent weaknesses in performance skills. There are a series of strategies you may wish to explore to help you decide if the performer's problem is so severe that it will influence your casting. Some problem-solving approaches are discussed below.

The performer is so nervous that the reading is badly damaged. Avoid discussing nervousness: The performer is already self-conscious enough about it, thank you. You may decide the humane thing to do is to let the actor finish reading and retreat to a seat. Or you may talk with the performer about personal items on the audition form, helping the actor over the nerve hurdle by thinking of something other than self. When you return to the script, decrease the size of the challenge by giving the actor a brief passage to read. Finally, because physical activity often decreases problems with nervousness, assign an audition passage that includes rapid movements on stage. Nervousness is common and is not necessarily the sign of a weak performer.

You have reason to be concerned about the performer's projection in the auditorium. Try walking further away from the performer and then stopping the reading by asking questions — the topic is not important — to make the actor focus on talking to you in the distance. If the actor now becomes audible, you have learned that the apparent difficulty with projection can be overcome, and you can feel confident about getting that projection ability transferred to the script during rehearsals.

The performer seems physically stiff. Give the performer specific actions such as, "You are hunting for a piece of paper on which is a message you must find in order to escape before the guards return. Quickly go to the corners of this tiny cell, look for the paper, turn that chair over to see if the paper is taped to its bottom, go to that desk . . . ." Then combine the line readings with the comparable movements. If the stiffness persists, you can conclude that corrections may be difficult to achieve during rehearsals and you may be reluctant to cast the performer in a major part.

The performer "pumps" out words with body movement, hand gestures, bending at the waist. This characteristic usually results from inexperience and poor training. Simply ask the performer to stop doing it. If the pumping continues, give the performer other physical activity. If the performer no longer has those mannerisms, praise him or her and ask for a repeat. If the pumping continues, you are justified in not casting the actor in anything but a small role.

The performer deadens the lines, stumbles over them, makes no sense of them.

The problem may be due to a lack of understanding of the lines or, worse, the performer's vocal inflexibility. Talk through the character, situation, and lines with the performer, and then try the passage again. If the problem persists, have the performer recast the sentences into his or her own words. Praise any corrections, and try the readings again. If there is improvement, you have learned how to help this performer, and it is a safe bet that some improvement would continue during rehearsals, so you can consider casting the performer; if you hear no improvement, you would be wise to avoid casting this actor.

After reading for a minute or so, the performer makes all lines sound like carbon copies. The likely problem is that the performer is not adding emotional content to the reading. Stop the actor and suggest emotions for the role, such as "This character feels tightly imprisoned as if with imaginary chains wrapped tightly around her chest so she can hardly breathe and she wants to scream with pain and frustration, but even more she wants to hide all of that from her jailer." If that does not change the readings, invent other emotional qualities and have the actor try the speech again. Alternatively, tell the performer of the problem and ask for corrections. A lack of improvement suggests a poor risk for anything but the smallest role.

You wonder if the performer can enlarge the character. Stop the reading and have the performer imagine being at a football stadium — go into detail describing the size of the place — standing on the fifty-yard line and trying to get the attention of her favorite aunt down by the goal posts. If there is no increase, assume the performer currently cannot fill space, a limitation that may carry through most, perhaps all, of rehearsals and into production.

The actor reads lines in an ever-so-beautiful and ever-so-modulated tone of voice. Usually the performer has a badly mistaken concept of the essences of acting. Candidly, but gently and politely, tell the actor: "Stop acting. *Be* the character." If necessary, you may also want to tell the actor that the era of golden-voiced orators is past: "Do not use 'an actor's voice,' please." If there is no improvement, the actor is probably a poor candidate for a major role.

You are concerned about whether the performer will accept direction. Directors prefer to cast the cooperative team player over the actor who may be a "better" performer but will not become a member of the ensemble. The nondirectable performer will try your patience during rehearsals. Test the actor for directability by giving instructions. For example, assign the actor certain line readings or activities and see if he or she attempts to follow your instructions. If the actor refuses or argues, you may decide not to cast that performer.

These generalizations and suggestions may help you develop approaches to situations in your auditions. The underlying premise of these suggestions is that the director does not sit passively during auditions. On the contrary you should feel free to make suggestions that will help the performer do better. You may interrupt the performer, reassign audition passages, suggest different emotional content or motivational drives, and in general participate in the performer's audition — always with patience and good humor, taking pains to show that you share the performer's earnest desire to give a good audition. Often you will discover talent hidden beneath awkward audition techniques.

RECORDING NOTES

The director must take careful notes on performers during auditions. After a hard set of auditions lasting two or three days, your memory is fallible. You must have written notes on each performer. The notes should be reasonably extensive, covering a series of points.

- Directability: Is the performer a team player? Cooperative? Coachable? Available for rehearsals?
- Vocal range: Is the performer vocally flexible? Free of vocal mannerisms? Able to stress appropriate words and phrases?
- Physical flexibility: Is the performer free from physical mannerisms? Can the performer's body help suggest details of the character?
- Emotional projections: Can the performer project a range of emotions? Perceive the depth of emotions in the character?
- Image of the performer: Does the performer project the image of, say, a man of principle? A rebel? A conservative? A saint?
- Possible roles the performer can play in this script.

Your notes should be well organized. Develop a form that allows you to make quick entries on a chart so you do not have to spend a great deal of time writing. A helpful form is the cast list with half a dozen blanks on the right side where you can write in the names of performers who appear to be potential candidates for one or more roles. This cast list and your notes not only will help you cast the show but also may be necessary if one or more cast members leaves the company later and you must recast roles.

Exercises

The following exercises are designed to help you prepare for auditions of the play you will direct.

1. Prepare an audition announcement, less than one typed page in length, including such details as (1) play title; (2) playwright; (3) director; (4) audition place, times, and dates; (5) general rehearsal schedule; and (6) production dates. Briefly describe the characters and any special qualities needed (i.e., gymnastic ability, musical skills, and the like). If advance preparation is required, indicate where performers can obtain scripts. Briefly describe how you will conduct auditions. Include quotations from critical reviews that praise the play.

2. Select audition passages either from the play you will direct or from other plays. Prepare an ample supply of audition materials to give to performers.
   a. Select passages that you can use to audition candidates for each major leading role.
   b. Select passages that you can use to audition (1) one male and one female, (2) two males, and (3) two females.

3. Assume that for auditions you will have an assistant outside the audition hall, ready to welcome performers, record their names and addresses, and help them by answering questions. Write detailed instructions to give that assistant, attempting to answer all foreseeable questions.
4. Prepare an audition form for performers to fill out.
5. Prepare a director's evaluation summary form on which you will record each performer's ability to play roles in your play. Such a form may look like this:

SUMMARY EVALUATION OF AUDITIONS

Actor's name	*is a viable candidate for*					
	Character name	Character name	Character name	Character name	Other (name)	None (don't cast)
1.						
2.						
3.						
4.						

We who evaluate performers and pass judgments on their abilities will do well to remember how other judges have viewed performers. Here are three classic opinions.

Marilyn Monroe

"You'd better learn secretarial work or else get married." (Emmeline Sniveley, Director of the Blue Book Modeling Agency, counseling would-be model Marilyn Monroe, 1944.)

Lucille Ball

"Try another profession. *Any* other." (Head Instructor of the John Murray Anderson Drama School, giving professional advice to would-be actress Lucille Ball, 1927.)

Ronald Reagan

"Reagan doesn't have the presidential look." (United Artists executive, dismissing the suggestion that Ronald Reagan be offered the starring role in the movie, *The Best Man*, 1964.)

—CHRISTOPHER CERF AND VICTOR NAVASKY
The Experts Speak

CHAPTER TWELVE

Casting

I regard the theatre as the greatest of all art forms, the most immediate way in which a human being can share with another the sense of what it is to be a human being.

—THORNTON WILDER

quoted in Malcolm Cowley, *Writers at Work*

Perfect casting is an ideal that engages every director's attention. The term refers to placing the best available performer in the most appropriate role for the per-

former's personal growth and the production's best interests, ensuring that the group of performers will work well together to create an ensemble, training performers to enrich the theatrical organization's long-term development, and achieving the director's vision of the production. Casting is a delicate process requiring you to walk a slender tightrope of decisions. Experienced directors often say that casting may account for as much as four-fifths of the production's ultimate quality, because a mistake can lead the production into grave difficulties, but an inspired insight can elevate the company to unexpected heights.

The ideal of perfect casting is seldom attained because the casting process is filled with confusion. There are more questions than answers and often there are several solidly acceptable, though completely different, answers to casting questions. Still, directors being basically optimistic, quite likely you will adapt quickly to the cast you have put together, and by the time the production opens you will be convinced that perfect casting was achieved after all. Although casting is one

For a show with a large cast that includes many different types and ages (including young children) the director must pay careful attention to casting to achieve the desired dramatic effect. *Unto These Hills* tells the story of the Cherokee Indians, first in conflict with DeSoto's soldiers in 1540 (opposite), and then forced to leave their homes to travel the infamous "trail of tears" to the west in 1838 (below). William Hardy directs this outdoor drama, presented each summer in Cherokee, North Carolina. — *Photographs by Ed Hunnicutt Studio*

of the director's most significant decisions, an organized and methodological approach can ease your burden.

Analysis of the Character

To cast a role correctly the director first carefully analyzes the demands of the role. Character analysis is discussed in detail in Chapter Five, and we need not repeat the steps of analysis or discuss the playwright's various approaches to writing the characters, all of which influence directorial decisions. You may wish to refer to that chapter to refresh your understanding of character analysis.

You must have an accurate understanding of the demands of each role in order to cast performers correctly. It is helpful to divide the broad topic of characterization into smaller points: the emotional qualities of the character, the desired audience response to the character, vocal demands, and physical aspects (age, special height or weight, athletic skills, and the like).

EMOTIONAL QUALITIES

Drama is communicated with emotions. Of all aspects of character, emotional tonality may be the most important and most easily overlooked during the casting process. Quality theatre mandates that the director cast performers with the emotional ranges the roles demand. You must fully understand the emotional demands of the role and then judge the performer's capacity to project those emotions. Casting a performer with limited emotional range shrinks the role; as the role is decreased, the play's emotions are lessened, and its thought is lost.

For example, imagine *Fiddler on the Roof*'s Tevye without the necessary warm emotional range — a close kinship with his Creator, good humor despite adversity, love for his family, flexibility in dealing with the dilemmas his daughters bring him, attempts to be the stern disciplinarian, and more. An actress cast as Nora in Ibsen's *A Doll's House* must have the emotional dimensions to be both the docile "little lark" and the firm-minded independent soul who leaves her domineering husband. An actor unable to capture the emotional size of Macbeth would decrease the tragedy into a petty affair. Drama depends on the emotional ebb and flow of dimensional characters, and directors depend on performers with the emotional depth to make those characters credible and alive.

THE DESIGNED AUDIENCE RESPONSE

Playwrights often expect a specific audience reaction, almost always emotional, to various characters. The design of the play depends on creating those audience responses. Without performers capable of awakening such response productions would fail. To illustrate this point, imagine a *Fiddler on the Roof* starring an unlovable Tevye, an *Othello* in which Iago seemed to be a better human being than Othello or Desdemona, a *Glass Menagerie* with a Laura who evoked no sympathy, or a *Doll's House* whose Nora was so irritating you devoutly prayed she would fail in any activity she attempted.

As you make casting decisions, you attempt to estimate audience response to performers. What will the audience subconsciously feel about this or that individual? Here you are looking not only at acting talent but also into the performer's persona. This inner quality is a matter of "heart" or "soul"; casting a "heartless" performer as Tevye is no less a directorial error than casting a tone-deaf singer

Among the director's concerns while casting a play is the actor's persona, a somewhat intangible factor that has to do with the individual's overall personality. The actors' personal standards can influence how they approach roles such as the Christus in the *Black Hills Passion Play* at Spearfish, South Dakota (below). Josef Meier, founder of the Passion Play in 1938, has portrayed the Christus in more than 7500 performances, winning many honors including a knighthood from Pope Paul VI — *Photograph courtesy of the Black Hills Passion Play of America*

Certain plays often demand special performance
talents. *The Miracle Worker*, for example, requires a
young girl to play the deaf, blind, and mute Helen
Keller. The director of such shows must pay careful
attention to casting. George Black directed the
production illustrated above for the Heritage
Repertory Theatre of the University of Virginia.
— *Photograph courtesy of the Heritage Repertory Theatre
of the University of Virginia*

in the role. An actor cannot change his or her inner nature simply by putting on
a wig and saying someone's lines.

Empathy — the phenomenon of the audience "feeling in" with the emotions
on stage — is a powerful theatrical effect. A performer with internal warmth will
evoke warmth from the audience. A performer who is bitter, prone to rumor-

For certain productions the director's casting decisions are influenced by concerns about the performers' physical abilities. Outdoor dramas frequently require performers to play several roles, such as an Indian dancer and then (after quick costume and makeup changes) a soldier, a citizen, and perhaps other roles. Because such productions are typically presented five or six nights a week for several months in the summer and take place outdoors without benefit of air conditioning or protection from weather conditions, performers' endurance and stamina often are factors in casting. Above is the spectacular "Eagle Dance" from *Unto These Hills*, presented in Cherokee, North Carolina, each summer and directed by William Hardy.
— *Photograph by Lou Harshaw*

mongering, cruel, and quick to blame others may create an uncomfortable feeling in the audience. Such an actor would be a disaster as Tevye but acceptable as a minor character not designed to evoke audience warmth. Your task is to estimate the performer's empathic communications and cast the production accordingly.

VOCAL DEMANDS

A vocally dead performer can change a lively and exciting character into a painfully dull one; a monotone performer who speaks at an unchanging volume and rate can make an exciting scene dreary and boring. Your responsibility in casting is to analyze the vocal demands of the role and select a performer who has a good chance of mastering them. The ideal performer has comfortable vocal variations of rate, pitch, volume, and timbre.

Some playwrights are more demanding of performers' vocal ability than others. For example, playwrights such as Shaw and Fry, because of their wordiness, need performers who can keep the play alive and correctly paced with colorful vocal variations; playwrights like Shakespeare demand performers who have correct breathing techniques to handle the long, inverted speeches. Certain roles demand special vocal strength — Hamlet and Cyrano, for example — or attention to accents — Amanda Wingfield in *Glass Menagerie* and Sam Shepard's "western" characters, for example. To cast the show correctly you must judge the performers' vocal abilities against the characters' demands.

PHYSICAL QUALITIES

The physical qualities of the character generally are relatively unimportant unless you are casting a physically demanding role in which physical aspects help define the character. You will of course carefully note the playwright's descriptions of the characters' physical appearance, but you generally place little priority on such matters as color of hair or eyes, height, or weight. Such matters are usually ignored or trusted to the talents of the costume and makeup crews.

This is not to say that you should ignore physical qualities completely. Certainly it would be counterproductive to cast a very short actor to play Abe Lincoln. You must also consider demands for physical agility in such characters as Cyrano de Bergerac or endurance in characters such as Sweeney Todd. Age is also significant; although theatrical history is full of elderly performers essaying such tender roles as Romeo and Juliet, quality productions will not grossly violate age when it defines the characters.

Considering the Performer

CREATING AN "ENSEMBLE"

For a critic or audience member to say that a given production had a strong "acting ensemble" is high praise. The director tries to cast individuals who will create an ensemble, a tightly knit performance unit that preserves the unique qualities of each individual while emphasizing the collective whole in a well-matched production.

In casting to build an ensemble you consider performers' attitudes to theatre, especially their definition of their relative importance in theatre, and whether they expect to give to theatre or take from it. An ensemble company does not exclude mavericks or eccentrics, but it does require performers who are willing to dedicate their talents and their inner selves to the production and each other. Ensemble playing demands performers who are willing to work together closely to grow both individually and collectively. The ensemble cannot have performers locked into their own notions of stardom; it requires actors prepared to give to others while developing their own artistic abilities.

COOPERATIVENESS

Experienced directors know that a performer with a proper attitude about working in theatre will often be a better choice than the performer who appears to have greater performance talents but a less cooperative attitude. You will enjoy working with performers who are directable, dedicated, eager to learn, and capable of enough self-discipline to do their homework before rehearsal and be quietly prepared, on time, and supportive. Directors do not enjoy performers who have insufficient respect for theatre as an art, who collaborate poorly with others, or who have so little regard for their talents that they will not work to improve.

The "cooperativeness component" presents you with difficult choices. Although you do not want to cast the "superstar" who will not cooperate with the work of others, remember that this is not a popularity contest: You cannot dismiss the "star" too easily, and often you must cast for talent not cooperation. The superstar who gives little to others in the company may make the performance more vital. The dependable and cooperative, though unfortunately less talented, performer will give to others and make working on the production a better experience. There is no easy solution here, but many directors decide to cast the performer who appears able to grow to make the production vital, instead of the actor who tries to exploit the production by dominating the stage.

A SENSE OF THE THEATRE

Look for the performer with dramatic flair and style, a sense of theatre, a certain fire, enjoyment of dramatic communication, and boiling energy. The performer with that magic has outstanding vocal emphasis, dynamics, and interesting stress patterns that bring the lines to vivid life. The performer with a sense of theatre typically has a smooth poise and bearing on stage, an expressive face with strong eyes, and effective gestures. Even at auditions such a performer visibly listens to others' lines. The dramatic performer will dig out the conflict in the script and use it to make sparks fly.

TYPECASTING

Typecasting results from a narrow view of a performer, a consideration of surface image rather than inner depth. The narrow view might lead one to conclude that an actress who looks young, sweet, and virginal will be better for Juliet (even though her acting abilities are somewhat limited) than another actress who looks more jaded and carries herself with a certain worldliness but has greater performance talents. If the first performer lacks the acting ability, you might be left with a good image but no substance. The second performer may be able to convey the character's exterior qualities with acting skills (makeup and costume will help) and at the same time give a more inspired performance. Typecasting is generally unimaginative and repetitious: This actor played the tough cop in the last three shows, so he will be a tough cop in the next production. The performer grows stale without new challenges.

CHARACTER PROJECTION

Performers often project certain character qualities. This young man communicates a rebellious fire, that young woman is the girl next door, this man appears to be gravely concerned about morality and justice, this woman is grandmotherly, and so forth. You should note such qualities during auditions and consider them in casting as an aid to character portrayal.

EDUCATIONAL CASTING

Casting for the performer's potential artistic growth in the role is educational casting. This casting method is dedicated to the individual's well-being and therefore is immediately appealing, especially in university or college theatres. When applied carefully, educational casting benefits performer, production, and theatrical organization.

In one aspect of educational casting, the director thinks of the individual who "deserves" to be cast. For example, suppose that performer A has auditioned frequently and worked backstage but has been discouraged about never getting a role. If he is not markedly a lesser candidate than others who audition, educational casting would give A the nod. He has "paid his dues."

In another aspect of educational casting, the director thinks of the long-term interests of the theatrical organization and the individual. For example, suppose performer B is a college freshman who looks promising with talents more or less on a par with some of the upperclass students who auditioned. Educational casting would give B the nod, an investment in the theatre organization's next four years. New people must be worked into productions so they will be next season's veterans. Alert community theatre directors also cast newcomers in order to preserve their theatre's growth.

Carried to extremes, however, educational casting can be harmful. Suppose performer J has shown fine growth over the years, playing roles W, X, and Y, so we now cast her as Z because that is in her best interests. Obviously the process is helpful to performer J, but her advantage is performer S's obstacle. Jealousies may result, particularly if S seems to be an equally good or better candidate for the role. This is not beneficial to J or S and can be harmful to the company's morale because the resulting ill-will damages the production and the theatrical organization.

LEVEL OF ABILITY

Casting actors under their abilities can injure their morale and artistic growth; casting them over their abilities can be destructive of both performer and production. As a director you necessarily face mixed priorities when casting a production. To a large degree you intend to put together the best possible cast to ensure a rich production. Often this will require you to consider casting a performer in a role that simply does not fit his or her abilities.

Should you cast a performer in a role markedly less demanding than other roles the performer has done well? Although no single answer is applicable to all cases, you may solve the dilemma by asking yourself if that performer's talent will lead him or her to create more character, call the character to the audience's attention, or overwhelm the leads. A performer skilled at creating character may expand a small role until it competes with the principal parts and makes the play lose focus. You would then have to use a variety of subtle or direct techniques to subdue the performer and maintain an artistic unification. Can you establish sufficient rapport that the performer understands your focus? If you believe that the production will be significantly improved by casting this talented performer in an undemanding role, in most instances you should do so. Usually the problem can be solved if you perceive it in advance; candid discussions with the performer are important.

More significant are the problems of casting a performer distinctly over his or her personal and performance abilities. You should not be reluctant to cast an experienced, talented performer in a role that somewhat exceeds his or her current level, because the actor will find the challenge artistically stimulating. But if the performer is less experienced and cannot grow to meet the demands of the role, the results can be unfortunate on a number of levels. The performer will suffer the pain of failure; others in the cast may feel the actor is causing the production to suffer and therefore may treat the performer badly; in rehearsals you may focus on the struggling performer to the exclusion of others; the performer's friends and relatives who come to see the show will be embarrassed; and the total production will suffer. The performer's growing awareness of the complex reactions will exacerbate the problem.

The difficulty is not restricted to the performer's artistic abilities. Often a performer, especially one with little experience, is not comfortable with a role demanding profanity or suggestive sexual activity. Some become distressed if you insert unexpected religious, political, social, or sexual overtones into the production. Experienced performers know that the character, not the performer, speaks those lines or does those acts on stage, but beginning actors may not have learned to separate themselves from the character.

Should the director cast performers "over their heads?" As a guideline, cast performers who have, with some stretching, a decent chance of handling the role; do not cast performers so far over their heads that they will fail badly. Learning to distinguish between the two is always difficult, but keep foremost in your mind the concept of protecting the performer.

AVAILABILITY FOR REHEARSALS

Inexperienced directors may wonder why availability needs to be considered as part of casting — after all, don't performers who audition intend to be available for every rehearsal? No. Too often directors discover, after the casting process is completed, that Ms. Jones simply cannot rehearse Friday nights, Mr. Smith wouldn't think of rehearsing weekends, and the Johnson brothers have to go out of town every Tuesday and Thursday. If you do not get commitments from performers before casting, you may be frustrated by your inability to get the full cast together to build an ensemble. The director who knows of schedule conflicts but is confident "we'll be able to work around them" will be sadly disillusioned and fatigued by opening night. Given a choice between two performers, other aspects being relatively equal, you would be wise to consider casting the available performer instead of the somewhat more talented but less committed actor.

Despite the pettiness, the egomania, and the persecution complexes of stagefolk, they are more amusing, more generous, and more stimulating than any other professional group.

—RICHARD MANEY
Fanfare

Other Aspects of Casting

PRECASTING

Casting one or more performers outside the regular audition process is called precasting. The process generally involves casting one or more leading roles before auditions. If that fact is kept secret from those who audition and performers try for roles not knowing that some parts are already cast, the director has participated in a fraud and richly deserves the censure he or she undoubtedly will receive once the truth comes out. No ethical director dupes performers by pretending all roles are open when in fact some have already been filled. Precasting is acceptable only if there is an open announcement of it.

Performers who fail in auditions often claim that they would have been cast if the director had not precast the show. It is a serious charge. If the performer has no evidence and is simply distributing sour grapes, he or she is guilty of unethical behavior and deserves censure for damaging the director's reputation, the theatrical organization, and theatre art. Many directors will avoid casting such a performer in future shows because the performer's habit of blaming others for personal failures may make rehearsals difficult and uncomfortable.

The understudy is less important in fact than folklore would have us believe. As legend has it, half an hour before curtain on opening night the leading actress suddenly develops a mysterious disease, and a young actress steps forward and shyly says she knows the lines. She takes the role; the show opens on schedule; she is amazingly perfect; a star is born; and the show is saved. At Sardi's everyone gives her a standing ovation.

The story made a number of cute 1930s movies, but in fact productions seldom bother with an understudy. If you elect to cast an understudy (why not two or more?), he or she must be prepared to step in should an emergency occur. Preparation demands that the understudy must have at least minimal rehearsals with the other performers, thereby reducing the principal performer's rehearsal time. As the understudy rehearses, there may be confusion about interpretation of the role. Finally, if you have an understudy who works diligently throughout rehearsals, are you then obliged to give him or her a chance to perform at least once? Will that lead to a quality production?

But if I did not cast an understudy, what happens if my lead is unable to perform? You may have to cancel a performance. It seldom happens. In some two hundred plays and musicals I have directed, only once were we unable to perform because of a problem that an understudy could have solved. Out of several hundred student productions I have supervised, only twice was an understudy needed. The odds are against your needing an understudy.

You do have a viable alternative to casting an understudy. Because you and your directorial assistant know interpretation and blocking, either of you can step in as replacements, carrying scripts if necessary, and the result can be an effective production. In amateur theatre at least it's probably best to forget about casting an understudy and focus on working with the regular performers.

DOUBLE CASTING

Double casting means putting together two complete, or at least partially complete, casts for one production. The casts take turns performing. School administrators urge high school directors into double casting because it allows more youngsters to participate, but those same administrators would never suggest putting together two separate football teams to take turns playing opponents. Double casting presents a number of difficulties and no educational, artistic, or theatrical advantages. There is no point in allowing more people to participate in what will almost certainly be a disaster because neither cast is adequately prepared.

THE TENTATIVE CAST LIST

Experienced directors know that adjustments may be necessary in the final cast list, and they reserve the right to make changes for a short time after rehearsals begin. There are many valid reasons for changes. For example, two performers may simply not merge properly or one cast member may be badly miscast.

To be sure the cast understands your option to make changes, post the cast list with the announcement, "This cast list is tentative for the next XX days." In amateur theatre you can expect a short trial period, perhaps five to seven days; in professional theatre five days is standard due to rules concerning payment to performers. If you do not make some sort of announcement when you post the cast list, it is virtually impossible to make changes. Although you have the power to change the cast, the process will never be easy. If you are convinced a change is necessary, do it without delay and brace yourself to weather an uncomfortable storm.

Exercises

1. Drawing on your experience as a participant in a theatrical production that achieved ensemble playing, define the term and list the factors that created a working ensemble. How did the director's casting influence the creation of an ensemble? Discuss the group dynamics leading to the construction of an ensemble. What do you perceive are the participants' advantages in a close-knit ensemble? Did the ensemble positively influence your work in the production?

   Consider your experience in a production that lacked ensemble playing. What factors inhibited the creation of the ensemble? How did the director's casting prohibit an ensemble? What group interactions prevented building an ensemble? Did the lack of an ensemble adversely affect your work in the production?

2. Describe the empathic communications of several performers you know well, from your view as an audience member or as a working partner on stage. Analyze the reasons one seems to evoke positive responses from the audience while another apparently does not. Based on your awareness of the performers' personal qualities that create those audience responses, what generalizations do you discover about empathic qualities in performers? How do your conclusions influence your casting decisions for the play you are to direct?

3. Discuss the desired audience reaction to each major character in the play you are to direct. What personal qualities will you seek to match performer to role?

4. Describe the emotional qualities of each major character in the play you are to direct. What emotional ranges are necessary for each role?

5. Describe the vocal demands of each major character in the play you are to direct. What vocal qualities would you seek in possible candidates for each role? What vocal standards must individual performers meet to be cast in each major role?

6. Describe physical qualities of each major character. What physical attributes will you seek in performers?

The director is the kind of lover who draws his talent, invention and joy in his work from the talent, invention and joy which he borrows from or inspires in others. To direct a production means to gather together all the people and things that make up a perfor-

mance and to create, through them, a certain atmosphere, arousing and serving their capabilities and their personalities. In the setting — the whole play's material surroundings — such things, for example, as wood, paint, nails and light are not, as one might suppose, lifeless, inorganic things but formidable entities whose favor toward the play and its interpreters is to be won only by a secret and long-premeditated accord.

—LOUIS JOUVET
"The Profession of the Director,"
in Cole and Chinoy, *Directors on Directing*

CHAPTER THIRTEEN

Planning the Rehearsal Schedule

One of Jerome Robbins' great strengths is his ability to ask anyone any question, no matter what. Sheldon Harnick, the lyricist for *Fiddler,* who worked with Robbins on that musical, says this: "Any show should be one man's vision. When Robbins takes over a show, it's his vision in every department. He drives the set designer crazy, he drives the orchestrater crazy, he has a total vision of what he wants. He presses and presses you on every point, no matter how trivial, until it isn't trivial anymore."

—WILLIAM GOLDMAN
The Season: A Candid Look at Broadway

The director plans the production's rehearsal schedule with the meticulous attention of a skipper planning a campaign to win the America's Cup. You and the skipper have in common a major vision, and you share the responsibility for constructing an effective master strategy that will achieve the goal. Like the skipper, you are in charge of designing each step to lead to the fulfillment of a master plan, calculating the correct amount of time to complete each production element, and steering the correct course to achieve the desired outcome. In play direction, as in sailboat racing, victory goes to the well-prepared.

A production without an effective rehearsal schedule is doomed to chaotic attempts to catch up, with directorial attention diverted to the clock rather than significant goals. In contrast, a well-planned, efficient schedule creates a positive working atmosphere that encourages all participants to unleash creative energies and do their best work. Because it is the director's responsibility to ensure a correct environment for creative effort, construction of a proper schedule is a significant part of the director's craft.

The goal of rehearsals is to unify all elements of the production into one artistically cohesive, well-prepared whole that realizes the director's vision. Rehearsals allow director, performers, designers, and technicians to experiment creatively to find an approach that will bring the play clearly and vividly alive for the audience. No one automatically knows from the outset how to do a play correctly. Intensive periods of search and experimentation are essential. You design re-

Directorial vision of the production is achieved with a detailed rehearsal schedule that carefully allots time for development of characterization, scenic effects, costumes, lighting, properties, makeup, and sound and other effects, as for this production of *The Front Page*, directed by Edward Amor at the University of Wisconsin, Madison. — *Photograph courtesy of the University of Wisconsin, Madison*

hearsals to facilitate that searching process. The final success or failure of a given production is dictated by the director's rehearsal design; properly conducted rehearsals will be filled with the excitement of discovery for cast and director alike.

Factors in Making an Effective Rehearsal Schedule

You consider many factors in constructing the most effective rehearsal schedule possible. Is this a relatively simple production, such as a small-cast, one-act play in a studio theatre, or is it a complex show, such as a mainstage, full-scale musical or Shakespearean play? Does the play need lengthy technical rehearsals for scene and lighting shifts? Is this a play, like *Hamlet* or *After the Fall,* that demands additional time to develop rich characterization? Does it require the development of a correct sense of style like *The Miser* or *The Importance of Being Earnest?* Does it call for special rehearsals to achieve the desired intensity of the secondary characters like *Marat/Sade?*

Will the cast be veterans, able to create their roles efficiently, or will they be so inexperienced that you must allow additional time for coaching and instruction? Will you be working with children, who have short attention spans and need abbreviated rehearsals? Will your cast consist of college students, whose energy and devotion allow long rehearsal hours? Are you directing in a community theatre with adults who have full-time occupations and family commitments that prevent them from rehearsing every evening? Are you working within a professional organization, directing well-trained performers who are available for full-time rehearsals?

Answers to questions such as these will help you design the best rehearsal schedule for your particular play. As these questions indicate, no single timetable is applicable to every play, every theatre, and every director. Wise directors avoid copying old rehearsal schedules when starting a new production and design a special schedule based on careful examination of the unique qualities of the play and the qualifications of the performers.

A Sample Rehearsal Schedule

The following schedule assumes an "average" full-length play, written in prose in the realistic convention with a moderately small cast of six to eight characters. The sample schedule further assumes that the cast is relatively experienced, that there are no unusual production requirements, and that no special technical effects are needed. We assume that the play is average in difficulty, although one is wryly aware that all average plays are equal but some are more equal than others. Of course, no matter how average a play appears to be, once in rehearsal its apparently ordinary problems can become mountainous hurdles.

Given that caveat, the following information will guide you in constructing your own rehearsal schedule. This timetable is based on the premise that your play opens on a Thursday night. The discussion further assumes that you start rehearsals on a Monday, that the first block of time is a week and a half long, and that subsequent rehearsal periods are a week long.

FIVE AND A HALF WEEKS BEFORE OPENING: ESTABLISHING MEANING AND GOALS

In order to make the public listen to the fine shades of your feelings you have to experience them intensely yourself. To live through definite intelligible feelings is easier than to live through the subtle soul vibrations of a poetic nature. To reach them it is necessary to dig deep into the material which is handed you for creation. To the study of the play we shall devote jointly a great deal of work and attention and love. But that is little. In addition you have to prepare yourselves independently.

I speak of your personal life, observation which will broaden your imagination and sensitiveness. Make friends of children. Enter into their world. Watch nature and her manifestations surrounding us. Make friends of dogs and cats and look oftener into their eyes to see their souls.

But our first step in this great work is to live in the play. Hence, to work!

—CONSTANTIN STANISLAVSKI

"Stanislavski to his players at the first rehearsal of *The Blue Bird* (1908)"

Rehearsal goals. Attitudes, relationships, discipline, working habits, and significant determinations about the production's ultimate quality are established by the end of the first week and a half of rehearsals, five weeks before your show's opening. You therefore plan carefully to establish the proper working atmosphere during early rehearsals. In the above quotation Stanislavski tells his performers to capture the intrinsic quality of childhood essential for Maeterlinck's play *The Blue Bird*. That concept of "the child" applies to a salient aspect of good theatre: a wide-eyed delight in pretending, in make-believe, in creating and inventing. "Make friends of children" is excellent advice, and one of your goals in early rehearsals should be to engender a spirit of creative playfulness, to let loose the child's imagination locked within the stern, inhibited adult.

Creative warm-ups can free that delightful spirit, not only preparing the performers' vocal and physical tools but also reaching into the imagination and awakening sensory memories. Warm-ups stretch the spirit as well as the body. You begin every rehearsal with fifteen to thirty minutes of warm-ups, including physical and vocal stretching, theatre games, and improvisational exercises.

During the first week and a half you have three other basic goals. Be sure everyone in the cast has a clear understanding of the play's overall meaning — its subject and theme — as well as each individual action unit's primary thrust. Open doors for the cast to develop characterization. Finally, create the proper working environment for the coming weeks of rehearsals.

Day-by-day schedule. Monday. Your first rehearsal sets working patterns for the rest of the working period. Start precisely on time to show the cast that rehearsals must begin promptly; don't wait for late-comers to arrive or repeat announcements to those who come late.

The careful director is well prepared, indicating to the cast that all aspects of rehearsals are ready. Before the cast arrives your production stage manager sets up the rehearsal hall with appropriate furniture and tape on the floor to represent the stage areas. Rehearsal schedules, materials about the play and playwright, and other production information are ready to give the cast. Scene, costume, and lighting designers are present to show the cast their designs for the production; publicity people have forms ready for the cast to fill out, and a photographer takes posed or candid shots.

Without turning the rehearsal into a lecture, communicate your vision of the production; the reasons you selected the play; its subject, theme, and primary appeals; the effects you intend it to have on audiences, and the main line of action that links the events of the play. To set basic parameters for the cast, give your interpretations of the characters' motivations and drives as they act and interact throughout the play.

Have the actors read the entire play. Some directors read the play to the cast, but it is difficult to imagine a single advantage to such a process. Let the actors begin their work. A dull first reading should not concern either you or the cast; such a reading simply proves the need for rehearsals.

When the cast has read through the play, the director leads investigations into the characters. What is the character's through line of action? What are the character's superobjectives? Why does a character say this or do that particular action? What motivates the character here and here? How do you envision the character? What emotions and subtexts do you sense under the surface? If the character appears happy, can you find opposites and contrasts? What color is the character, what flower, what music? Where has the character been before entering? How does the character feel about other characters? When does the character evolve and change? How is this character different from others? To encourage the actors to begin work on their characters, they, not you, should answer these questions.

At the conclusion of this and all rehearsals, set goals for the following rehearsal by telling the cast what they are to prepare. For example, one performer should come to the next rehearsal with a hat that might represent the character, another performer should work to find the character's voice, and so forth. All should begin writing a character biography. Allow time for their questions. Conclude by expressing your optimism about the play and this particular company.

Tuesday. The second rehearsal runs much like the first; however, if the cast was sitting for the first rehearsal, tonight they should be walking in the stage environment but ignoring blocking. Focus on the action units that divide the play into significant movements. Working with your cast, examine each action unit, finding primary objectives and giving each an identifying title.

Wednesday and Thursday. Examine the action units, beats, motivations, and emotions in the play, half the play each night.

Friday. Work scenes in the first act. Think of this as exploration and experimentation. Carefully avoid statements that suggest the performer is wrong — don't say, "No, that's the wrong way to read the line" or "Don't do it that way" — instead be supportive and help performers discover the characters. Keep in mind these are rehearsals, not a performance.

Saturday and Sunday. If you are directing a musical or a large-cast play, weekend rehearsals may be mandatory to allow uninterrupted work on complicated scenes.

Monday. Weekly Production Meeting. Present are all production personnel: your directorial assistant (who takes minutes); the production stage manager; designers of scenery, lighting, makeup, costumes, properties, and sound; publicity people; and all assistants. The first item of business should be a review of the overall production schedule, followed by a report from each production unit. Focus on problems and solutions. Be sure all problems are aired, all possible alternatives explored, and appropriate solutions considered.

Monday, Tuesday, and Wednesday. Work an act a night, looking at character emotions, objectives, obstacles, subtext, and beats. Carefully note the performers' instinctive movements as they read their parts and you will discover valid concepts for blocking the play.

FOUR WEEKS BEFORE OPENING:
BLOCKING AND CHARACTERIZATION

The ideal director . . . needs to have remarkable gifts besides the fundamental qualities of industry and patience. He should, of course, have sensitivity, originality without freak-ishness, a fastidious ear and eye, some respect for, and knowledge of, tradition, a feeling for music and pictures, colour and design; yet in none of these, I believe, should he be too opinionated in his views and tastes. . . . Players of tried skill sometimes have to be toned down in order to balance and harmonize with those of lesser accomplishment, while the less experienced may need encouragement in order to gain greater confidence and style. There must always be room to adopt an unforeseen stroke of inventiveness, some spontaneous effect which may occur at a good rehearsal and bring a scene suddenly and unexpectedly to life. Yet the basic scaffolding must be firm, the speech modulated, clear, and varied, the phrasing elegant and clear, constantly varying in pace and pitch. The movement should be simple (or apparently so) and calculated to put each speaker in the best possible position, so that the eyes of the audience are drawn inevitably to him at the right moment.

—JOHN GIELGUD
Stage Directions

Rehearsal goals. When does the director block the play? Opinions vary, some arguing that the director should have the play totally blocked before rehearsals begin, recording the notes in the prompt book; and others claiming the cast should create its own blocking during rehearsals as part of the organic growth of the whole. Regardless of the merits of each concept, there is no doubt that beginning directors should work privately to block the play before rehearsals begin, rather than attempting to block during rehearsals.

A key to successful blocking is frequent review. Rerunning action units helps the performers set the blocking in their minds and allows you to take a breath before moving on. Do not simply go through an entire act and expect the performers to have the blocking even reasonably mastered. You need to stop, back up, review, and so on. Budget time accordingly.

The following schedule for your fourth rehearsal week before opening is a rather luxurious expenditure of time for blocking. It can be condensed, but beginning directors in particular should not rush through blocking.

Day-by-day schedule. Thursday. Before rehearsals your production stage manager places furniture pieces and tapes the floor to simulate the stage and floor plan. Read through the first act, encouraging the cast to use doors and furniture as their characters see fit, recording in your prompt book all movements that strike you as appropriate. Tomorrow you will use those ideas as you begin blocking.

Friday. Block a major portion of Act One, action unit by unit. Because this is your first blocking, be especially patient with the cast and yourself. Tell the actors to write all blocking notes in their scripts — they should not trust these instructions to memory — and be sure they understand that blocking will be changed often during the next weeks of rehearsals, which means their notes should be in pencil. To help you check the effectiveness of blocking and the performers be sure they have grasped details, review frequently by backing up to the beginning of an action unit and running it again. Revise blocking as necessary — your assistant will record all changes in the prompt book — but avoid polishing work at this time.

Saturday and Sunday. For the typical play the director calls a rehearsal for only one of the four available rehearsal periods during the weekend, usually Sunday evening. For a musical, however, you should expect to rehearse all four periods: Saturday morning, Saturday afternoon, Sunday afternoon, and Sunday evening.

On Saturday, away from the cast, revise as necessary the blocking of Act One, based on what you learned from the first blocking on Friday night, and modify your preliminary blocking of Acts Two and Three as necessary.

Sunday evening. Review blocking of the first part of Act One. Work unit by unit to make the necessary changes, and then continue blocking the rest of the act. Run through the act again, now working primarily on characterization and secondarily on blocking. At the conclusion of the run-through, rework problem areas.

Monday: Weekly Production Meeting. All design personnel, production staff, crew chiefs, and promotion people should be present. Review the production schedule, and ask for progress reports. Promotion people should be sending stories about the cast and production, the costume shop should be measuring performers, and scene construction should be in progress. Urge the sound designer to let you audition sound effects this week; property crews should be providing simulated props for rehearsal.

Monday. Block Act Two for the first time, one action unit at a time, reviewing frequently.

Tuesday. Work Acts One and Two, stopping as necessary. Audition sound effects. Simulated properties should be available.

Wednesday. Block Act Three for the first time. When finished, rework trouble areas, then review Act Two.

Thursday. Work Act Three, going through the action units, stopping as necessary. Run the act. Run Act Two. Encourage the cast to work for characterization as well as blocking. Give detailed notes after the run.

THREE WEEKS BEFORE OPENING:
MEMORIZATION, CHARACTERIZATION, AND TEMPO

Reclining Figure gave me a crack at my first experience with a serious Method actor, Nehemiah Persoff. Nicky Persoff is now in Hollywood and stars in many television shows. But when I was directing him back in 1954, he was the kind of serious actor who didn't really trust a director who had done only musicals. It seemed to me he was doing too much heavy thinking, which slowed down his performance.

The style of acting called Method acting is a complicated one; and the methods of many Method actors differ. I felt that in certain scenes Nicky was working too slowly. He wasn't picking up his cues. That couple of seconds seemed interminable on the stage. But Nicky didn't like my pushing him by saying, "Nicky, pick up your cues." . . . He answered with a slight touch of contempt, "You mean you want me to talk faster?" And I answered him in the same tone, "If that'll help, yes."

The rehearsal schedule must allow time to handle special problems. Stage fights must be expertly rehearsed to safeguard performers from injury and achieve dramatic effectiveness. Above, fight choreographer B. H. Barrie (center) carefully rehearses performers for a fight sequence for the New York Shakespeare Festival Delacourte Theatre production of Shakespeare's *Henry IV.* — *Photograph copyright 1984 Martha Swope*

A little while later, Martin Gabel took me aside and told me, in a fatherly way, some of the things one could say to an actor who is deeply immersed in a certain school of acting: "Abe, don't tell him to talk sooner or pick up his cues. The words to say are 'take an earlier adjustment.'" In other words, when an actor is asked a question, he shouldn't stop to think of what the question was and what his answer will be. He should take theatrical license and be prepared to answer the moment he is asked the question, unless the author has written in the direction "a long pause." . . . The next time I had an argument about a pause with Persoff, I said in professorial tones, "Nicky, please take an earlier adjustment." And I was surprised that he laughed. Coming from me, that classical suggestion struck him funny. After that, his style became crisper and we became very good friends.

—ABE BURROWS
Honest Abe

Rehearsal goals. You have three major goals this week: memorization, characterization, and tempo. Use many techniques to develop characterization, including improvisations, sensory recall, playing extremes of characters, doing the character exactly wrong, cast members exchanging roles, encouraging enlarged emotional ranges, free use of props for characterization, constant examination of character motivations and objectives, playing obstacles, reading characters from other plays by the same playwright, trust and relaxation exercises to free the performer, and concentration on physical behaviors of the character. For the cast, this week should provide exciting progress in characterization as they develop the trust that enables them to let the mask of self down and begin "wearing" the characters. Memorization should allow the cast to discard scripts.

Help performers find playable emotions. Many performers — especially those at colleges, where intellectual pursuits are expected — need encouragement to conceive of performing as an exercise of emotions. For such performers, examination of a character's thought patterns may be more comfortable than digging into the character's feelings. Other performers hesitate to show emotion, and many are so afraid of overacting that they underplay emotions. But plays are constructed of emotions. Communication, even of the strongest abstractions, starts with emotion.

This week you will begin to see the whole and will be able to pattern sequences. Work on tempo and rhythm will begin to improve the production; stressing key plot points will shape the show.

Analyzing problems and seeking solutions will occupy your attention. You should consciously seek each problem's basic cause, find all possible alternatives, and finally select a proper solution. Do not expect to solve all problems as they occur — avoid the trap of believing the director must have a godlike ability to answer every question — and let the performers work out their own answers. Indeed, you may often have the answer but elect to put a question back to the performer. As the performers discuss ways they might play this or that quality of the character, your answer should be, "Okay, show me." It is all too easy to waste rehearsal time talking; remember that drama literally means "to do, to show."

With three weeks left before your production opens, begin putting pieces together. Conclude each evening's work with continuity rehearsals, running entire scenes nonstop to help you and the performers see the whole. As always, set goals for future rehearsals before dismissing the cast.

Day-by-day schedule. Friday. Run the entire show for the lighting designer. Likely you will be surprised that the run takes so long, but be comforted in knowing that future work on tempo will decrease playing time. Give notes after rehearsal, then meet with the lighting designer to discuss concepts.

Saturday and Sunday. On Saturday and Sunday afternoons, call the principals to rehearse significant action units; these should be memorized. On Sunday evening call the action units that most need improvement (Friday night's run will show you where work is needed). Conclude each rehearsal with continuity runs to help you perceive tempo and emphasis. Your primary goal is to ensure communication of the play's basic meaning while working to bring the characterizations to life. In particular help the cast perceive superobjectives throughout the play and objectives in each action unit. Continue evolving the play's blocking and visualization, and work on business and handling simulated properties.

Monday: Weekly Production Meeting. Focus on design progress reports from those in charge of scenery, costume, lighting, makeup, props, sound, and publicity. Does any unit require extra time or workers to catch up? Have unforeseen problems plagued progress? Does the future schedule need adjustments? Is the show on budget?

Monday, Tuesday, Wednesday, and Thursday. Work one act each night in stop-and-go rehearsals, going over scenes repeatedly as necessary, and then running the act with as few stops as possible. Seek to enrich characterization and vocal variations; work on tempo and pace. On Monday, you'll work Act One; Tuesday, Act Two; Wednesday, Act Three; Thursday, special scenes that need individual attention. Your cast should be off book. During each run establish which scenes need attention, and ask the cast to tell you their problem areas. Use that information to work individual scenes after each run.

TWO WEEKS BEFORE OPENING: TECHNICAL REHEARSALS

[Orson Welles formulated] a definition of the director as absolute "master." An explicit statement of that definition can be found in a speech entitled "The Director in the Theatre Today" that Orson delivered to the Theatre Education League in 1939. . . . "Someone eventually has to shut up," said Orson, who surely didn't have himself in mind. "The composer, the light man, the scene designer, the choreographer and the actors . . . cannot all decide upon individual conceptions of the play. That would result in chaos. The director must know what he wants of each of these; he must know what is right for that conception he has of the play." That is, whatever the myriad — and undeniable — contributions of the individual members of the company, finally a production must express the director's vision.

—BARBARA LEAMING
Orson Welles: A Biography

Rehearsal goals. Coordinating technical aspects of the production is your major goal two weeks before your production opens; working with technical personnel, you ensure artistic unification of technical effects with playscript and performers. Technical rehearsals bring into the production all costumes, scenery changes and flying effects, color and intensity of lighting plus running cues, sound effects and music, makeup, properties, trap doors and elevators, smoke or fog, and other special effects. They are for designers and crews what working rehearsals are for director and performers.

Essential qualities for successful technical rehearsals. "Murphy's Law" — if anything can possibly go wrong, it will — has a corollary "Tech Rehearsal Law," which says Murphy was an optimist. Despite that disturbing pessimism, sound theatre management and an effective technical director can make technical rehearsals work smoothly.

Five basic principles will help keep the tech rehearsal law at bay:

1. Everyone involved in the production must carefully examine the feasibility of all aspects of the production during design conferences months before tech rehearsals. The week of techs is a poor time to discover that the original design of special effects, scenery, costumes, or lighting was too complex to accomplish within the time available.

2. Each necessary ingredient must be ready according to a logical pattern of need. Lights must be hung before scenic walls are erected, scenery must be in place before lights can be focused, scenery must be painted and lights ready before costumes can be checked, and so forth.

3. On the sound premise that technicians need to rehearse as much as actors, good technical theatre practice demands that crews conduct "dry tech rehearsals" on their own — running all lighting cues, scenery shifts, special fog effects, and the like — before rehearsals with the performers.

4. You and the technical staff should work out all details of the tech schedule in advance with a clear statement of priorities. Avoid letting a given problem monopolize attention, time, and energy to the detriment of other equally important aspects of the production.

5. All possible technical matters should be solved before tech week. Properties and sound effects should be working effectively days in advance of scenery shifts and lighting cues, as should other matters such as quick costume changes and makeup.

Preparation of cast. The cast should be solidly prepared — lines memorized, scenes blocked, and characterization under control — before technical rehearsals. Your focus on running techs will distract you from performers; neither director nor performers can expect a great deal of work on acting during techs.

Avoiding cast-crew conflicts. Tech rehearsals too often treat performers like mere objects to be lit, clumsy obstacles in the way of moving scenery, or ill-shaped lumps without the grace to fit into designed costumes. A "we-they" adversary relationship can ensue, separating performers and crews. This is a recipe for friction and ill-will that, once started, can accelerate into destructive infighting. Sensitive directors and technical leaders help performers and crews treat each other with the respect due to partners dedicated to staging as perfect a show as possible. I have found benefits in leading the performers in applauding good work by designers and crews, or in delivering thank-you cards the actors have signed.

Day-by-day schedule. Friday. Begin preparing for technical rehearsal week. Run the entire show nonstop as much as possible, working for continuity, rhythm, and tempo; the cast will continue to work on character growth and emotional ranges. Work with all sound effects and properties; with real or simulated costumes, rehearse costume changes.

All crews should attend this rehearsal to learn as much as possible about the way cast and director are putting the production together. To avoid a negative crew-cast relationship, the wise technical director will encourage crews to support the performers' efforts. The tech director who "cannot find time" to bring crews or allows a wise-cracking attitude toward the work of the cast — apparently innocent little jokes have a way of growing into vicious put-downs that undermine performers' confidence — will create permanent frictions that undermine the success of the show. Equally you must not allow cast members to disparage the technicians.

Saturday. Unless there are strong reasons to conclude the contrary — scenes not blocked, memorization problems, unbearably rough spots — you will find the show improves if the cast rests away from the theatre in the morning and afternoon. If you do plan to rehearse, find a location other than the stage; technical personnel should be working there.

In the evening the first order of business is the costume parade, a display of all costumes on the stage under production lighting. Depending on the complexities of the costume plot, the parade will require approximately sixty to ninety minutes. You and the costumer will sit in the auditorium and examine costumes individually as well as collectively.

Following the parade, run the entire show nonstop. Give notes after the run. Work troublesome scenes as needed. Conclude as always by setting goals for the next rehearsals.

Sunday. If possible, avoid calling the entire cast in the afternoon. While you may not wish to call the full company, you might call principals to work given scenes, seeking to iron out problems with characterizations, emotions, relationships, or staging.

In the evening run the complete show with makeup, properties, sound, and costumes. Give notes after rehearsal and set goals for tomorrow.

Monday: Weekly Production Meeting. The primary focus should be on final planning of all details of running tech rehearsals. The meeting should produce a comprehensive schedule for the next week. Anticipate possible problems and prepare contingency plans.

Monday. Do a nonstop smooth run with costumes, makeup, properties, and sound effects. Because the next rehearsals are going to focus on technical demands, you want the performers to concentrate fully on characterization at this rehearsal while you work on tempo and pace. Rework problem scenes.

Tuesday and Wednesday. Before these rehearsals you should meet with the cast in a quiet room for relaxed warmups. Have the production stage manager make brief announcements regarding tech rehearsals. On Tuesday tech the first half of the play; on Wednesday, the second half. The rehearsals will be stop-and-go, cue-to-cue, with performers giving cues for each technical effect — this speech to cue that sound effect, this moment to begin that lighting change, this scene shift, and the like. Expect delays as crews reset sound effects or the lighting board in order to be able to run the show effectively the next rehearsal.

Careful attention to details during technical rehearsals
will result in a smooth-running production that
achieves the director's vision. Above, the Arena Stage
(Washington, D.C.) production of *K2*, set on one of the
world's tallest mountains. Two climbers, played here
by Stephan McHattie (left) and Stanley Anderson
(right), battle the elements in a life-or-death
confrontation with their past, present, and uncertain
future. Jacques Levy directed the production at Arena.
Note the lifelike representation of the mountain, snow,
and climbers' equipment. — *Photograph by Joan Marcus*

Following each night's rehearsal if possible run some of the half just worked
to allow tech crews and performers to begin to fit the pieces together. On the
other hand, if tech rehearsals become bogged down and cannot be finished in a
reasonable time, do not allow anyone to become confused about priorities: while
it is important to finish techs, it is more important to protect cast and crew members. Do not permit tech rehearsals to drag on into the early morning hours.

Thursday. Run the show with all technical effects. Your goal tonight is to
begin putting together all the pieces of the play. Depending on perceived difficulties, you may elect to omit makeup and costumes tonight and use the time for

During technical rehearsals all parts of the production
are put together so that the audience will be able to
enter the world of the play without distractions. The
more complicated the production, the more advance
planning is necessary for technical rehearsals to work
smoothly. Above, *Buried Child* at the Arena Stage,
Washington, D.C., directed by Gilbert Moses.
— *Photograph by Joan Marcus*

running other aspects of the production. If necessary to eliminate technical problems, tonight may be a stop-and-go rehearsal.

THE FINAL WEEK: POLISHING AND BUILDING CONFIDENCE

While a good director may often offer helpful criticism and valuable coaching or supply
interesting, even thrilling, interpretative ideas, perhaps his most useful contribution to
the work of rehearsal is not "artistic" at all, but consists of being a good chairman.

It is in this capacity that he arranges the agenda for each day's work, sets the pace
and determines the amount of time devoted to this or that. Above all, it is principally
from the director that a rehearsal takes its tone, derives its atmosphere.

—TYRONE GUTHRIE
A Life in the Theatre

Rehearsal goals. You have two major goals during the final week of rehearsals. Your first goal is to polish the show. You should not add substantial amounts of new materials — the final week is not the best time to introduce massive new blocking or make radical changes in characterization — and you should focus on eliminating rough spots. Polishing requires making corrective notes on even the smallest item — the director's microscopic attention to a gesture or scene shift will surprise those not familiar with final week polishing. You want to preserve what is artistically correct and repair areas that are wrong. Run the whole show without stopping.

Final rehearsals are run as if an audience were present. This demands full makeup, costumes, sound, lighting, scene shifts, properties, and all other aspects of production. Only by running with complete technical effects will you and your technical staff discover and correct problems in rehearsals. At each rehearsal you must insist on show discipline — the curtain must rise precisely on time, intermissions should be correctly timed, cast and crews must maintain silence backstage, and performers must be in the wings before their entrances.

Your second major goal is to build confidence. In the final week you prepare performers and technicians, mentally and physically, to do a quality production. To the extent possible, emphasize the positive, even when calling attention to mistakes.

Day-by-day schedule. Friday. In this rehearsal you will seek to run the show as a coherent whole and check all technical effects to be sure they work smoothly. You will also work on tempo and emphasis of key moments. In addition, rehearse for emergencies: A production that has not considered appropriate reactions to emergencies — audience or company member needing immediate medical assistance, fire, and the like — shows a lack of responsibility on the part of the stage management, and you should insist on a full emergency rehearsal.

After the run, assemble the cast and crews to give notes. Guard time carefully: Long-winded discussions following a full run can exhaust already tired workers. Some performers, perhaps apprehensive about their work, may question every note, thereby prolonging the meeting. Gently suggest they meet with you privately after you dismiss the company. Finish your notes with a statement of goals for the next rehearsal. Technical chiefs should then talk with their crews in preparation for their work the next day.

Saturday. If extra rehearsal time is needed, you may use the morning and afternoon periods as well as evening. You can accomplish significant work between nine and noon, and one and five, and these are the last rehearsal periods you can use to work on individual units of the play. Call a daytime rehearsal if you feel the play has major problems. If performers are still having memorization problems, for example, a line rehearsal is definitely necessary. If a given scene is incorrectly paced, a tempo rehearsal will improve its quality. Because crews will be working onstage, take your cast to a different rehearsal area.

Saturday Evening. The evening rehearsal's major priority is to polish the technical parts of production, solving all technical problems to ensure a smooth-running production. During the rehearsal you, the costume designer, the makeup chief, the lighting designer, and the technical director will sit together in the auditorium, and after the rehearsal you will discuss necessary corrections.

Tonight you should block the curtain call. Many directors dislike doing the curtain call too early in the rehearsal period because the final bows suggest completion and the show is not "finished" until opening night. But if you wait too late to work out curtain calls, they will not receive adequate rehearsal with crews.

Sunday. If rehearsals of scenes or acts are needed, hold them Sunday afternoon, but dismiss performers early enough for them to take a break before the evening's call. Evening rehearsal should be full dress, operating on the same schedule as a performance. To build performers' confidence, establish a series of routines: Company call, and all other performance processes, should be followed as they will be on performance nights. Ritual can be reassuring. This should be a nonstop run.

Monday and Tuesday. These should be full dress rehearsals run precisely as if the audience were present. You may eliminate makeup on Tuesday if it has been correct for earlier rehearsals — cast members appreciate an opportunity to let their skin "rest" a night — but you will want performers to wear all wigs or beards. Reserve time to work special problem areas at the end of the run-through.

Wednesday. For this final dress rehearsal, run the production exactly as it will be on performance nights. There is an old adage that says "a poor final dress means a good opening night." Nonsense. Undoubtedly that bromide was coined by a producer whose show had just finished a horrible final dress rehearsal. A bad final dress is not a disaster, but it doesn't give performers any reason to feel assured that things will go well on opening night. You want to build confidence, not increase worries.

Assemble cast and crews after the curtain call to speak briefly about significant aspects of the rehearsal. Give the cast a list of specific goals they should work on in preparation for opening night. You might lead the company to think of giving to the audience, sharing talent like an act of love. You might also stress that the "show is ready for an audience," to build confidence and encourage the cast to look forward to playing to the audience. This conclusion of the rehearsal process is an excellent opportunity to thank cast and crew for their contributions and cooperation and tell them to enjoy the experience of entertaining the audience the next night.

Exercises

Construct a full rehearsal schedule for the play you will direct. Be detailed, following the outline below.

1. List all times and dates for rehearsals.
2. For each rehearsal specify every event in half-hour increments. For example:

> 7:00–7:30: Announcements, warmups, and statement of goals for the evening.
> 7:30–8:00: Read through action units 1 and 2.

8:00–8:30: Discuss action units 1 and 2, including intent and title of each unit and each character's emotion and objective.

8:30–9:00: Read through action units 3, 4, and 5.

3. For every rehearsal specify directorial goals — what you want to achieve — and performers' goals — what you want each performer to achieve.

4. Include such details as when you expect the cast to be off book; when you will begin using props, sound, makeup, and costumes; time assigned for techs and dress rehearsals; and everything else involved with the rehearsal process.

5. Anticipate special difficulties for performers or technical personnel. Discuss various solutions and contingency plans to overcome such problems.

6. When you have completed the full schedule, tally the total amount of time you plan to rehearse each individual action unit, scene, and act. If some appear to receive insufficient time, revise the schedule as necessary.

PART FOUR

Rehearsing the Production

CHAPTER FOURTEEN

Working with Actors, Part One: Guidelines for Rehearsals

Although the performing arts are still unwelcome at many major American and English universities — it was a professor at Harvard who declared a course in acting to be equivalent to a course in butchering meat — I believe that without the performing arts no university can be complete. If a library is a quintessential research facility, where students of Hellenistic poetry or Idealistic philosophy can investigate the primary and secondary sources of their disciplines, then surely a theatre or concert hall is a living library, where the works of drama or music are in a position to find their true, significant form. It is true that many of these performances are of poor quality; so are many works of scholarship. The important thing is that both scholar and artist should be striving to achieve the highest standards of excellence.

—ROBERT BRUSTEIN
Who Needs Theatre: Dramatic Opinions

Productive rehearsals are essential to bring the intangible directorial vision to concrete existence on stage. In rehearsals the director, cast, and production personnel work together to interpret the play accurately; find the most effective means to communicate that interpretation; learn to work together cooperatively to build a close-knit ensemble; examine characters for emotions, objectives, motivations, and reactions; learn subtext under the dialogue; experiment to find the best staging techniques; establish rhythm and tempo; use blocking, business, and movement meaningfully; and ensure that audiences will be able to see and hear the stage action. Additional time is required to ensure smoothly effective technical effects such as scenery, costumes, lights, sound, makeup, and properties. The price paid for an artistically integrated production is an intense and complex rehearsal process that the director must control effectively.

Aware of the many rehearsal goals, directors face a number of questions. How often should a play rehearse? What guidelines govern rehearsals? How many hours of rehearsal are necessary? When should the cast have lines memorized? What is the most effective maximum length of rehearsals? Minimum? How can the director avoid an overrehearsed or underrehearsed play? What is appropriate

Steps allow characters to be open to the audience and
still relate to each other and also provide interesting
composition, as in this scene from John Neville-
Andrews's production of *King Lear* at the Folger
Shakespeare Theatre — note that the upstage
performer touches the seated actor while he tilts his
head to listen to her. During rehearsals the director
experiments with levels and steps to achieve
directorial vision of the production. — *Photograph by
Julie Ainsworth*

discipline? How does the director ensure that rehearsals are a period of artistic growth?

This chapter examines these questions and other operational rules that are applicable to the rehearsal of any production. Here we look at some mechanics of rehearsals; the following chapter discusses working with actors.

Estimating Length of Rehearsal Period

A rule of thumb suggests that for an amateur production of an "average" play, you should rehearse approximately an hour for every minute on stage, which suggests that a 45-minute, one-act play should rehearse some 45 hours; a full-length play running 2 hours and 10 minutes would require about 130 hours of rehearsal. According to this guideline, and assuming a four-hour per evening schedule, the average full-length play needs at least thirty-three days of rehearsal.

An experienced director with an experienced cast needs less time to achieve satisfactory results; an inexperienced director will need more. Regardless of the director's experience, more rehearsal time is necessary for plays with additional difficulties and complexities, such as poetic diction; large cast; classic dimensions of tragedy or comedy; and the technical demands of scene shifts, elaborate costumes, and complicated lighting effects.

Musicals require time to rehearse not only actors but also singers, dancers, and orchestra members; the musical's complex technical requirements of scene shifts and lighting effects demand still more preparation time. Instead of one hour of rehearsal per minute of stage time, a better estimate for the musical is approximately two hours. If the so-called average play requires five weeks of rehearsal, the musical needs eight weeks; but because they are seldom given that much time, directing a musical is an excellent test of the director's ability to organize complex elements with simultaneous rehearsals for dance, voice, and acting.

Frequency of Rehearsals

In the amateur theatre each week has eleven rehearsal periods: seven evenings, two weekend mornings, and two weekend afternoons. To avoid exhausting performers, directors typically rehearse five or six periods and seldom use all eleven periods, although complicated plays and musicals may need nine or ten. On the other hand, rehearsing only two or three times a week prevents intensive work and can retard dynamic growth; infrequent rehearsals may also imply to the cast that the director is indifferent about the production.

Given a five- or six-week rehearsal period, many directors in amateur theatre schedule five evening rehearsals a week for the first two to four weeks. If the play is difficult, directors often use weekends to rehearse principals or special scenes.

The last two weeks of rehearsal, which bring in technical effects, usually demand evening rehearsals on Saturdays and Sundays.

Duration of Rehearsals

A typical rehearsal begins with ten minutes of general preliminaries and twenty minutes of warm-ups, and concludes with approximately fifteen minutes of summation, notes, and goal-setting. This means that you can expect to expend approximately forty-five minutes of each session in activities not directly related to rehearsing. Therefore, for a one-act play you should plan to rehearse not less than an hour and a half at a time, which allows only forty-five minutes' actual rehearsal of the play. Two to three hours is a minimum for a full-length play.

The maximum length of rehearsals ranges from four to six hours. Professional performers are protected by Equity regulations that prevent them from rehearsing more than eight and a half hours, with ninety minutes reserved for a recess. Amateur performers have full-time jobs or classes and academic assignments that divert energy. Rehearsals that extend beyond four hours begin to overload the performer; as fatigue increases, the performers' ability and learning curve decreases. However, it is possible to rehearse all day and evening if individual performers receive substantial breaks away not only from the stage but also from the theatre building, and you carefully husband your own energy and have loyal assistants to shoulder much of the load.

Creating a Creative Atmosphere

Creativity flourishes brilliantly in the correct atmosphere but languishes in a negative environment. More than any other individual you are responsible for setting the proper tone. Partners to creativity are commitment and a sense of play: One must take one's art seriously, but not oneself. You lead the performers in dedicated serious commitment to theatre art, enhanced by laughter and childlike enjoyment of the work.

Beginning directors are often unaware how much the prevailing rehearsal atmosphere communicates about the environment they have created. An experienced director visiting a novice director's rehearsals can easily perceive the working conditions not only of the current rehearsal but also of past rehearsals. The mood at rehearsals conducted by the open and honest director is free and relaxed; the atmosphere created by the closed or suspicious director is rigid and tense; loud and raucous cast behavior bespeaks a director with little self-discipline; and an air of enjoyment with genuine concentration on the task at hand indicates a director who encourages creative development.

A director who seeks to blame others for mistakes — the playwright's script is flawed, the actors won't do as they're told, and so forth — creates an uncom-

Director-choreographer Bob Fosse (at right, with cigarette) rehearses with dancers of the New York production of *Dancin'*. Note the director's facial expression showing total absorption in the dancers' work. Rehearsals require intense concentration, which can be as fatiguing for the director as the physical work is for the cast. — *Photograph by Martha Swope*

fortable atmosphere. Once started, such scapegoating snowballs and can damage the actors, the production, and ultimately even the director. The director comfortable with his or her personal educational process — and all directors, whether veterans or novices, find that rehearsals teach them a great deal — will create an atmosphere that encourages all to learn; the director unwilling to admit lack of knowledge will create a tense atmosphere that inhibits growth.

As the director, you create the proper atmosphere during rehearsals. Your excitement about doing this play with this cast will be contagious; your eagerness to experiment, learn, and grow creatively will be shared by the performers. Your commitment will be matched by the performers' dedication; your energy and enthusiasm will create similar qualities in performers; and your respect for the performers' abilities will be returned.

When you start to rehearse with other people something begins to happen. What it is exactly I don't know, and don't even want to know. I'm all for mystery there. Most of what happens as you develop your part is unconscious, most of it underwater.... you get taken over by some force outside yourself. Something happens.

—KIM STANLEY
Quoted in *The Player* by Lillian Ross and Helen Ross

Setting Goals

A principal key to successful rehearsals involves setting goals twice each rehearsal session. You begin each rehearsal by setting goals for that period's work. For example, if directing Shepard's *Fool for Love,* you might say, "Tonight we'll work the scene where Eddie taunts Martin. May, we'll look at your subtext and reactions during this scene, and you should extend your emotions, even overplaying them, until we find the correct size. Martin, force yourself to work primarily on concentration and emotion while Eddie is taunting you. Eddie, work on correct physicalization of the character and objective: let's see how your body can communicate your intention. Then we'll run that scene several times to remove the blocking kinks that you said were bothersome the last time we worked the scene." The goal-setting process concentrates performers' attention on significant areas.

You set goals for the second time at the conclusion of rehearsals. You might say, for example, "Tomorrow night we're going to run the first six scenes. Before tomorrow's rehearsals I want you to pay special attention to your characters' activities when not on stage, before entering or after exiting. We'll work on your motivations and emotional attitudes for entrances and exits. Any questions?" Record these goals in your prompt book and refer to them at the beginning of the next rehearsal.

The cast benefits from the focus that goal-setting provides. You also profit because setting goals forces you to concentrate on priorities and helps you recognize which scenes need work. Each night after the company has left, sit quietly with your assistant and record the progress of the rehearsal, then discuss major problems and future solutions. From that examination will come further goals for you and for the performers.

[Elia] Kazan has said: "I put terrific stress on what the person wants and why he wants it. What makes it meaningful to him. I don't start on *how* he goes about getting it until I get him wanting it." Think of this as step one in a three-stage process in the rehearsal of actors. Consider that it accounts for Kazan's famously energetic productions. ("All my actors come on strong, they're all alive, they're all dynamic — no matter how quiet.") ... Step two in the process introduces the actor to "the circumstances under which he behaves; what happens before, and so on" — what Stanislavski called the "given circumstances." ... the opposition of given circumstances to a character's desire [is] the source of dramatic conflict and the stimulus of a character's action. "I will say nothing to an actor that cannot be translated directly into action," Kazan said in 1944. Twenty years later, he was still expressing the same thought: "The life of a play is in behavior." So the third step in the rehearsal process sets the actor loose to try to accomplish his desire: "I try to find the physical behavior without preconception on my part, if possible, but from what the actor does to achieve his objective under the circumstances."

—DAVID RICHARD JONES
Great Directors at Work

Providing Leadership and Maintaining Discipline

How does a director establish leadership? What should a director do to maintain cast discipline? These questions plague all directors from time to time because a group art cannot succeed without discipline; the more your attention is diverted to discipline problems, the less you are able to work on the production. Beginning directors, naturally enough, are concerned about leadership and discipline. As you undoubtedly have discovered from your past work as an actor or technician, chaos and unfocused effort are predictable results of a lack of group discipline, and meandering rehearsals and muddy scenes are evidence of a lack of directorial leadership.

Discipline helps create teamwork. Consider the sailors on a racing yacht: Without discipline, crew members might argue about who is responsible for handling the headsail sheets when tacking and thus make coordinated maneuvers impossible. Ultimately such a boat will run hard aground while the crew continues to argue about who should have avoided the disaster. A theatrical production can also run aground if the director does not take the helm. A well-disciplined theatrical company, like the well-trained sailing crew, is a joy to watch, each person aware of personal responsibility and all totally dedicated to making every moment work perfectly. Discipline creates a smoothly oiled machine, controlled and always focused on the final goal. Without discipline there is no teamwork; without cooperative teamwork, theatre art cannot exist.

A fundamental tenet of leadership holds that if you must tell a group you are in charge, you're not. Therefore, instead of making speeches about directorial power, you should maintain a positive mental set and operate on the premise that the cast quite naturally recognizes your authority. "I'm the director and we'll do it my way" is wrong-headed leadership for three clear reasons:

1. The statement sets up a confrontational situation by throwing down a gauntlet that asks for rebellion.
2. It may inhibit performers from making individual creative contributions.
3. It is simply not the most effective way to establish personal authority.

You obtain positive results when you *demonstrate* authority; talking about your leadership suggests an officious pretentiousness that most theatre workers dislike. You lead by example. Negative examples cause negative results. If you have temper tantrums or pouting fits, you can expect equally immature behavior patterns in your cast. If you show you respect your cast members as people and as performing artists, you will experience little difficulty.

We can describe some attributes of effective leadership:

■ Effective leaders learn from others. If you intend to make a career as a director, establish correct working habits early. Ask a director you respect to come to your rehearsals and critique your work. Listen to others' opinions. Study other directors' work. Volunteer to serve as assistant to a director of quality productions; you can learn a great deal if you approach such apprenticeships with a strong desire to study directorial techniques.

- Effective leaders are well-prepared and well-organized for the task at hand. You should come to rehearsals with a clear set of goals and rational approaches to achieve those goals.

- Effective leaders are flexible. Even though you may have important goals for a given rehearsal unit, circumstances may suggest changes. Plan alternative problem-solving approaches.

- Effective leaders are sensitive to the needs of the cast as a group and as individuals. Each cast has a different chemistry, and each individual has unique qualities.

- Effective leaders do not waste time. A cast can be demoralized by inefficiency and exhausted by waiting to rehearse. Tech volunteers who wait in vain for someone to tell them what to do may become discouraged and leave; they will be sorely missed when a work call goes out. Do not allow other business to distract you from your primary goal at rehearsals, but delegate responsibilities to keep the various aspects of the production running efficiently.

- Effective leaders know when to push and when to pull. Effective leaders also know when to do neither: Deliberately doing nothing is often precisely the right action because it encourages others to use their own initiative.

- Effective leaders operate on the premise that everyone in the production sincerely wants to improve performance techniques in order to achieve excellence.

- Effective leaders conscientiously give equal attention to all members of the group. The larger the cast, the more difficult it is for you to give notes to each individual, but every performer deserves attention. To be sure no one feels slighted, consider assigning an assistant to maintain a checklist of notes to the cast each night with instructions to inform you if individuals are not given notes.

- Effective leaders know that *critique* does not necessarily mean "find fault with." Part of your role is to identify faults to correct them, but an equally important portion of your job is to praise good work to preserve it.

- Effective leaders seek to create a team. Theatre is a collaborative art, not a one-man show.

- Effective leaders listen well, encouraging members of the team to make suggestions.

- Effective leaders are self-actuated. Actors who become directors are often surprised to learn that the director receives few words of appreciation. Most actors sense a great deal of reinforcement in rehearsals, but they may not realize that the director initiates the praise; when such actors turn to direction, they often become subconsciously irritated at the lack of positive comments. Prior awareness of this situation will help you find direction less frustrating.

- Effective leaders take the art seriously, but not themselves. Laughter is a vital part of the creative process; you should approach your work with good humor and an ability to laugh at your own errors.
- Effective leaders establish clear rehearsal rules. Be sure all members of the cast know the rules governing rehearsals. If you assume your cast will automatically follow "standard rules of operation," you will be forced to state rules after each infraction, thereby appearing to be an arbitrary tyrant. You can avoid problems by clear and early communication. The following list suggests sample ground rules you may wish to employ.

SAMPLE REHEARSAL RULES

1. All cast members should arrive before the stated time of call, certainly never later than announced call. Rehearsals begin on time as scheduled; cast members who will be unavoidably late should notify the director or the director's assistant.

2. Performers should always bring a pencil (not a pen) to rehearsals because blocking and other notes are subject to many changes.

3. Nothing is permitted to distract from rehearsing the play; rehearsal is a time for work, not social encounters and parties.

4. The actor sincerely interested in learning performance art and craft will be in the rehearsal area to observe the work of others.

5. Performers should not use rehearsals for memorization.

6. Smoking and eating are not allowed in the rehearsal hall.

7. No drugs or alcohol are permitted in the rehearsal hall. Performers should be discouraged from using such substances before rehearsals or before performing.

8. Performers should keep an actors' journal, bringing it to each rehearsal and making frequent entries about their questions, discoveries, and progress.

9. No visitors are permitted at rehearsal without the director's prior permission.

10. While the cast is working there must be no noise in the rehearsal hall; actors experience enough difficulties getting into character and concentrating on the play without having to overcome distractions. Actors who wish to chat should leave the rehearsal area.

Promptness

Starting rehearsals on time is one significant aspect of proper discipline, and both beginning and experienced directors often have to address the problem of tardy arrivals. The performer who arrives late disrupts the flow of rehearsals. Furthermore, each scene depends on growth and interplay between characters, which is impossible if any participant in that scene is absent. Performers attempting to develop characterization are severely hampered if their partners are not working the scene with them.

The tardy performer is bad for morale. The director has to deal with the discipline problem, and the results can have a long-range adverse effect on the company. The person who arrives late seems to be saying that other things are more important than the production. Often the tardiness means you cannot rehearse a scheduled scene.

The usual strategy of directors dealing with tardiness is to have an earnest talk with the cast about all discipline matters before rehearsals begin. These talks can start at auditions and be emphasized at callbacks; at the first rehearsal you should specify rehearsal regulations. To help forestall cast tardiness, you must never be late; ideally you should be at rehearsals at least fifteen minutes early. You must start rehearsals precisely as scheduled; delays discourage promptness.

If a performer is late several times, take him or her aside privately, out of the rehearsal hall, and discuss the problem. For this first talk you should listen to any explanations, not hector the performer or create unpleasantness. If you are reluctant to speak privately to the performer about the problem for fear it will be awkward or you are upset at the damage the performer is doing to your production, force yourself to conduct the talk. Your reluctance indicates that your own attitude may be contributing to the problem. If the performer continues to be late, a second private talk is necessary. This time you will need to be quite firm about the performer's personal responsibility for work in the show.

If all else fails, you may be forced to remove the performer from the cast. First be sure that you have an adequate replacement and that you have weighed the overall advantages and disadvantages, including company morale for this production and ramifications for possible future productions. You should not replace a performer if you have contributed to the problem — if you have often been late, for example, or have not talked frankly with the performer more than once — but you should feel free to replace a performer whose lack of self-discipline hinders the production.

Warm-Ups

When I first started directing, I avoided warm-ups thinking they were merely a waste of time: I wanted to get directly to rehearsing. Later I directed musicals and at the urging of choreographers and musical directors I rather grudgingly conducted warm-ups for singers and dancers. That made me belatedly aware of what other directors already knew: Warm-ups are an important, even essential, part of the rehearsal process for both musicals and plays, novices and experienced actors (although professional actors may prefer to do warm-ups on their own).

Warm-up exercises are the first order of business at rehearsals, before announcements or goal-setting discussions. Exercises benefit performers' creative, mental, physical, and vocal abilities, and make their work in rehearsals more effective. Because the entire group participates, exercises engender a team spirit that is a valuable first step in building an ensemble. In addition, physical stretches and exercises make the body more limber, which protects performers against accidental damage, and vocal exercises warm up the vocal mechanism, which helps performers develop correct vocal techniques while protecting them against damage to that delicate instrument.

Warm-ups are also an important "transition zone," because they help performers refocus from daily concerns to the play's rehearsals. Performers come to the theatre full of thoughts about a disagreeable day at work or family tensions and the like. Warm-ups bring the performers together into the universe of the play, and improvisational games establish a spirit of imaginative, childlike playfulness that performers can use in developing characterization.

Your favorite acting book will list a number of exercises. With experience you will develop personal exercises that you feel are most effective. Encourage individual members of the cast to bring their favorite exercises to warm-ups. However, perhaps one word of warning is appropriate here: These exercises may be so enjoyable that they become longer and longer, so set a time limit for warm-ups.

Deadlines for Line Memorization

At what stage of rehearsals should the director require actors to know their lines? No single rule is applicable for all casts at all times. If the cast is experienced, memorization takes place smoothly; inexperienced performers need time to learn the tricks of memorization. Memorization comes more easily with nightly rehearsals; infrequent rehearsals make memorization more halting, which explains why leads often have their parts memorized well before those who have only a few lines and thus rehearse less frequently. In general you will find that grade school and high school students typically need prodding to learn lines, college and professional actors are usually quick to memorize, and adults in community theatres often experience difficulty memorizing lines.

Early memorization can be disadvantageous. Insisting on line memorization by the second week of rehearsals tells performers that mechanical matters are more important than concept and characterization. If you communicate that in rehearsal, the production will be mechanical and stilted, with narrow characterization but fine memorization. Further, because physical movements aid memorization, it is not reasonable to expect actors to know lines until they also have blocking, and few directors want to block the play during the first week of rehearsals.

Rigid insistence on early line memorization may create discipline problems, and you may expend a great deal of energy hectoring your actors about lines. That energy could be better spent developing a rich understanding of the play, meaningful characterizations, and variations in line readings.

You should not allow performers to set their own memorization schedule, however, because some will learn lines early and others will procrastinate until opening night looms. This erratic process will cause other uneven qualities — performer A will be thinking of lines today and calling for cues while others are working on characterization; performer B will hold tightly to the script when others are off book and working with props — and you will be unable to work on tempo or develop cohesive unification.

Given a five-week rehearsal schedule, you may want to call for line memorization according to acts. For example, you can ask for Act One to be memorized by the middle of the second week, Act Two by the beginning of the third week, and Act Three by the end of the third week. We rehearse each act many times before asking the cast to go without scripts.

Lines should be securely memorized well before tech rehearsals. A cast plagued with memorization problems at dress rehearsals will be uneasy. Actors who do not have their lines will be uncomfortable; those who share scenes with them will worry about possible disasters; and you will be unable to shape the production's tempo.

STRATEGIES TO ENCOURAGE MEMORIZATION

What steps should you take if the cast doesn't memorize lines on schedule? The problem may be more in your imagination than in fact; most performers learn lines with little trouble, providing rehearsals are conducted effectively, and you do not want to invent problems where none exist. But you may be justifiably concerned about line memorization if, for example, you have had unfortunate experiences with similar casts, or all signs indicate this particular cast is slow. In such cases the following strategies may help:

1. Be sure your schedule is reasonable. One director canceled a production because the cast did not have the entire play memorized after two weeks of rehearsal. However, the cast was rehearsing no more than two or three times a week, had blocked only half the play, and had read through Act III only twice. The director was markedly unfair to insist that lines be memorized at that point.

2. Communicate the schedule early and with proper emphasis. It is patently unfair to announce on Wednesday that you expect lines by Friday and no less unfair for a director to focus consistently on characterization, blocking, and business and then suddenly insist on line memorization. Performers understand your priorities by what you emphasize during rehearsals.

3. To help individuals with memorization problems, have your assistant go over lines with them outside of rehearsal. If the actor lacks memorization experience, emphasize the value of repetition. New actors should also learn to assign themselves reachable goals, mastering one page, then one scene, at a time, instead of a broad target such as "tonight I'll memorize the whole play." Beginning actors also need to learn to recognize cues — not by memorizing the last word of the preceding speech but by knowing the entire speech — and to have a full breath when the last word is said. Teach actors to inhale on, say, the fifth word from the end of the cue speech because inhaling after hearing the last word will create ineffective pauses.

4. Go over scenes repeatedly to help the cast with memorization. Performers should work on lines outside of rehearsal, but repetition during rehearsal is markedly effective. Rehearse an act several evenings in sequence before

the performers are due to go without books. Remember that physical movement is directly related to line memorization: Before asking for memorization, you should have blocked that part of the play, and the cast should have had repeated opportunities to work the act.

Avoiding the Underrehearsed Production

It is easy to recognize an underrehearsed play by its general air of discomfort and tension, not at all similar to the normal intense production anticipation. Performers are not relaxed in their roles; lines and business are muffed; blocking is scrambled; and most action is extremely quick as if all participants want nothing more than to get through the whole business. In the underrehearsed production there is no control of rhythm and tempo, the play lacks shape, and the playwright's structure is lost in the confusion. The underrehearsed production is an ordeal for the audience: Tensions from the nervous cast infect the audience, who will be glad when given the opportunity to escape. Often the director complains that the cast forgot essential qualities they had mastered and added many new things never before seen.

An underrehearsed play is not necessarily caused by too few rehearsals. The problem with most underrehearsed plays is simply poor use of available rehearsal time, usually the result of failure of leadership: The director has not successfully led the company to pursue salient goals but has allowed rehearsals to wander aimlessly. The solution is to conduct "quality" rehearsals, in which the group uses its time wisely, working at a high level of efficiency and creativity. In quality rehearsals the director is similar to an efficient chairman, setting significant goals, keeping the company properly focused on the business at hand, and ignoring distractions.

Avoiding the Overrehearsed Production

An apparently overrehearsed play is like a diamond covered with an unpleasant film. Everything is there, but the sparkle is missing. Performers seem to be saying lines by rote, without thinking of meaning; no one is listening because they've heard it all before. One feels the production is on automatic drive.

Although most directors conclude that an overrehearsed quality necessarily results from too many rehearsals, the more probable cause lies elsewhere. The play that appears overrehearsed usually has grown static in rehearsals with no new ideas from cast or director, no growth, and no suggestions for changes. Everyone has been wrung dry. That quality can appear at the tenth rehearsal or the fiftieth. Too many nonstop run-throughs can contribute to the difficulty if there are not sufficient directorial notes following each one.

You can avoid the problem of an overrehearsed play by aiming high enough to stimulate both yourself and the cast. The lower your target, the sooner the goal is reached; a more lofty target forces everyone to work harder. Instead of settling in, keep yourself and the cast off balance, seeking new approaches to replace the comfortable older techniques. Continually strive for dimensional characters, new concepts in characterization, and complex personifications. Experiments are helpful. Continue to set goals at each rehearsal's beginning and end.

Rehearsal Atmosphere

An act of creation has nothing to do with either external comfort or conventional human civility; that is to say, working conditions in which everybody is happy. It demands a maximum of silence and a minimum of words. In this kind of creativity we discuss through proposals, actions and living organisms, not through explanations. When we finally find ourselves on the track of something difficult and often almost intangible, we have no right to lose it through frivolity and carelessness. Therefore, even during breaks after which we will be continuing with the creative process, we are obliged to observe certain natural reticences in our behavior and even in our private affairs. This applies just as much to our own work as to the work of our partners. We must not interrupt and disorganize the work because we are hurrying to our own affairs; we must not peep, comment or make jokes about it privately. In any case, private ideas of fun have no place in the actor's calling. In our approach to creative tasks, even if the theme is a game, we must be in a state of readiness — one might even say "solemnity."

An actor has no right to mould his partner so as to provide greater possibilities for his own performance. Nor has he the right to correct his partner. . . . Intimate or drastic elements in the work of others are untouchable and should not be commented upon even in their absence. Private conflicts, quarrels, sentiments, animosities are unavoidable in any human group. It is our duty towards creation to keep them in check in so far as they might deform and wreck the work process.

—JERZY GROTOWSKI
Towards a Poor Theatre

As director, you create the rehearsal atmosphere, choosing between the cathedrallike solemnity Grotowski describes above and a quite social environment. Beginning directors, usually overconcerned that the actors "enjoy" rehearsals and often quite desirous of their casts' affection, tend to think of cast parties and comparable "fun" activities not related to the business at hand. More experienced directors, however, are aware of performers' motivational drives to excel and know that actors' enjoyment of rehearsals is directly related to progress toward perfection; these directors have discovered that "fun" is a factor of performers' development.

In particular you will be wise to heed Grotowski's warnings about actors telling their colleagues how to play a scene or develop a character. Such "backstage directors" create ill-will and chaos. Actors who coach other actors in line interpretations, blocking, or characterization, are violating a cardinal precept of his or her role in the production; such actors are ignoring their own concentration and characterization. Performance skills suffer.

"A maximum of silence and a minimum of words" suggests a serious attitude toward creative development and artistic and educational growth. The opposite indicates a close-minded and self-centered attitude accompanied by a lack of desire to learn and improve. To illustrate the importance of this attitude, we in theatre would be wise to observe rehearsals of professional ballet or symphony companies. Actors and directors who have watched the working processes of such companies report they are amazed to discover the effectiveness of their serious attitudes, and how unproductive our noisy and chaotic theatre rehearsals are in comparison. Many experienced theatre directors conclude that theatre workers, because they typically are highly verbal and gregarious, especially need to adopt the "maximum of silence" concept Grotowski recommends. We are trying to learn how to create a work of art, an awesome process that deserves the solemnity Grotowski describes, but always accompanied by the childlike delight Stanislavski recommends.

Exercises

1. Drawing on your experience as a participant in theatrical productions, describe rehearsals clearly marked by a creative atmosphere leading to growth. What are the characteristics of a creative atmosphere in rehearsals? Describe the director's techniques that established that positive atmosphere.

   Describe, in contrast, rehearsals that at best only infrequently had an atmosphere that encouraged creative work. What do you think dampened creativity? What do you believe were the director's failures?

   List experiments you intend to use to build the proper rehearsal atmosphere. An ideal list will be based on two premises: "If this technique doesn't succeed, I'll try this," and "if this system is effective, I'll add to it by doing this."

2. Again using your personal experience as a member of a team (not necessarily limited to theatrical productions), identify strengths and weaknesses of leaders with whom you've worked. What do you conclude are effective leadership techniques? Ineffective techniques?

3. What do you anticipate will be your personal strengths and weaknesses as a leader?

4. Prepare vocal, physical, and character warm-up exercises to use during rehearsals. Specify your goal with each exercise.

5. Prepare a written list of rehearsal rules for your cast.

[To illustrate what can happen in a poorly-rehearsed production, actress Fanny Kemble describes playing Juliet opposite a Romeo with whom she'd not rehearsed before. Imagine a modern production with these problems!]

The play went off pretty smoothly except they broke one man's collarbone, and nearly dislocated a woman's shoulder by flinging the scenery about. My bed was not made in time, and when the scene drew [that is, when the curtains "drew" back to reveal the set], half a dozen carpenters in patched trousers and tattered shirt sleeves were discovered smoothing down my pillows and adjusting my draperies. . . .

The last scene is too good not to be given verbatim:

ROMEO

Rise, rise, my Juliet, And from this cave of death, this house of horror, Quick let me snatch thee to thy Romeo's arms.

Here he pounced on me, plucked me up in his arms like an uncomfortable bundle, and staggered down the stage with me.

JULIET

(aside)

Oh, you've got me up horridly! — that'll never do; let me down, pray let me down.

ROMEO

There, breathe a vital spirit on thy lips, And call thee back, my soul, to life and love!

JULIET

(aside)

Pray, put me down; you'll certainly throw me down if you don't set me on the ground directly.

In the midst of "cruel, cursed fate" his dagger fell out of his dress; I, embracing him tenderly, crammed it back again, because I knew I should want it at the end.

ROMEO

Tear not our heart-strings thus! They crack! They break! — Juliet! Juliet!
    (dies)

JULIET

(to corpse)
Am I smothering you?

CORPSE

(to Juliet)
Not at all; could you be so kind, do you think, as to put my wig on again for me? — it has fallen off.

JULIET

(to corpse)
I'm afraid I can't, but I'll throw my muslin veil over it.
    You've broken the phial, haven't you?
    (Corpse nods)
Where's your dagger?

CORPSE

(to Juliet)
'Pon my soul, I don't know.

—FANNY KEMBLE
Diary

CHAPTER FIFTEEN

Working with Actors, Part Two: Developing Character

Acting begins with a tiny inner movement so slight that it is almost completely invisible. In early theatre rehearsals, the impulse may get no further than a flicker. For this flicker to pass into the whole organism, a total relaxation must be there, either god-given or brought about by work.

—PETER BROOK
The Empty Space

Working with performers is, most directors find, our most artistically fulfilling and personally enriching activity: Sharing actors' victories in creating characters and commiserating with their defeats, constantly experimenting in rehearsals to solve problems, relishing the performers' ambitious drive for perfection, and watching characters come to life. As a director you are uniquely both participant and objective observer at rehearsals; you watch your cast members evolve from raw beginnings through what Peter Brook calls the first flicker of characterization to fully developed characters. The actors' creative growth process is exciting to perceive. I believe that watching an actor develop a skeletal sketch in the script to a multifaceted person is an honor, rather like being permitted to watch Michelangelo create one of the figures of the Sistine Chapel, and that the director's vision of the production is like Michelangelo's ability to envision richly detailed figures where only a bare ceiling exists.

Performers' Motivational Drives

Helping you through the process are the performers' basic motivational drives that compel them to do their best. These drives in turn make the actors expect a great deal from their director. Actors' drives and expectations include the following:

216

- As artists they want recognition for talent and labor, and seek appreciation for their achievements; they expect the director to treat them with professional respect and praise them for their progress.
- They want to belong to a company that achieves the unique, the extraordinary, the beautiful; they expect the director's work to lead the company toward perfection.
- They need to do truthful performances; they expect the director to help them recognize the truth and discard the artificial.
- They want to achieve a level of perfection that creates a sense of pride; they expect the director to help them achieve that level.
- They want to improve their proficiency; they expect the director to help them better their art.
- They want the production to have the greatest possible impact on the audience; they expect the director to have an artistic vision and an effective organizational plan that will help them communicate effectively with the audience.
- They want to overcome personal feelings of doubt and insecurity; they expect the director to help them feel secure about their work.

Actors should be handled not as employees (even though they are) but in much the same way a prize fighter is handled, or a bullfighter. They are the creatures (finally) who must appear before the crowd and hold the attention of the crowd. They are the gladiators of the arts.

—WILLIAM REDFIELD
Letters from an Actor

Character Analysis

STEPS TO ANALYZE A CHARACTER

Performers begin with character analysis (discussed in more detail in Chapter Five). During initial rehearsals you can help the actor lay a firm foundation by suggesting a process of character analysis based on the following steps:

1. Talk about the playwright — other plays or novels by the writer, biographical information, critical views, and the like. Your goal is to broaden the actors' concept of the play.
2. Make available the playwright's other works for the cast to read.
3. Bring to rehearsal background information about the play's time and place. This is particularly helpful for a script dealing with other countries or times, such as *Uncle Vanya* or *The Crucible*.
4. Bring photographs, actual clothing, music, periodicals, and everyday items that help identify the time and place of the play.
5. Carefully talk the cast through an analysis of the play, its structure, style,

genre, and especially its subject and theme. Then discuss the essences of characters, showing how the playwright develops and uses each of them.

6. Ask each member of the cast to maintain a "performance journal" in which they write daily detailed notes about rehearsal progress, what is learned about the character, personality sketches of the character, the character's superobjective, intentions, subintentions, and beat breakdown throughout the play.

7. Ask performers to read through the script repeatedly to discover what their character wants, that is, the character's goals and motivations. These and all other discoveries should be recorded in the performance journal. To help performers perceive these qualities, during rehearsals you will continually ask, "What do you *want?* Why do you want it?"

8. Ask performers to discover all clues to the character's emotional tonality, or emotional profile. You seek to help the actors perceive the characters' primary emotions and changes in emotional attitude during the action.

9. Ask performers to find all conflicts and obstacles that are in the character's path or that the character puts in the paths of others. You want the performers to feel the impact of those obstacles and see how each character's determination to achieve particular goals makes him or her work to overcome obstacles.

10. Performers should find changes or evolutions in the character as the action progresses. You want the performers to think of their characters in dynamic movement.

11. Performers should examine the visual aspects of the character — manner of walk and gesture, physical handicaps, favorite fabric and color, clothing, mannerisms, and the like.

12. Ask the performers to discover the vocal attributes of the character.

13. Ask the performers to think of metaphors — such as a spring breeze, an angry lion, or an antique English clock — that help define the character.

In addition, ask each performer to start:

1. Writing a biographical story of the character's on- and offstage life, carefully drawing out specific implications from the script and trying not to go too far afield.

2. Dividing the character's scenes into beats.

3. Identifying the character's reason for being in the scene.

4. Seeking the character's nonverbal subtext (often included as part of the definition of intention), what the character is actually feeling, thinking, and saying under the text.

5. Deciding the character's emotional responses to other characters, particularly the character's changes in emotional attitudes throughout the play.

Starting rehearsals with inquiries into these areas will help actors delve deeply into characterization. These and comparable other questions will continue during rehearsals.

Newspaper writing seeks to answer the questions — Who? What? Where? When? Why? How? The performer, too, seeks answers to these questions to put flesh on the bare bones of the character. You encourage the performer to ask the questions — the process of asking is often more significant than the answers — and you may at times prompt the performer's imagination by asking additional questions. You can start the process in early rehearsals with questions such as the following:

- Who are you? Who are your relatives? Who are your friends? Enemies? Who are you in terms of social, economic, hereditary, environmental, experiential, and educational influences?

- What do you want? What are you doing? What are your emotional variations during the play? What does the character want, and how strong is that desire? What will your character do to achieve his or her goals? What will your character do to overcome barriers in the path of that goal?

- Where are you? Where is the action of the play? Where have you been before you enter? Where are you going when you exit?

- When must you do these things? When does the play take place?

- Why did the playwright put you in the scene? Why are you unhappy? Why are you cruel? Why do the others want you to leave? Why do you want the money? Why must you take actions now (instead of yesterday or tomorrow)?

- How do you try to achieve your goal? How do you move when you are happy? How do you react when you encounter an obstacle?

Careful directors may prepare lists of such questions for each character, recording them in the prompt book to ask during rehearsals. Often the most significant questions are those asking *why,* because the answers lead actors to think about motivation.

[HELEN] HAYES. I know I suddenly, when we were rehearsing *A Touch of the Poet,* blurted out once to Harold Clurman — and this may sum up what I want from a director — "Stop telling me what everything means. Just tell me how to do it." I think that's it! . . . The director should help me in my grasp on the spirit of the character. He should have those things ready to supply to me, so that my grasp of the character's whole being could be enlightened. But I think the directors are too often today taking over the actors' business of interpretation of the character and forgetting about their business as directors.

INTERVIEWER. In other words, the director should be the absolute master at rehearsal. He should be able to say, "I want you to do it this way," and he should decide whether it is satisfactory; and if it isn't satisfactory, to say, "Now do it this way."

HAYES. Yes. I think the director ought to know something more about the mechanics of putting a thing on the stage — which is very, very important. Because, heaven help you, you can be expressing something so miraculously, but if you're way off in the wrong part of the stage, and if something else is happening on this part of the stage that detracts from you there — If some mechanical thing is against you, you can be acting your heart out, feeling and understanding, and everything can be happening inside of you — and yet you can never make it happen, because the director's part of it — the picture which he sees from the front, the overall picture — has not aided you in conveying that.

—HELEN HAYES
Lewis Funke and John E. Booth, *Actors Talk About Acting, I*

Internal and External Approaches to Characterization

Performers typically use one of two basic approaches to creating a character: the "outside-in" or the "inside-out" approach. The former is an external technical approach favored by performers such as Helen Hayes; the latter is an internal psychological approach associated with the teachings of Stanislavski and favored by performers such as Marlon Brando. The technical approach constructs a character by exterior appearance and actions, which indicates inner motivations; the internal approach delves inside the character's motivations and history and builds outward to the character's actions. Although the approaches differ, each shares the common goal of honest depiction of character through actions and emotions.

Fervent arguments separate proponents of these two acting methods because many acting teachers and performers believe the two approaches are diametrically opposed. Those differences are more significant to actors than to audiences: When watching two equally talented actors, one using the inside-out and the other the outside-in approach, even trained theatrical observers have difficulty identifying which performer is using which acting method. Actors often use aspects of each approach.

INTENTIONS (OR OBJECTIVES) AND MOTIVATIONS

Crucial to both the inside-out and outside-in approaches is the concept of *objectives* or *intentions,* terms used interchangeably to refer to a character's active determination to achieve a major goal or behave in a specified manner. Just as your life follows a master goal, so dramatic characters have superobjectives; and just as you have smaller day-to-day goals that are part of your life goal, so dramatic characters have secondary intentions or subobjectives. Superobjectives govern the character's existence; secondary objectives are smaller scene-by-scene steps toward the superobjective. The superobjective dictates the character's through line of action, from the play's beginning to the end. Character creation begins with defining the character's superintention in the play, then finding each of his or her subintentions in the individual scenes.

To illustrate this vitally important concept of objectives, consider Blanche in *A Streetcar Named Desire.* She has a visibly strong superintention or superobjective. We find it by asking — What does she *want?* What does she *need?* What is her emotional stake? What does she intend to accomplish, more than anything else? On what do her emotions center? Those questions lead us to see that

Blanche's superobjective is an urgent drive to obtain security, refuge, love, and warmth; all other actions are related to that basic superintention. Does Blanche have other options? No. She has exhausted all other possibilities and now she is desperate. Because this is her last chance, a strong sense of urgency makes her emotional stake in her superobjective as strong as any question of life and death. All scenes show aspects of her drive to achieve that superobjective.

Knowledge of Blanche's superobjective leads to an understanding of the complex character revealed by her secondary objectives. For example, suppose you and the actress try to understand why Blanche lies to Stanley. Does she want to lie? No. Then why does she concoct falsehoods? Because her lies are subobjectives, intended to help her achieve her major goal. Does she want to put on airs? No. Why does she? She intends to portray herself as desirable. Why? So men will want her. Do we conclude she is a prostitute? Not at all; she uses her sexual appeal to draw men to her so they will satisfy her superobjective, even if they only temporarily give her the warmth and shelter she wants. As this brief discussion of Blanche indicates, director and actor have many opportunities for meaningful creative dialogue in discussions of the character's intentions.

ACTORS MUST MAKE DISCOVERIES THEMSELVES

To ensure that the actors have discovered the superintention, you repeatedly ask questions that encourage them to search for their characters' intentions. Remember that actors must discover characterization qualities themselves: Although your detailed study of the play will have given you answers, you cannot spoon-feed them to the actors. For these insights to be meaningful and part of the internal structure of the characters, the performers must make these discoveries through their own creative processes. Properly led performers are likely to develop more accurate and more sensitive concepts of the character than the director; spoon-feeding the actors would inhibit that detailed growth. Your job is to lead each performer by asking questions, not by supplying answers.

For the same reasons you do not allow other actors in the company to discuss objectives for characters other than their own. Often your discussion with one actor leads other actors to want to volunteer answers. During the director's questions to one actor about objectives and motivations many actors apparently feel they are in a "class" and need to comment. They seem to find it easier to speak about another actor's character than to work out the details of their own. You need to focus their enthusiasm away from others' work and on their own characters.

THE CHARACTER'S SPINE

To the director spine is the play's main action, what the playwright intends the play to communicate; to the actor spine is the individual character's major motivational force or dominant action throughout the play. Your obligation is to bring to life the play's overall action; the actor's task is to perceive and bring to life one character's active desire. To fulfill your responsibility for artistic unification and achieve your vision, you ensure during rehearsals that each character's spine is compatible with your concept of the play's spine.

Much of your work with actors is designed to help them discover characters' spines. The Stanislavski-trained actor, believing that effective characterization results from understanding active movement, and not passive mood, expresses a character's spine with an infinitive verb or phrase such as "I want to be king" (Macbeth), "I want to avenge my father's death" (Hamlet), or "I want to make my sons respect me" (Willy Loman). To work collaboratively with the actor you ask leading questions that help the actor encounter the character's spine. Here the director's favorite question is — What do you want? Because the dramatic answer should deal with the essences of the character rather than superficial qualities, you may need to ask the question repeatedly until the actor has a clear concept of the character's primary desire.

OBSTACLES

Inherent in the definition of a character's superobjective must be the concept of the obstacle: If there were no obstacle, the superobjective would be achieved easily and therefore undramatically. Obstacles are for the actor what complications are for the playwright. The writer knows that a play cannot live without complications; they are the lifeblood and heartbeat of the play, creating fire and dramatic tension. A play without complications would be a dreary series of non-dramatic incidents. Obstacles are also the source of conflict and dramatic tension for the actor. For example, if Stella and Stanley accepted Blanche into their haven despite the dangers she poses to their relationship, Blanche's intention would be easily accomplished, and the play would be over. With no complications and obstacles, *Streetcar* would be a short, uninteresting playlet with one-dimensional characters. In contrast, lively dramatic productions result from performers playing character obstacles.

You help performers find and play intentions and obstacles by asking questions such as — What does Blanche want? What stops her from obtaining it? What is Blanche trying to accomplish in this scene? What force opposes her? How does she react to that force? Obstacles may be interior or exterior, physical or psychological, but they must be visibly present in every beat.

BEATS

The "beat" is a performer's unit of measurement, referring to one basic intention from beginning through middle to end. A minor utilitarian character may have a simple beat. For example, the butler who enters to announce, "Dinner is served," has one beat consisting of his intention to announce dinner. It begins when he enters; its middle is the announcement; and it ends as he steps aside to indicate the guests can enter this door for dinner. For clarity, the actor must play each of the three parts one at a time: beginning, middle, and end. Each small subintention of the whole must be played at its time before the next piece can begin; if the subintentions overlap, the intention will be buried in confusion.

When an actor plays more than one intention in a particular beat the performance is muddy; when the actor plays one dynamic intention in a beat, the performance is strong. A great dramatic performance is the product of an actor's playing the single dynamic intention in one beat, linking that subintention to the superintention, and all the while struggling against one or more major obstacles.

Your role is to help performers avoid muddy lack of clarity and aim at the great performance. Throughout the play, every beat's subintention must be played within the framework of the superintention. The actor should play only a single intention at a time in a given beat. To play more is to distract from the basic goal of the beat.

MOTIVATION

Performance art requires every action to be motivated. You want no speech, no silence, no action, no inaction on your stage without its motivation. Further, all motivation must be clearly communicated to the audience. The performer's goal is not merely to know or feel the motivation but also to ensure that the audience consciously or subconsciously perceives the reasons for the character's behavior.

Imagination

INTERVIEWER. How does a director help an actor?
[VIVIEN] LEIGH. By giving him confidence; because most actors, I think, are lacking in confidence. By helping him with his own particular gifts.
INTERVIEWER. And imagination is one of these gifts, isn't it?
LEIGH. Indeed. Imagination really means how to present an idea in the most interesting way, in an imaginative fashion. It may be very eccentric, it may be art, but, well — just that the imagination can take flight, and in acting every performer should take flight, so that you do things in an imaginative way as opposed to a pedestrian or an ordinary way.

—VIVIEN LEIGH
Lewis Funke and John E. Booth, *Actors Talk About Acting, I*

The child's imaginative games are the actor's profession. To create a character, actors select; to create selections, they use imagination. Effective actors use their imaginative powers to create dozens of choices; ineffective actors invent too few choices. One of your first responsibilities is to find ways to encourage your cast members to apply their imaginations. Your effectiveness depends on the degree to which you stimulate the actor's invention of choices to build a dimensional character.

For example, consider one small piece of business. Assume the script's stage direction says the character "pours a glass of wine, drinks." If the performer simply follows those instructions, no character is created and the scene is dull because the actor is not using imagination to discover dozens of ways to do the action. You help the actor by asking questions to indicate some of the possible options. Where has the character been before this scene? Why does the character want wine? Why at this particular moment? Is the character merely thirsty? Is he or she drinking wine in order to offend someone in the room? Would he or she prefer a better wine? Does the character look for some other drink but settle for the wine because it is available? Does the character hold the wine bottle up to the light? Nod appreciatively? Grimace? Shrug? Read the label? Do the character's lips move while reading the label? Does the character sniff the cork? Gesture to the others in the room, inviting them to have a glass? Gulp it without enjoyment? Sip the wine, rolling it over the tongue, and breathing over the wine to taste it? Does the character like the wine or dislike it? Is the character surprised by the taste? Does the taste make him or her pick up the bottle to read the label?

You have two basic ways to help the actor develop imaginative choices. You can either give the actor specific instructions or ask questions. For example, given the direction, "pours a glass of wine, drinks," you might simply instruct the actor to pick up the bottle, blow the dust off the side, quickly pour a glass of wine, grin at the others, and chug it down. You expect your instructions to give a base of activity that will help the actor fill in the details. Alternatively, you can ask the actor such questions as — What would your character do when picking up the bottle? Does the character know good wine? What does the character *want?* What are the character's emotions? — to help the actor use imagination to think of other choices. Don't let the questions imply that you want intellectual answers only. Ask the actor to demonstrate answers. "How would the character walk to the table? Show me." "What is the character's objective? Show me."

ASKING WHAT IF?

Rehearsals must be a time to experiment. Avoid the temptation to turn each rehearsal into a miniperformance. You and the actors must be free to do things absolutely wrong, to explore all the outer parameters of characterization and interpretation, to try staging concepts that may or may not work. A "what if?" attitude should dominate early rehearsals. What if a line were read this way instead of that? What if a performer imagines an obstacle here? What if the character continued talking without interruptions? What if there is total silence now? What if the character laughs there? What if the character moves away abruptly (or doesn't move at all)? What if a complex piece of business takes place during that exchange?

No single acting stimulus is effective for all performers at all times, but few are more stimulating than the question — What if? Well-designed questions prompt wide-ranging answers: "What if the character doesn't know a thing about wine but wants to pretend to be an expert? Show me." The effective "what if" question speaks to the character's emotions, desires, motivations, and obstacles. "What if you have to tell others you are leaving town, but fear their reactions because you owe them money, and so you use the wine as a device to delay telling them? Show me how you would get the wine." The "show me" part of your questions should prompt the performer to find answers that can be shown in concrete actions.

ISOLATIONS

One goal of rehearsals is to explore possible ways of developing characters into dimensional humans. Rather than seeking to achieve that goal directly, take a circuitous route to explore interesting avenues. You might try the strategy of playing *isolations*. For example, in *The Glass Menagerie* Amanda is a mixture of a number of attributes: She is strong, weak, selfless, selfish, comic, totally lacking in humor, cunning, and more. It is a mistake for the performer to try to play all aspects of this complicated personality at once. Instead you can encourage the performer to experiment with isolating one attribute: Rehearse one scene with the actress playing Amanda as totally strong; repeat the same scene with her finding Amanda nothing but selfless; do the scene a third time showing Amanda as laughing at herself and her children; and so forth.

With this experimentation behind her, the actress will better perceive the various qualities of Amanda, know when in the play each aspect of her personality is likely to dominate, and understand that she should not attempt to show all the complex qualities at once. As a result the characterization will appear crisp and sharp, not muddy and confused.

THE JAMES-LANGE THEORY

A century ago psychologists William James and C. H. Lange developed a theory that explains emotions as results of action. According to the James-Lange theory, we feel sad because we do acts of sadness, we experience the emotion of happiness because we laugh, or we feel brave at night in a dangerous neighborhood because we stride boldly, chin up and shoulders back. The physical act creates the emotion: Walking in the woods we come across a bear, and we turn and run, thus becoming afraid.

The theory is based on the premise that physiological behavior causes an emotional response, and although some acting teachers (and some psychologists) disagree about the concept's validity, I believe it can be effective when it is one of several tools to develop characterization. I have found this external approach valuable when used with Stanislavski's more internal techniques. It is, I think, especially helpful as one of various warm-up exercises, a stratagem to help unlock an actor's line readings, and a very convenient "quick fix" to establish aspects of character in members of crowd scenes.

Most of us apply the James-Lange theory in daily life without conscious awareness of the theory. A frightened soldier often does more acts termed brave than the unfrightened one; the former seeks the opportunity to remove fear by doing acts of bravery. A tired prizefighter bounces on his toes around the ring in the tenth round, as if not at all tired, in order to feel energetic. Undoubtedly you have at times felt depressed, exhausted, and unwilling to attend a rehearsal where you

The director must be able to speak clearly about the essences of the production to help build morale and keep the performers focused on their roles. Kim T. Sharp (right), director of *Trumpet in the Land*, gives last-minute notes to the cast prior to the opening performance of the outdoor drama at Dover, Ohio.

were responsible for the moods of others. To get over feeling "down," you actively pumped your energy higher, tried to walk with a bounce, applied a smile, and in that process eliminated your depression.

The James-Lange theory can be a vital part of your working technique. Suppose an actor is reading his lines meekly as if frightened, and you want him to be bold. Do you assign him movement to back away from the stimuli? Hardly; that will make him read the lines more meekly. Instead, applying the James-Lange theory, you place the actor in the up left corner, put another performer far down right, and have the first actor make threatening gestures with his fist while moving rapidly, directly, and aggressively downstage toward the other performer. Will he now read his lines more boldly? Yes. Has he lost some meekness? Certainly.

Experience with the James-Lange theory leads to an acting exercise that calls for the performer to "walk as the character."

- Start in a large rehearsal hall. Ask performers to be themselves, walking casually from one side of the room to the other, first with relatively simple instructions. "Be yourself in a hurry to get to lunch."
- Build in obstacles. "Be yourself trying to get to lunch but stopped by someone you do not know who asks you for directions; if you are late you won't get lunch, but the person is quite lost."
- Try different activities. "Be yourself in a bookstore wanting to look at a book with graphic photographs of the sexual act without letting anyone you know see you, and someone you respect is coming."
- Try to reproduce ordinary real-life experiences. "You're walking from a store to your car, but standing next to your car is someone who always asks you for something you cannot give. How do you walk to the car?"
- Gradually get the performers walking like their characters. "Your character is walking down the street. He sees a friend. How does he go to that friend?" "He sees someone he doesn't want to talk to. What does he do?" "He smells cooking vegetables." "He hears a gunshot." "It is late, dark. He is afraid. Does he show it? What frightens him?"
- Begin to draw scenes from the play: friendly encounters, angry confrontations, desires achieved, desires frustrated. Use the specifics from the scene, then expand the situation to include activities just offstage. The exercise is perhaps twenty minutes long, conducted two or three times a week the final weeks of rehearsal as part of warm-ups.

These examples illustrate the applicability of the James-Lange theory to theatrical practice. They also demonstrate the importance of proper blocking, as we shall discuss in a later chapter.

The James-Lange theory is an outside-in acting approach. The Stanislavski inside-out technique, applied to meek performers you want to behave boldly, has the actors use sensory recall to remember how they felt and behaved when angry. When performers have gone through that preparation, they read the line more boldly.

Is the James-Lange theory "better" or "worse" than the Stanislavski system? Neither. One performer may benefit from the James-Lange concept, and another will be enriched by the Stanislavski approach. Neither will be a better actor than the other simply because of the approach used. Pragmatic directors experiment with both techniques, staying with one or the other as long as it remains effective and switching when appropriate.

Perhaps the most significant aspect of theatre games is that you will learn to teach yourself by creating a situation similar to the one in which your character finds himself.

—LOUIS JOHN DEZSERAN
The Student Actor's Handbook

IMPROVISATIONAL EXERCISES

Improvisational exercises are rehearsal techniques that allow the director and actor to discover character traits and motivations. The James-Lange exercises help the performer find the exterior of the character; improvs help the performer look inside the character. Spontaneous responses to hypothetical situations, improvs challenge the actors' imaginations and call for characters' reactions. An improv should not take on undue importance because it is an exercise, a tool, not an end in itself.

At their best, improvs flesh out the playscript, adding scenes full of emotions and conflicts that help actors better perceive characters and react to other characters and complications. Mediocre improvs, on the other hand, are mere games, entertaining for some members of the cast but only passingly educational. Improvs that depart too far from the script tend to be ineffective because the actors will develop characterizations that have no basis in the play and may add dimensions counterproductive to the whole. At their worst, improvs give the performers silly instructions — "Show your character as an oak tree shedding leaves in the fall but anxious to preserve its acorns" — that are not related to the script.

Effective improvisational exercises help performers discover new aspects of their characters. For example, if you are rehearsing a production of *The Glass Menagerie,* you might help the performers playing Tom and Laura to explore the depths of the brother-sister relationship by having them do an improv that starts in the middle of Amanda's criticism of Laura for not attending business school. To start such an improv have Tom enter just as Amanda is leaving Laura and ask, "What's wrong, Laura?" Now what does Laura say? And then Tom? The exercise should help each actor explore relationships with the other. You would guide Tom to ask what Amanda said; Laura replies; Tom sympathizes; and as the improv progresses you and the performers will see if Laura and Tom understand Amanda's real motives for wanting Laura to go to business school: Amanda's fear of what will happen to Laura when her mother is gone. A second improv from the same scene would have Tom ask, "What's wrong, mother?" Now what does Amanda say? This improvisation should bring out Amanda's deep concern for her daughter's future.

[Regarding participating in theatre games and improvisational exercises.] Growth will occur without difficulty in the student-actor because the very game he plays will aid him. The objective upon which the player must constantly focus and towards which every action must be directed provokes spontaneity. In this spontaneity, personal freedom is released, and the total person, physically, intellectually, and intuitively, is awakened.

—VIOLA SPOLIN
Improvisations for the Theatre

CROWD SCENES

Performers cast as members of the crowd seldom know how to build a character; most expect the director to give them a year's acting lessons in a few nights of rehearsals. As a result, the typical group of ten to forty "citizens" or "soldiers" can be an antidramatic unmoving lump on stage, distracting attention from the principals. Worse are the members of a musical's chorus, usually not experienced actors, who tend to stand full front to see the musical director in the orchestra pit. A combination of James-Lange action exercises and improvs may help you develop the best performance from these "extras."

The James-Lange walking exercise helps you use rehearsal time efficiently by working with all the crowd members at once; judicious use of the James-Lange concept helps the performers work physically; and careful improvisational exercises give each individual a single quality. Design assignments that speak to what the character *wants* but cannot achieve because of obstacles. You might tell one performer to walk "like an old man who wants to get to the soup kitchen and is afraid someone will steal his admission ticket"; another to walk "like a young girl excited to be away from home the first time and anxious to see everything that is happening but at the same time hiding from the police and frightened of the males who look at her"; a third to walk like "a soldier with a minor injury who wants to get to the cafe for a drink but also wants to hide from his superiors who would make him return to the war"; and so on. Improv exercises then put the individuals through aspects of the scenes. Performers should each play a single essence, not a complicated character; when all extras are side by side on stage, the audience will perceive the complexity created by all the different characterizations, which will lead them to think all the characters are dimensional and complex.

THE "ILLUSION OF THE FIRST TIME"

Crucial to the success of any performance is the actors' ability to convince the audience that everything on stage is happening spontaneously for the first time. It is one of theatre's paradoxes: Despite many hours of rehearsals, the actors must appear to be freshly experiencing the actions on the stage, saying lines they never said before and newly discovering aspects of others and themselves. The alternative is to go dully through the motions, reacting before a stimulus actually occurs and playing the scene repetitively.

Quite possibly this one quality marks the difference between a production that the audience happily accepts and one in which they simply cannot believe action or characters. In the latter production the alchemy of empathy will lead the audience to feel the actors' boredom as their own.

You should work for spontaneity during the polishing rehearsals, emphasizing the need for that "illusion of the first time." Look for a number of specific danger signs. Are performers actually *listening* to cues or merely replying by rote? Does an actor anticipate a cue, beginning the response before the stimulus? Does the actor say lines as if on automatic pilot, not knowing what was just said? Is the actor playing the scenes as carbon copies of previous rehearsals? As you repeatedly draw performers' attention to the problem, encouraging them to strive for that magical aura of the first time, they will begin to increase concentration and energy levels, focusing more on the action.

A fight rehearsal for *War of the Roses* at the New
Jersey Shakespeare Festival pits Joan of Arc (right,
played by Lisa Barnes) against the Earl of Shrewsbury
(played by Ed Dennehy) while other combatants
practice in the background. Fight Director Paul Barry
(right) watches carefully. — *Photograph by Nicholas J.
de Gregory*

CRITICISM

The director's job includes giving critical comments to all involved in the
production. This is not confined to negative comments; it includes compliments
for jobs well done. You handle negative criticism delicately because it can be
destructive if given at the wrong time; positive criticism can also be counterproductive unless the performer readily perceives that you are sincere. Be sensitive
to each performer's mood and needs to temper your comments accordingly.

A valid guiding rule for criticism can be stated simply: Criticize the work, not
the individual. Further, criticize the specific, and do not let your comments be
too general. It is perfectly valid to say to a performer, "Your diction in this scene
was sloppy." It is, however, invalid to be personal or sweepingly general: "You
are sloppy" or "You do sloppy work." Good criticism is honest, direct, and carefully designed to explain the problem and offer possible solutions.

Edith Evans was playing Lady Fidget in *The Country Wife,* and one day Edith was carrying
on like a maniac up there, like one demented — posturing, waving imaginary fans, doing
crazy things with them — when, from the back of the auditorium, came the voice of

Tony Guthrie, who was rehearsing us. And he said, "Edith, what in God's name are you doing?" And she went down to the footlights and said, "I'm trying things — I'd rather be an ass in front of my fellow actors than do nothing on opening night." Now, see, of this I approve.... Of course, nine times out of ten it's terrible. That's what I mean by the process of elimination: I do all the wrong things, and then I finally get down to what's right — I hope.

—HELEN HAYES
Lewis Funke and John E. Booth, *Actors Talk About Acting, I*

No chapter — indeed, no book — can ever adequately describe director-actor working relationships. The chemistry is as complex as humanity, the variables as changeable as human nature. Directors deal with individuals who are unique, excitingly eccentric, and creative. Given the mercurial nature of theatre you cannot direct by a predesignated formula. Discussion of the process can only lead you to be sensitive to the relationship; although this chapter addressed some areas of concern, many questions are left unanswered. The purpose was not to dictate what you must do in a given situation but to indicate methods of finding possible solutions.

You can obtain more details from a number of excellent books, such as *Acting in Person and in Style* by Jerry L. Crawford and Joan Snyder, *Acting Is Believing* by Charles McGaw, *The Actor at Work* by Robert Benedetti, *The Stanislavski System* by Sonia Moore, *The Use and Training of the Human Voice* by Arthur Lessac, *Method or Madness?* by Robert Lewis, *Acting Power* by Robert Cohen, and *Respect for Acting* by Uta Hagen.

In particular you should carefully read the books that establish the standards for modern performers: the Stanislavski approach. Stanislavski's *An Actor's Handbook* gives insight into his method of acting. His *An Actor Prepares* and *Building a Character* together present a total view of the Stanislavski system, but the reader should bear in mind they were published thirteen years apart. *Creating a Role* is a collection of Stanislavski's teachings; *My Life in Art* is his autobiography.

Can the theatre exist without costumes and sets? Yes, it can.

Can it exist without music to accompany the plot? Yes.

Can it exist without lighting effects? Of course.

And without a text? Yes; the history of the theatre confirms this. In the evolution of the theatrical art the text was one of the last elements to be added. If we place some people on a stage with a scenario they themselves have put together and let them improvise their parts as in the Commedia dell'Arte, the performance will be equally good even if the words are not articulated but simply muttered.

But can the theatre exist without actors? I know of no example of this. One could mention the puppet-show. Even here, however, an actor is to be found behind the scenes, although of another kind.

Can the theatre exist without an audience? At least one spectator is needed to make it a performance. So we are left with the actor and the spectator. We can thus define the theatre as "what takes place between spectator and actor." All the other things are supplementary — perhaps necessary, but nevertheless supplementary.

—JERZY GROTOWSKI
Towards a Poor Theatre

Exercises

1. Drawing on your performing experiences, describe in your own words how you applied essences of the "outside-in" and "inside-out" acting approaches to developing a character. Did you find that the external approach was better for certain aspects of developing the character and the internal more effective for other aspects? If so, what made the differences? Why was one approach more effective than the other?

2. For the play you are to direct, draft a number of significant questions you will have ready to ask the performer playing the protagonist. You will need general questions that pertain to the character in the play as a whole, plus specific questions for the character's major scenes.

3. Draft questions like those in exercise 2 for the performer playing the antagonist.

4. Write a planned James-Lange exercise to help performers develop character. List all the steps of the exercise.

5. Write several planned improvisational exercises to help performers in crucial scenes of the play you are to direct.

CHAPTER SIXTEEN

The Floor Plan

In the original production [of *The Seagull* at the Moscow Art Theatre in 1898] the window in the third act was placed to one side and the landscape was hidden; when the characters entered the hall in galoshes, shaking out their hats, rugs and scarves, one pictured autumn, a fine drizzle, and puddles in the court-yard covered with squelching boards. In the revival [also at the Moscow Art Theatre, in 1905] the windows . . . faced the spectator so that the landscape was visible. Your imagination was silenced, and whatever the characters said about the landscape, you disbelieved them because it could never be as they described it; it was painted and you could see it. Originally [in the first production], the departure of the horses with their bells jingling (the finale of the third act) was simply heard offstage and vividly evoked in the spectator's imagination. In the [later revival], once the spectator saw the veranda from which the people departed, he demanded to see the horses with their bells, too.

'A work of art can influence only through the imagination. Therefore it must constantly stir the imagination.' (Schopenhauer.) But it must really stir it, not leave it inactive through trying to show everything.

—EDWARD BRAUN
translator and editor, *Meyerhold on Theatre*

A well-designed, carefully thought-out floor plan (also called a ground plan) will make the blocking process flow easily. Your play analysis will help you design an appropriate floor plan for a set that: (a) is organically part of the play and the action, (b) demonstrates the play's psychological areas and conflicts, (c) helps actors bring characters to life, (d) represents the environment, (e) communicates the mood or atmosphere, (f) makes good theatrical use of the stage, and (g) can be constructed within the limits of the available manpower, time, and financial resources. The floor plan must include all necessary details, but bear in mind Meyerhold's advice that a set should avoid showing so much that the audience's imagination is inhibited.

For major productions, directors may originate floor plan concepts, or scene designers may start the process. A collaborative approach may be the most satisfactory, with both director and designer working to discover the floor plan, shar-

The director starts with a floor plan that will bring visual story-telling devices to the production, and uses blocking and composition to create a meaningful and aesthetically pleasing stage picture. Director Douglas Campbell brings to life the tedious existence of the crew of the S. S. Glencairn in this scene from *The Moon of the Caribbees* at the Guthrie Theater. Note how lighting draws the composition together and creates an aura of mystery with the dark shadows on the character at the top of the triangle. — *Photograph by Act Two*

ing ideas at frequent meetings, and keeping the process open to creative input from lighting and costume designers. Although this chapter discusses the director's work with the floor plan to help you learn by doing, it should be clearly understood that in actual theatrical practice you work closely with your design colleagues. Your completed floor plan design will improve communications with the scene designer.

Start making your floor plan by drawing many sketches until you have a viable concept. Then draw the floor plan to scale or, for a complicated set, make a three-dimensional model of the set. Laying out the floor plan on the stage or rehearsal floor, with real or simulated furniture, will help you achieve an effective plan and will show you height and bulk that are not shown on a two-dimensional floor plan. Put one copy of your completed floor plan in your prompt book or, better yet, insert many copies in the script to use for sketches of blocking notes and characters' positions.

Figure 16-1 illustrates a proscenium arch stage's floor plan, which is a two-dimensional scale drawing of the stage and audience area as viewed from above. It shows furniture, doors, windows, platforms, stairs, and other aspects necessary to stage the play. This particular floor plan indicates that you can use the right and left corners of the stage because they are within audience sight lines (as we discuss later, raking the set can overcome problems with sight lines). An upstage "crossover" space, hidden by masking flats, allows actors to cross from one side of the stage to the other without being seen; if your stage lacks a convenient crossover space, you will need to plan entrances and exits carefully so actors are not trapped on one side of the stage when they need to enter on the other side. Note that doors are hinged on their upstage edges and swing offstage, thus masking the offstage area.

Figure 16-1. Sample Floor Plan

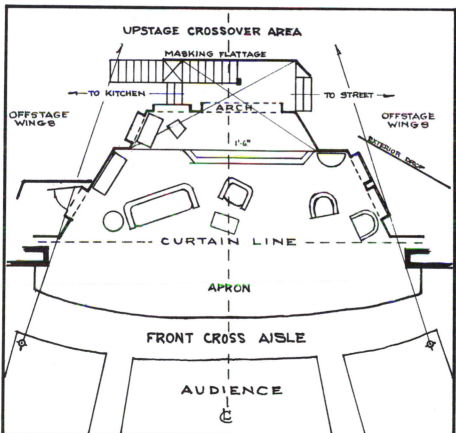

Balance

Two imaginary fulcrum lines help you perceive a balanced floor plan. The primary fulcrum line runs from DC to UC. A secondary fulcrum line runs along the center plane from L to R. Dotted lines in Figure 16-2 indicate both fulcrum lines for initial consideration of stage balance, which is important to your floor plan and subsequent blocking and composition.

Figure 16-2. Fulcrum Lines

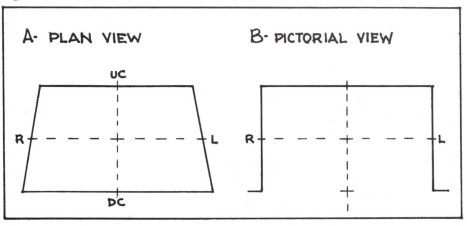

Figure 16-3. Symmetrical Balance

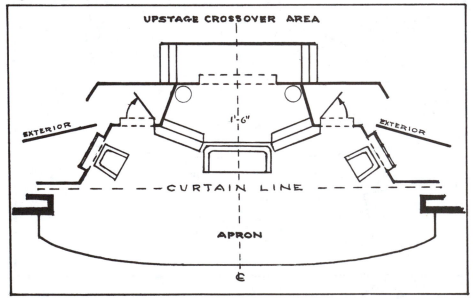

Symmetrical, Asymmetrical, and No Balance

The floor plan may be in either symmetrical or asymmetrical balance, both of which are quite viable according to the needs of the play and the director's vision, or out of balance, which is seldom acceptable.

Symmetrical balance, shown in Figure 16-3, keeps equal weight or bulk on either side of the two fulcrum lines, which run from stage left to stage right and from downstage to upstage. Asymmetrical balance (Figure 16-4) moves heavier items toward the fulcrum points. Either form of balance can create a usable floor plan.

A floor plan that is out of balance (Figure 16-5) is virtually unusable because it will tend to make you place actors on the lighter side (stage right in this illustration) to offset the bulk on the heavier side; it will inhibit placing actors on the heavier side because they will increase the balance problem. Thus an unbalanced floor plan sharply limits your use of the set.

Architectural Logic versus Theatrical Needs

Some directors prefer to draw the entire house before working out the floor plan for a given room, but architectural logic should not be overemphasized. Theatre

Figure 16-4. Asymmetrical Balance

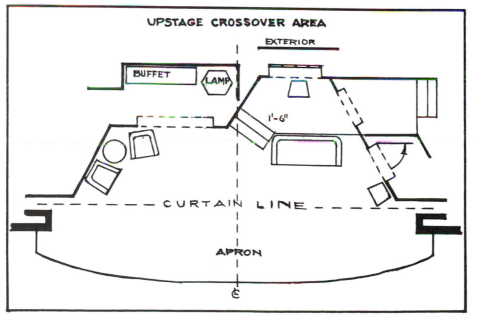

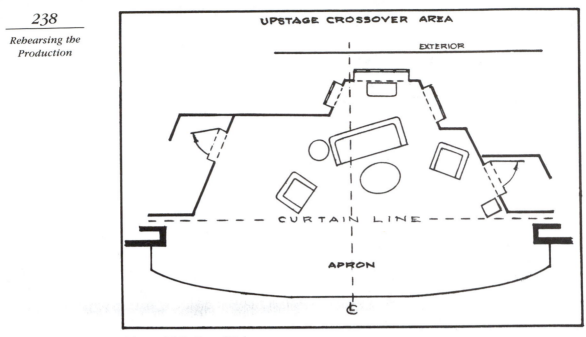

Figure 16-5. Out of Balance

is not real life but an artistic representation of life; a set is not a real home but a symbol of that environment. Theatrical concerns are no less important — many directors think they are more important — than architectural verisimilitude, and theatrical needs may require judicious violations of the rules for constructing an actual home. Of course windows should not look into what are clearly offstage rooms, and doors must not lead through stairways, but for most plays a reasonable floor plan is functional and plausible though not necessarily totally true to life.

Entrances and Exits

Play analysis helps you judge whether entrances or exits most affect the play's action. A downstage door is a strong exit because the actor going to the door will be moving toward the audience and remaining relatively open, but it makes a somewhat less effective entrance because the actor coming in will be in profile or closed. An upstage door provides a dynamic entrance because the actor will be full front when entering, but usually it is a less effective exit because the actor will be moving away from the audience and in a closed position. In either case, a jog in the wall and platforms or steps will increase the strength of the door's position.

Symmetrical balance is shown in this photograph from *The Merry Wives of Windsor,* directed by John Neville-Andrews at the Folger Shakespeare Theatre. Note how the center level, simple and direct, contributes to the visual effect of the stage picture. — *Photograph by Joan Marcus*

Raking the Set

"Raking" the set can mean elevating the upstage areas or placing the set at an angle rather than parallel to the curtain line. Both changes can improve playing areas and the strength of door positions. Figures 16-6 and 16-7 illustrate changing a full-front set to a raked set. Jogs and angles add emphasis and interest.

Furniture Placement

Ask questions as you consider furniture. What pieces are essential for the action? What nonessential pieces are necessary to suggest the environment? How many

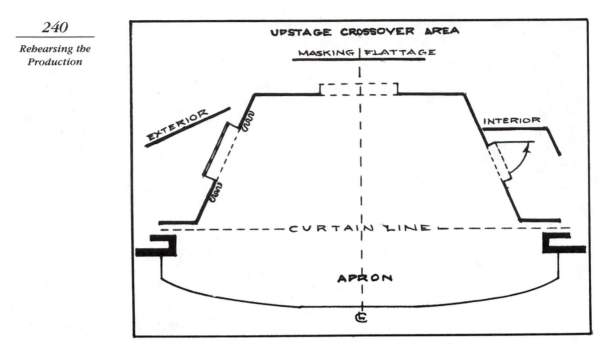

Figure 16-6. A Full-Front Set

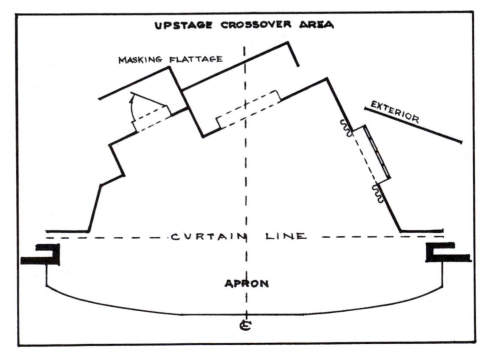

Figure 16-7. A Raked Set

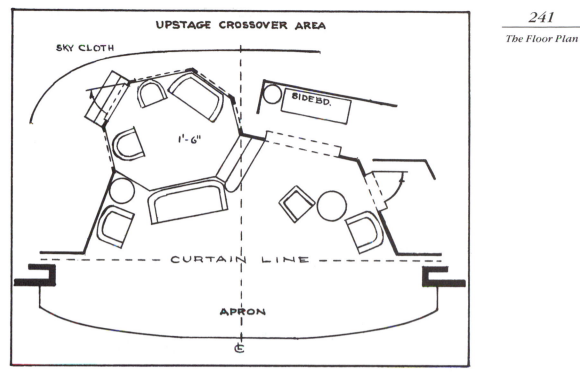

Figure 16-8. Poor Furniture Placement

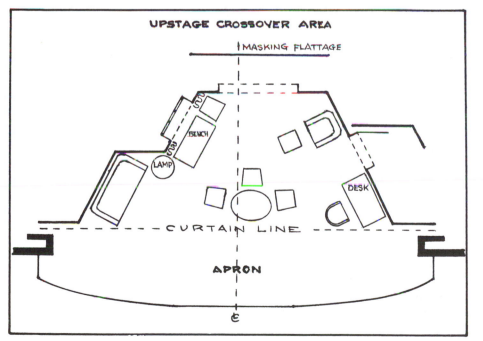

Figure 16-9. Improved Furniture Placement

seats do you need? Are furniture pieces sufficiently separated to permit characters in conflict to remain apart? Does the placement appear logical? Will furniture placement help or hinder your use of the stage? Is furniture grouped in acting areas?

Figure 16-8 illustrates incorrect choices. Pieces against the walls prevent interesting movements behind or around the sofa, chairs, and table. Entrances and exits will be quite weak because the performers will be figuratively cut in half by the pieces masking the doors. Chairs and sofas are placed without regard to their relation to each other. This floor plan would make blocking difficult, uninteresting, and nontheatrical.

Compare Figures 16-8 and 16-9. Note the increased playing areas in the latter. Eliminating furniture in front of doors adds strength to entrances and exits.

Furniture Problems

DINING TABLES

You may direct a play, such as *Brighton Beach Memoirs,* that requires a dining table large enough for a sit-down dinner involving many people. Avoid long rectangular tables because they do not permit flexible arrangements and you cannot easily shift actors to positions within audience sight lines. Your best choice is likely to be an oval table, which will allow you to keep actors more visible.

OVERSTUFFED CHAIRS AND SOFAS

Select furniture that actors can use. Although a play like *The Cherry Orchard* might use overstuffed chairs that swallow anyone sitting on them, actors often experience so much difficulty getting out of such seats that characterization is damaged. Chairs with low seats are also awkward.

BEDS

Curiously, the sight of an actor lying with head upstage and feet downstage may make some members of the audience giggle, perhaps because the feet appear to dwarf the head. To avoid that unintended humor, position beds across the stage or on a diagonal.

TABLE AND FLOOR LAMPS

Many directors have been surprised to find that end tables overnight sprouted tall lamps with large shades while bulky floor lamps suddenly surround chairs and sofas. Prop crews, busy with last-minute set dressing, may not think of lamps as obstructions that can hide upstage actors, but the director does. To avoid such surprises at final dress rehearsal, carefully specify lamp size and location in advance so they will not interfere with sight lines or actors' movements.

SOFA ALIGNMENT

Before positioning a sofa, consider how it will be used. Sofas must be raked so they can be used by two or three actors. A sofa with an up and down stage alignment is virtually unusable because an actor sitting on the downstage part must face away from the audience to talk with an actor on the upstage seat. Moreover, the upstage actor will be masked by the downstage actor.

Special Problems and Solutions

Consider carefully the location of special units as you design your floor plan. All units should give your set strong theatrical playing areas.

BOOKCASES AND FIREPLACES

Pieces such as bookcases and fireplaces belong next to walls. If placed far upstage, they will be more ornamental than useful because the actors going to them, or playing a scene at them, will be closed or too far upstage for viable exchanges with other characters. Located downstage they are convenient magnets that draw the actors to them, making motivated movement easier, keeping the actors open, and encouraging dynamic blocking.

IMAGINARY WINDOWS AND MIRRORS

Beginning directors are fond of placing imaginary windows and mirrors along the curtain line and having characters move downstage to pantomime looking through the window or at the mirror. Such devices may be convenient, but most often they simply become distracting, calling attention to themselves: Audiences are apt to become so conscious of the actors' technique in miming the imaginary window that the sense of the action is lost. If the rest of the set is realistic, the pantomimed windows and mirrors quite likely will be incongruous. Only in exceptional cases will the imaginary downstage window or mirror be effective.

DOWNSTAGE AREAS

Rather than using only the stage center area, you will want actors to move DL or DR to open the stage and create variety. One way, of course, is simply to block them to the downstage corners, hoping they will find sufficient reason to move. Experienced directors make motivation easier by placing appropriate furniture in those areas. Chairs and end tables are useful — they must be small to avoid obscuring upstage areas — and motivational movement will be increased if you use the tables for such props as a telephone, ashtrays, books, magazines, papers, and the like. Downstage furniture pieces also have an aesthetic value in that they anchor the design in place.

STAIRS

Stairs make excellent entrances because the actor coming on the stage will be facing front. Exits on stairs, however, are difficult and require careful timing; usually the exiting actor faces front while saying part of the final speech, pauses to turn upstage and go up several steps, and then turns back to say the last line. A landing often makes a very useful playing area.

Levels and Platforms

Major contributors to effective blocking and composition, levels and platforms can be part of most realistic and abstract designs. In the realistic set, such as a

Well-planned levels, platforms, and stairs provide excellent performance areas for the large cast in this production of *Measure for Measure* at the Oregon Shakespeare Festival, directed by James Edmondson and designed by Jessie Hollis. Such good design factors facilitate directorial work with blocking and composition, which is especially important in staging crowd scenes. — *Photograph by Henry Kranzler*

living room, you can use stairs and landings or raised platforms. An abstract set can be constructed totally of platforms.

My entire artistic career, all my productions have been nothing but constant self-criticism. I never approach a new production without first shaking myself free of the previous one. The biography of every true artist is that of a man tortured ceaselessly by dissatisfaction with himself. The true artist becomes an artist not merely through using the gifts with which he has been endowed by nature, but also by dint of the colossal labour of perfecting those gifts.

Only the dilettante is pleased with himself the whole time and is never plagued with doubts. The master is unfailingly ruthless with himself; complacency and conceit are alien to him.

—EDWARD BRAUN

editor and translator, *Meyerhold on Theatre*

Exercises

1. Design a floor plan for a hypothetical play that requires (a) stairs, (b) a door leading outside, (c) a door leading to another room, (d) a fireplace, (e) a window, (f) a dining table with four chairs, and (g) a conversational grouping that includes a sofa and two chairs.
2. Design a floor plan for a hypothetical play that requires platforms, levels, and stairs.
3. Make a scale drawing of the floor plan for the play you will direct. When you have finished, check your plan by putting real or simulated furniture pieces on the stage you will use.

CHAPTER SEVENTEEN

Blocking the Play, Part One: Principles

I believe that the theatre makes its effect not by means of illusion, but by ritual.

People do not believe that what they see or hear on the stage is "really" happening. Action on the stage is a stylized reenactment of real action, which is then imagined by the audience. The reenactment is not merely an imitation but a symbol of the real thing. . . . the priest in Holy Communion reenacts, with imitative but symbolic gestures and in a verbal ritual, the breaking of bread and the pouring of wine. He is at this moment an actor impersonating Christ in a very solemn drama. The congregation, or audience, is under no illusion he really *is* Christ. It should, however, participate in the ritual with sufficient fervor to be rapt, literally "taken out of itself," to the extent that it shares the emotion which the priest or actor is suggesting.

—TYRONE GUTHRIE
A Life in the Theatre

As you translate your vision of the play into visual images, you can think of blocking as similar to a moving picture consisting of stopped-action frames. In each frame the director uses *composition* to position the performers in aesthetically pleasing arrangements that depict character relationships and imply the play's story. The whole blends together in a series of physical actions, or *movement,* from one area of the stage to another, which add to the director's statements about characterization, relationships, and situation. During rehearsals the director designs composition and movement in the process called *blocking*. The visual aspects of the stage combine to supply the director with expressive story-telling techniques that are as communicative of a vision as the playwright's script or the actor's voice and body, and no less significant.

The director's vision can lead to a dynamic, theatrical, and artistic expression of the play, using principles of movement and composition that give visual life to essences of the play's characters, plot, conflicts, and style, as shown in this scene from Bob Fosse's New York production of *Pippin*. Ben Vereen is the Leading Player, the commentator who maintains contact with the audience. — *Photograph by Martha Swope*

The Significance of Movement

Movement tells the story of the play, shows character attitudes and relationships, and emphasizes the dramatic conflicts. Used by a director with an imaginative vision, keen stage sense, and delight in theatre, composition and movement contribute to the production's meaning. The director plans movement that will tell the story and depict characters' qualities. The movement is designed to focus audience attention on significant action and away from the extraneous, hence the wisdom of advice to "block for the protagonist." Properly designed theatrical visual qualities give the audience the same aesthetic pleasure as painting or sculpture.

The theatrical truth of the bromide, "Actions speak louder than words," is borne out by the fact that audience members say they will go *see* a play, not *hear* one. Poor composition and illogical movement will disturb audiences, who may then complain that the play simply is not dramatic, that "nothing happens" even though the play is well written and strongly acted.

For the actor, well-assigned movement is essential for the expression of emotions, reactions, attitudes, and thoughts. Movement and character are closely connected. For example, if the director requires an actor to remain motionless for an impassioned speech, the speech will lack strength. Such mistaken blocking affects more than just the single speech; that isolated moment may make the actor feel required, usually unconsciously, to change the character in the entire play to justify the incident. On the other hand, if the director gives the performer movement that communicates not only the text but also the subtext of a passionate speech, that particular moment will be enhanced and the actor will have a better grasp of the total character.

The visual often communicates far more effectively than the spoken. Tyrone Guthrie's comments about the priest's actions illustrate the point: In order for the congregation to be "taken out of itself," the priest must move precisely here at this exact moment to perform this specific action, hold motionless at the next moment, and then move in a certain manner to another location. The movement and gesture of the mass communicated to the congregation even when the priest spoke in Latin. In a theatrical production the director assigns, or blocks, each such action. Even when the performers create their own blocking, the director alone is responsible for deciding whether the blocking is artistically acceptable, theatrically proper, and stylistically correct.

Developing the stage composition and movement patterns in time and space is one of your most satisfying directorial tasks. Composition and movement are your tools as visual artist, helping you communicate important aspects of the play in your various roles, including:

Psychologist, drawing emotional and intellectual motivations from playscript and performers and showing them visually.

Sculptor, positioning the performers in aesthetically pleasing configurations.

Magician, in effect saying "watch this hand" while the other hand subtly prepares the next stage device, thereby focusing the audience's attention on the significant action while hiding the unimportant.

Painter, using the panoply of costumes and properties to show character relationships.

Choreographer, moving performers through their stage universe.

Master storyteller, combining effects to show the audience the story, situation, and plot.

Your compositions give the performer important acting aids and the audience aesthetic pleasure, most often communicating to each actor's and audience member's subconscious. Blocking is an intellectual challenge like that of chess. It re-

In this scene from *Cyrano de Bergerac* the director
uses movement and composition to tell the scene's
story, imply characterization, and suggest conflict. The
director uses a number of techniques to give stage
focus to Cyrano: All other performers look at him, he
has moved downstage to center; and he is the only
performer gesturing, thus holding stage due to
contrast. The composition is enhanced by the subtle
use of levels: The heads of the three men stage right
form a stairway leading the eye to Cyrano, with the
third man's body not directly facing Cyrano ("indirect
focus") to make the stage picture more subtle and
therefore more interesting. Note that those on higher
upstage platforms, normally a position used to receive
focus, are arranged in nondistracting poses. James
Blendick is Cyrano in this production directed by
Michael Langham at the Guthrie Theater.
— *Photograph courtesy of the Guthrie Theater*

quires careful preplanning of each move to accomplish a long-range goal, and each victory becomes a personal pleasure.

Principles Governing Stage Movement

The application of four basic principles will answer most blocking questions you may encounter; armed with a knowledge of these principles you will find that blocking becomes both easy and enjoyable. The principles can be expressed simply:

1. Movement attracts the audience's attention.
2. Movement is not permitted unless it is, and appears to be, motivated by the character's drives.
3. Movement communicates a sense of the style of the play, of the director, and of the character.
4. Movement must be organic, plausible, possible, probable, and true to the logic of life, the play, and the character.

ATTRACTING THE AUDIENCE'S ATTENTION

Movement draws the audience's attention. It is such a powerful attention-getting technique that the audience will look at the moving character even if another character is speaking, more brightly lighted, standing on an elevated platform, or located in a more dominant area of the stage such as center.

Rules affecting movement. Certain basic rules govern the effective use of movement.

- A performer should not move during another performer's lines because that movement distracts from the lines.
- Performers move only on their own lines.
- A performer's (in contrast to the character's) random or careless movement — idle shifts of weight, aimless pacing, busy fidgets — will attract attention, so you must carefully eliminate such unassigned movements.
- Movement is so powerful that you should usually avoid moving a character on his or her significant plot speeches or important character revelation lines.
- Movement is an essential aid for the performer to express emotion, attitudes, and thoughts.
- Because movement captures attention, use it to emphasize entrances, speeches, or business; for example, if you block the performer with a

The director uses movement and composition to draw attention to Lady Teazle, center stage, in this production of *The School for Scandal*. She is moving, drawing audience attention to her; the other characters look at her; she is separated from the others; she is the only one with empty space around her. Note, however, that your eye will briefly go to the character on the left. Why? Because he is somewhat separated from the others and he is full front. His partner restores focus to center stage because she faces Lady Teazle. The production was directed by Allen Belknap for the Folger Theatre. — *Photograph by Joan Marcus*

strong movement and then have the performer hold still momentarily to speak a line, the speech will be emphasized by the movement.

Exceptions to the rules. The few exceptions to the above rules can also be stated briefly. First, performers may move during another character's lines providing audience focus remains on the speaking character. Second, regular movement during dialogue can be used with telling effect. For example, the inmates in *Marat/Sade* will be moving during the entire production — one cannot expect the insane to hold motionless for long speeches — and their regular movement can be intensely dramatic. For another example, while Cyrano is talking to Roxanne in the last act of *Cyrano de Bergerac,* the director might have nuns walking from side to side along a far upstage plane. Providing the nuns' movement is metronomically regular and they make a closed turn (thus keeping their backs to the audience) to walk in the opposite direction, they will contribute to the effect, not distract. Use these exceptions judiciously, always with an awareness of the important principle that movement captures attention.

MOVEMENT MUST BE MOTIVATED

Movement without motivation looks ineffectual, stagey, and implausible. Such movement may embarrass the actor and, by extension, the audience. Moreover, the motivation must be clear to the audience. Once you grasp this concept, you can bring to the production clear and powerful movement that helps performers, enhances characterization, and appears smooth and natural.

Guidelines for motivated movement. The following guidelines will help you ensure that all movement is motivated; your goal is for the movement to appear to originate from the character, not from the director or the performer.

- Motivation must be based on script, character, or situation. If the performer cannot find the motivation, and the movement looks awkward and stagey, stop the rehearsal and work with the performer to find adequate motivation for the movement; eliminate the movement if it continues to lack visible motivation.
- Motivation must be playable and played, not kept internal.
- Motivation must be readily recognizable by the audience.
- Motivation must be plausible.
- Movement for technical reasons — perhaps you wish the performer to clear the doorway to prepare for another character's entrance — must appear to originate from within the character, not from the director.
- Movement for the performer's personal reasons — for example, standing with upstage foot slightly advanced in order to keep the body more open and improve projection of character and voice — must appear to originate from within the character, not from stage technique.

MOVEMENT COMMUNICATES STYLE

As you develop your directorial vision of a play you will sense the style of the movement patterns that distinguish your play from others. For example, the essence of *Medea* calls for movements that are different from those that evoke the spirit of *The Importance of Being Earnest,* and the mood of *The Lower Depths* suggests different movements from those you would use for *The Cherry Orchard.*

Revealing the character's inner self. In *The Glass Menagerie* Laura's personality prevents her from moving directly to another person except in certain emotionally charged situations. Cyrano de Bergerac's soul prevents him from retreating from another person except under the most unusual circumstances. Therefore you would block *The Glass Menagerie* with an awareness of Laura's inability to confront a person directly, except perhaps when she goes to Tom. You would block *Cyrano de Bergerac* with Cyrano moving boldly to stare down all who oppose him, except for backward steps when Christian challenges him by talking about his nose; because Cyrano has promised Roxanne to protect Christian, he cannot take his usual course of dueling with anyone who dares mention his nose. Thus typical movements depict character; atypical movements amplify emotional changes.

The sound of a dumb waiter beginning to move in a
supposedly empty building suddenly demands the
attention of two apprehensive gangsters waiting to fill
a contract to kill an unknown victim. Movement not
only is motivated but also communicates the
motivation and expresses the character's emotions and
relationships. — *Photograph courtesy of the William and
Mary Theatre*

Movement defines the play's basic style more effectively than an essay. It tells
of each character's unique place in the world of the play more eloquently than a
psychologist's report. Movement conveys the directorial interpretation of the play
more clearly even than the director's own verbalized statements.

MOVEMENT MUST BE PLAUSIBLE AND LOGICAL

Movement must be plausible, possible, probable, and true to the logic of life,
the play, and the character. Movement and composition must be organic to the
play, not devices tacked on for their own sake. Whether the play is a fantasy like
Peter Pan or a naturalistic drama like *The Lower Depths,* all production devices
including movement must remain true to the logic of the play.

The Life & Adventures of Nicholas Nickleby proved
that superior directorial vision could bring innovations
to the stage — an 8½-hour running time, a large cast
of 42 Royal Shakespeare Company performers playing
138 speaking roles, $100 ticket prices, and a
dedication to bringing all of the Charles Dickens novel
to the stage. Trevor Nunn and John Caird directed the
imaginatively staged production. — *Photograph by
Martha Swope*

Some directors violate this principle because they mistakenly think of a play
as pure theatre rather than an artistic representation of life. For example, some
beginning directors like to have a character suddenly spring up to stand on a sofa
or a table in a fit of ecstasy, or fall under a table in a paroxysm of despair; but
such movement is so extreme that it will appear implausible, improbable, and
illogical unless equally strong motivation can be found and shown. Other beginning directors like to have characters running rapidly about the stage to demonstrate an emotion such as happiness or frustration; but because people seldom
run through a room in real life, that kind of blocking defies the logic of life unless
the motivation is quite powerful. Such extravagant blocking is seldom valid. The
experienced director avoids movement for the sake of movement, or ever-so-
imaginative effects for the sake of effects, or movement designed to demonstrate
the director's clever imagination.

The director seeks movement and composition that appear plausible, possible, probable, and true to the logic of life, the play, and the character, as shown here in this scene from *The Comedy of Errors* as staged at the Houston Shakespeare Festival. Director Sidney Berger captures a spirit of fun and excitement, gives full stage focus to Antipholus of Syracuse (played by Richard Hill), and motivates the other characters to be sitting with their backs to the audience because they want to attend to the demonstration. The result is excellent use of the stage without the appearance of theatricality for its own sake. — *Photograph by Jim Caldwell*

These principles solve many questions and problems you will encounter. Considering the significance of these bedrock concepts, they are easy to understand and remember; with experience, they become easy to use.

For some directors, grouping and moving characters on a stage is no more exciting than directing traffic or solving jigsaw puzzles, but for Brecht . . . blocking was the heart of the enterprise; blocking was the action on stage. "The grouping and movement of the characters has to narrate the story, which is a chain of events." So he put photographs in his modelbooks to illustrate explicitly the logic of his blocking as his conception of the action. "If a scene didn't seem to work in dress rehearsal," Weber has said, "the first thing reworked would be the blocking." According to Weber, Brecht believed that "ideally . . . the blocking should be able to tell the main story of the play — and its contradictions — by itself, so that a person watching through a glass wall, unable to hear what was being said, would be able to understand the main elements and conflicts of the story." A visual correlative, we might call it.

—DAVID RICHARD JONES
Great Directors at Work

First Steps in Blocking

DOES THE DIRECTOR BLOCK PRIVATELY OR SPONTANEOUSLY?

You may block privately or spontaneously. Some directors believe they should complete all details of blocking privately, working at home with a scale model of the set and cardboard figures or chess pieces to represent characters, and writing all blocking in the prompt book before rehearsals. These directors believe such advance planning is a matter of doing one's homework; they also find that the complexities of blocking are more effectively solved away from the pressure cooker of rehearsals.

Other directors believe in spontaneous blocking during rehearsals, the performers actively contributing to the blocking process. Here the premise is that the rehearsal atmosphere facilitates more creative blocking and that the performers have valuable ideas about their characters' blocking needs. These directors believe that developing blocking with the cast during rehearsals creates organic blocking that is better for the production.

No evidence suggests that one approach is intrinsically better than the other. Inexperienced directors, however, should work alone to block the entire production; their unfamiliarity with blocking requires careful, time-consuming planning. The beginner trying to block spontaneously with the cast will spend a great deal of rehearsal time that would be better devoted to working on characterization and will probably not achieve quality blocking.

The private work technique is also recommended for more experienced directors working with inexperienced performers, who cannot be expected to contribute significantly to the blocking process; a complicated set of levels or many entrances; or a large cast of, say, more than fifteen performers. When the director has enough blocking experience — after directing perhaps twelve productions — the spontaneous technique may deserve consideration, although the process will be markedly less efficient than doing blocking alone. Even the spontaneous approach, however, requires the director to work out basic traffic patterns privately, because they are too complicated to trust to spur-of-the-moment processes during rehearsals with the cast.

BEGIN WITH ENTRANCES AND EXITS

A logical first step in the blocking process is establishing basic traffic patterns, that is, entrances and exits, where characters must go when they enter, and where they will be before they exit. Go through the entire script marking each entrance and exit with a colored highlight pen. Then make a simple chart that identifies the offstage location of each entrance or exit — bedroom, kitchen, front door, and the like.

Lacking any specific reason to the contrary, when characters exit through a particular door, their subsequent entrance will be through the same door. In a complicated production with a large cast, keeping track of such matters can be confusing. Part of working out the traffic pattern, then, involves recording where each performer exits to ensure that the later entrance will be from the same area.

Entrance-exit areas defined by use should remain congruent throughout the play. For example, if characters enter a living room from DL, brushing snow off their clothing and blowing on their hands, obviously the DL door leads outdoors. The effect is disturbing if you later have someone enter through that door dressed in nightclothes, yawning, and fresh from bed. And you cannot alleviate the problem by explaining to the cast that the door leads to a foyer that leads to a bedroom in one direction and to the outside in another direction because the audience, after all, will have no reason to know that there is a foyer. A chart of the traffic pattern will help you maintain logical and congruent use of entrances and exits.

BLOCK REQUIRED MOVEMENTS

The second logical step in blocking is to locate movement required by the action, such as to the telephone, bar, cabinets or drawers containing necessary properties, and the like. Use a colored highlight pen to call attention to these movements, and record them in the margins of your prompt book.

BLOCK THE PROTAGONIST AND OTHER KEY CHARACTERS

Because the protagonist is the central character who both initiates and receives the major action in the play, a third logical step is to block the protagonist. Your play analysis has already shown you the protagonist's significant scenes, such as conflicts, implied or direct statements of goals, and stimulus-response interactions with other characters. Go through the script and mark these key protagonist moments with a colored highlight pen and plan to play them in a major area, such as center stage. Read these protagonist scenes repeatedly, using your imagination's stage to see the protagonist in action with other characters, and then use a model of the set to block the scenes. Write the movement pattern in your prompt book. You can decide later how to get the protagonist and appropriate characters to the proper locations to play these scenes.

Repeat the process with other key characters, paying special attention to the actions in the script that put focus on other characters. Plan where you will play these scenes, and write blocking notes in the margin of your prompt book.

BLOCK KEY SCENES

Your play analysis identified significant scenes, such as the point of attack, complications, direct or implied conflict, character transitions, reversals, and climax. Mark each scene with a colored highlight pen and then use your set model to block each scene and give it appropriate emphasis.

DECIDE HOW MUCH MOVEMENT TO USE

What guidelines help the director decide what amount of movement is correct? Answers are predictably vague; we can only say, "One uses as much movement as the play needs." Too much movement gives the stage a busy quality; too little is visually static and is ineffective use of movement's contributions of emphasis, focus, and storytelling. To distinguish between the two extremes the director can only apply common sense, experience, and a few guidelines.

One can mount a powerful production with great economy of movement. For example, for *The Investigation,* a coldly harsh docudrama by Peter Weiss, I placed the cast in wooden armchairs and limited blocking to a few small area movements, maintaining visual dynamics with small movements in the chairs — leaning forward, making a gesture, crossing the arms or legs, shaking the head, for example. The result of this restricted movement was a tension-filled, highly theatrical experience.

In contrast, your production may also be quite powerful if you use a great deal of movement. For evidence one only has to learn from well-presented musicals. The combination of blocking and choreography creates an exciting stage picture that enhances the theatrical experience for director, performers, and audience.

No minimums or maximums can be stated. One is pragmatic. If it works, it is correct. You learn by watching the work of other directors and then applying concepts to your own productions; and you learn from experimentation in your own work.

AVOID EXCESSIVE BLOCKING

How can the director recognize an overblocked play? What is "too much" movement in a production? No formula can be stated — we cannot say that "six pieces of blocking per page are acceptable but eight will be excessive" — but we can specify basic guidelines, remembering that in art the economical is preferable to the extravagant.

More specific guidelines help identify excessive blocking.

- Blocking is excessive if there is movement on every speech.
- More than one basic movement per short speech is a symptom of over-blocking.
- Excessive blocking forces the performer to travel long distances on short speeches, such as from DL to DR, on a simple five-word sentence.
- If the blocking looks like blocking, it will appear excessive; art consists of hiding technique.

- Movement for its own sake — unmotivated movement — will *appear* excessive, even if the production factually uses less movement than you have seen in other productions.

- A common error in overblocked productions is "backtracking," calling for the performer to stand, sit, say a line, and stand again. Ask yourself, "Why did he sit if he's going to stand again in a moment?" If there is no valid answer to the question, the blocking is excessive.

- As common as the sit-stand-sit blocking is go-come-go movement in which the performer goes from C to UR, back to C, and soon UR again.

- Movement that is actor motivated rather than character motivated appears excessive. Especially noticeable is the actor who jitters back and forth, moving to release nervous energy.

- Unimaginative movement appears to be excessive blocking. If the director's blocking is pedestrian and plain, it quickly grows tiresome. Often such pedestrian work is a result of spontaneous blocking or blocking that has not been carefully refined, revised, and polished. Meticulous advance consideration of blocking usually permits more imaginative and theatrical work.

- Movement that violates the production's ground rules will appear excessive. If much of the production has tightly controlled blocking but there are random scenes with sprawling careless blocking, the latter will appear excessive.

- Movement that uses only a limited amount of the stage area — blocking only in the DR area, for example — will appear excessive.

BLOCKING ABBREVIATIONS AND SYMBOLS

The following are standard blocking abbreviations and symbols that you undoubtedly know from your previous performance experience.

Area identification
Upstage is away from the audience; Downstage is close to the audience; Right is the actor's right when facing the audience; Left is the actor's left when facing the audience.

C, CS: Center, Center Stage	DC, UC: Down Center, Up Center
U, US: Up, Upstage	D, DS: Down, Downstage
R, RS: Right, Right Stage	L, LS: Left, Left Stage
LC: Left Center	RC: Right Center
DLC: Down Left Center	URC: Up Right Center
UR: Upstage Right	UL: Upstage Left
DR: Downstage Right	DL: Downstage Left

Movement
X: Cross	XDR: Cross Down Right
XUL: Cross Up Left	XL3: Cross to the Left 3 steps
S: Sit	R: Rise
Kn: Kneel	Lie: Lie Down
Ent: Enter	Ex: Exit
Ent UR: Enter Up Right	Ex DL: Exit Down Left
Ent UC X DR, Kn: Enter Up Center, Cross to Down Right, then Kneel	

Line readings

Slight pause: /	Longer pause: //
Pause for approx. 5 secs: //5	
Break speech, interrupt: - - -	Take breath here: B
Build (crescendo): ↗	Decrease (diminuendo): ↘
Increase tempo (faster): T+ +	Decrease tempo (slower): T--
Stress underline (emphasize word, phrase, sentence): _____	
Top (building on top of previous line): T	
Undercut (lowering below previous line): U	

Exercises

Use the following experiments, or create others of your own, to test the validity of the principles of movement.

MOVEMENT ATTRACTS ATTENTION

1. Place three actors on the stage on a plane along the curtain line, one far left, the second center stage, and the third far right. Equalize all such matters as costume, lighting, and levels. Have the stage right actor step forward, turn left, and cross to the actor at center. Who did you watch?
2. Place the actors as above. This time, give lines to the actor center stage. Again the actor stage right moves, as above. Who did you watch?
3. Place a two-step level for the actor center stage, give her special lighting, and have her speak. Again the actor at stage right moves. Who did you watch?

These experiments show that movement is a powerful device that commands attention, even when other stage focus devices are at work.

MOVEMENT MUST BE MOTIVATED

1. Assign an actor to enter from DR, hold motionless while silently counting to ten, cross quite slowly to C, hold motionless for a count of twenty, turn and move rapidly to the door DR, stop at the door for a count of ten, and then exit.
2. Assign the same actor to be a thief entering a dimly lit room. The thief looks nervously around as if afraid someone is behind, cautiously crosses to C, moving slowly and looking around the room to be sure no one sees him, freezes when at C because he hears a noise from off left, holds motionless until he is sure that the person off left has moved away, apprehensively retreats to the exit DR, pauses there and cautiously looks out the door to be sure it is safe to leave, and then exits.

Of the two actions, which seemed stagey and artificial, and which showed motivation? Which would be acceptable in a quality production, and which should be rejected?

3. Assign an actor to enter from UR, cross to DC, and stand there for a timed sixty seconds until told to exit.
4. Assign the same actor to be a traditional British sergeant major, in full dress uniform with leather and brass shining. Bagpipes are playing. He enters from UR and marches to DC, making all turns with military sharp edges. Once at C he salutes, clicking his heels. He stands there at attention while the Queen and her guard pass by reviewing the troops. He imagines the ceremonies happening in front of him, remaining at attention until you tell him to exit.

Of these two experiments, which appeared to make the actor awkward, even embarrassed? Which seemed to communicate details? Which helped the actor become less self and more a character?

MOVEMENT COMMUNICATES STYLE

1. Block an improvised scene with movements that are dark and heavy, as to the beat of a kettle drum. Area movements are in direct straight lines. Overall there is not a great deal of movement.
2. Block a second scene with movement that gives the characters quick, bright, birdlike movements. Area movements are in gracefully curved lines. There is a great deal of movement.

Of these two productions, which communicates a sense of drama or tragedy, and which communicates a feeling of comedy? Which would be correct for *Macbeth,* and which for *Blithe Spirit?* What would be the effect if a director reversed the blocking, giving dark, heavy movements to the Noel Coward comedy and light, birdlike movements to Shakespeare's tragedy?

3. Improvise a short scene with a character who seldom moves directly to another person. Her movements and gestures tend to be awkward, full of hesitant starts and stops. One thinks of a wounded butterfly. However, when she moves to a case containing her treasures, the hesitancy disappears; as she talks to the inanimate objects in the case, her gestures are softly graceful.
4. Block a performer who strides, stands with legs wide apart, makes extravagant sweeping gestures, moves directly to other people, and looks at them directly. One thinks of a plaid sports coat, a bold tie.

Of these two movement patterns, which helps you envision the inner soul of Laura from *The Glass Menagerie?* Which helps you perceive the soul of The Gentleman Caller?

MOVEMENT MUST BE PLAUSIBLE AND LOGICAL

1. Place a table or sofa on the stage. Block a performer to jump up and stand on the furniture. Does it appear logical and plausible?
2. Work with the performer to find motivation to jump up on the furniture piece.

How large must the motivation be in order to make the movement appear plausible?

3. Improvise other scenes with performers running or doing comparably extreme movements. Experiment to find motivation. How large must such motivation be in order to appear plausible?

CHAPTER EIGHTEEN

Blocking, Part Two: Techniques

Arthur Hopkins, the producer and director, once said, "The reason for walking is destination." Let me add that the movement you create must come from carefully selected action which allows for the organic development of the character and the primary action of the scene.

Of course, the total animation of the body is brought about by a correct incorporation of surrounding circumstances, weather, time, character needs, relationship to the things and people that surround me, plus main needs and immediate needs. And so is the animation of the words of the character. They are the messenger of my wishes.

—UTA HAGEN
Respect for Acting

A vital portion of your director's vision is an awareness of emphasis. Just as the actor stresses the single most important word within a sentence and the salient sentence in a speech, so the director emphasizes the most important actions or speeches within each action unit, scene, and act. Movement, composition, speech, gesture, and tempo focus the audience's attention on significant action, character, speech, or business.

If the director does not focus audience attention on the principal moments, the inevitable consequence will be failure to communicate the play's key scenes. For example, the point of attack will be lost and the play's clarity obscured if the director blocks that crucial scene with the protagonist in a closed body position, in the far up left corner, half hidden by furniture, and competing with busy activity downstage. Instead you will place the protagonist more toward down center with all other characters watching intensely, thereby calling audience's attention to that critical action. Your play analysis showed you the major points of the play; your blocking technique will emphasize those points to the audience.

The director uses movement, composition, and placement of performers to focus the audience's attention on the salient action. In this scene from the Guthrie Theater's world premiere of *Hang on to Me,* Susan Browning, the actress center stage, has focus because she is (a) center, the strongest area of the stage, (b) separated from the other actors, and (c) in a full front body position. Had director Peter Sellars decided she needed more focus, he could have (a) had her stand, thereby making her the tallest on the stage, (b) assigned other performers to look at her, thereby in effect telling the audience where to look, (c) given her more separation from the others, or (d) given her gestures or area movements. — *Photograph by Joe Giannetti*

Blocking Techniques for Focusing Attention

A number of techniques help you focus audience attention on significant action. As we discussed in the previous chapter, powerful attention-demanding techniques include use of movement and gesture, levels, speech, and technical effects such as costume and lighting. With the caveat that these are *techniques* and that blocking must be organic to the play and always appear motivated, we now examine specific blocking techniques.

USING DOMINANT AREAS OF THE PROSCENIUM ARCH STAGE

The six areas of the proscenium arch stage have relative strengths, or dominant qualities, assuming consideration *only* of area and not other factors such as scene design, movement, levels, speech, costume, lighting, and the like. Figure 18-1 indicates that down center (DC) and up center (UC) are the strongest areas — audience attention is drawn more to an actor in the center area than to one placed elsewhere — followed by down right (DR), down left (DL), and up right (UR), with up left (UL) the weakest area.

There is no disagreement that center stage is a stronger area than the sides, but not all directors believe that DR is more dominant than DL. Those who do believe that because Western audiences read from left to right, they are more

Figure 18-1. Relative Strengths of the Six Areas of the Proscenium Stage

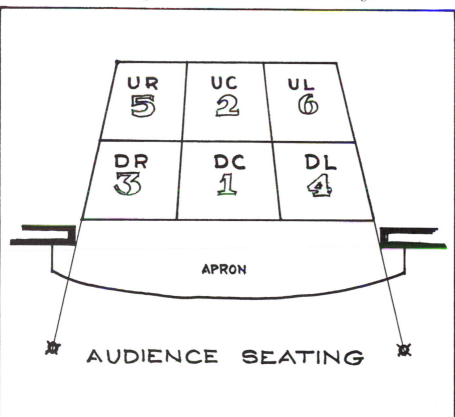

likely to look left first (stage right) rather than right. If that is true, one might say that movement from R to L "goes with the tide" and implies acceptance, and movement from L to R "goes against the grain" and suggests struggle. I believe that there is no perceptible difference between DR and DL, but, perhaps paradoxically, UL is the weakest stage area.

An actor's movement from a weak area to a dominant one will convey more strength and obtain more focus than the reverse move. To use stage areas for focus you could consider moving the protagonist from UL or UR to DC immediately before the character speaks a highly important line. On the other hand, should you need to place a character in a subordinate area, a movement to UL will serve your purpose well.

USING BODY POSITIONS

The actor's body position (Figure 18-2) may be open, profile, or closed. Full open is dominant over three-quarters open, which is stronger than profile, and

Figure 18-2. Actor Body Positions

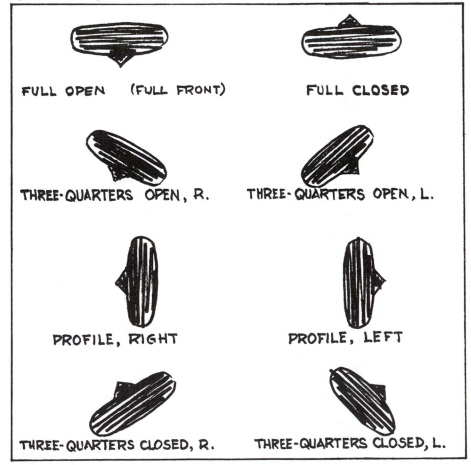

that in turn is more dominant than three-quarters closed. In certain circumstances, however, full closed may be as dominant as full open.

Judicious use of body positions helps you place focus on significant action and speeches. For example, you might shift a character to a full front position for an important speech, keeping other characters in profile or three-quarters closed; you might then move that character to profile when another character has an important speech.

USING SHARING, GIVING, AND TAKING STAGE

Associated with body positions are the techniques of sharing, giving, and taking stage. You can draw audience focus from one character to another with slight shifts of their positions from partially closed to full open, perhaps accompanied by small movements.

Figure 18-3 shows two performers *sharing stage*. Note that both are on the same plane and are in equal body positions. Neither is dominant due to body position. This position is appropriate when both are equally important.

In Figure 18-4 performer A has shifted to a more closed body position and moved slightly downstage, thus *giving stage* to B on stage left. You would direct one performer to give stage to another when the latter's speech or action deserves emphasis.

Figure 18-3. Sharing Stage

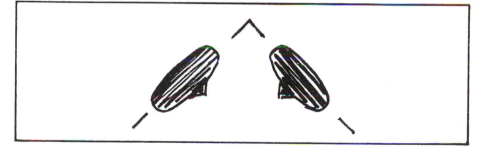

Figure 18-4. Giving Stage

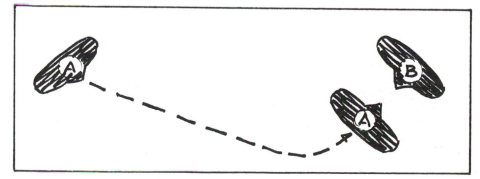

In Figure 18-5 A has moved to an open body position, thus *taking stage* because of the dominant body position. Note that the movement is subtle because it is slightly curved. You would block a performer to take stage for a significant reaction, speech, or business.

AVOIDING STEALING STAGE

Taking stage is easy: One character can obtain dominance over another with a simple change in body position, such as from profile to full open. It is an effective technique that helps you achieve emphasis and focus. But an actor can just as easily take stage at an improper time, *stealing stage* or pulling focus away from a significant character or scene. An actor may steal stage by making random or jittery movements, improperly sized gestures, shifts of body position, noise, and the like. During rehearsals remain alert for such distractions; when you observe them, carefully explain to the performer why those movements are not acceptable.

USING CROSSES

"Cross" may mean a character's area movement across the stage (as, for example, blocking an actor to "cross from RC to DL"), or a movement relative to another character or furniture piece, crossing downstage or upstage ("cross D of table"). Because movement is a powerful tool that captures audience attention, you will find you use many crosses.

In Figure 18-6 A has made a cross from UL to DL (commonly abbreviated XDL). Although no formal rule dictates a distinction between the words *cross* and *move,* most directors use the word *cross* for a relatively large movement from one area of the stage to another, and for shorter movements simply say "move left a couple of feet."

In Figure 18-7 A crossed B. Note that A made a strong downstage cross, staying in full view of the audience. However, C crossed D using an upstage cross that is weak because the moving character is covered by the downstage character. Usually you avoid an upstage cross of a standing character; an upstage cross of a seated character is acceptable.

Figure 18-5. Taking Stage

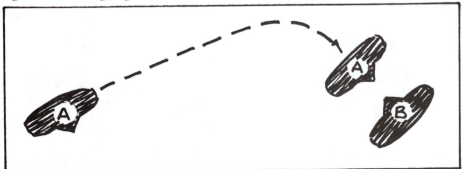

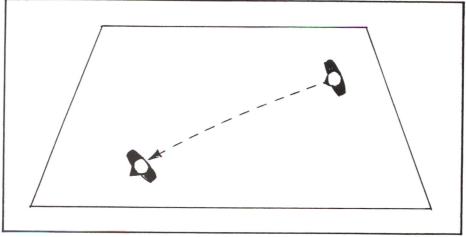

Figure 18-6. Area Cross

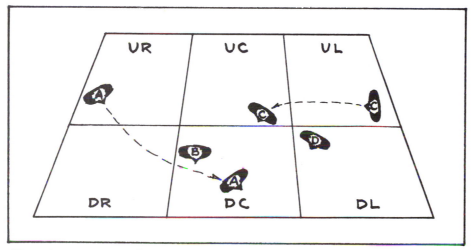

Figure 18-7. Cross in Relation to Other Characters

Figure 18-8 shows an upstage cross of a standing character that may be possible if it is carefully timed and A can find motivation to pause in line delivery. Think of a dead area, out of audience sight lines, in the shape of a large **V** upstage of the standing character. Performer **A** should not speak while inside that **V**. As shown in the figure, A says several sentences approaching that dead area, remains silent while in it, and resumes speaking when again in full view of the audience.

USING COUNTER OR DRESS MOVES

The character crossed by another makes a *counter,* also called a *dress* movement in the opposite direction, as B does in Figure 18-9. The counter helps bal-

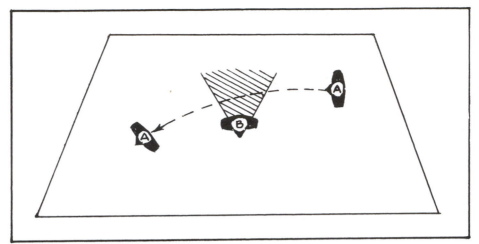

Figure 18-8. Upstage Cross in Relation to Another Character

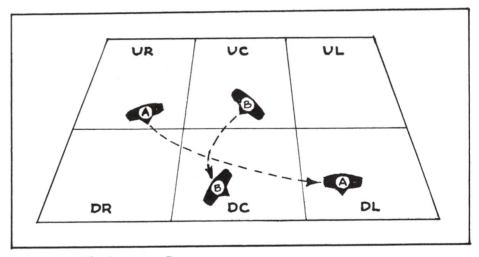

Figure 18-9. The Counter or Dress

ance the stage composition and maintains focus on the moving character. Note that the counter is a small, semicircular movement that will not distract audience attention from the moving character. Timing the counter is important: B should initiate the counter at the precise moment that A is directly downstage. Moving before or after that moment is sloppy technique and apt to distract from the moving character. Also important is motivating the counter: B should appear to want to watch A, listening carefully or otherwise reacting to A, and therefore staying closed or profile, not open.

USING THE SHORTEST TURN AND OPEN AND CLOSED TURNS

Movement necessarily includes turns: The character may turn at the beginning, middle, or end of an area movement, and often turns are part of movements in or out of chairs, at doors, and so on. *The actor should always take the shortest turn, that is, the turn that involves the least amount of turning.* A long turn is inefficient and calls attention to itself; the short turn is efficient and accomplishes the same goal more neatly. To avoid long turns, reposition the actor so the short turn will be easiest.

The open turn, illustrated by A in Figure 18-10, maintains focus on the character. On the other hand, B makes a closed turn that loses focus because the character faces upstage. Most movements require open turns; use the closed turn only if you deliberately want the character to be unobtrusive.

USING ACTORS' FOCUS: WHERE ACTORS LOOK

Focus has two different meanings. We have been using the word to refer to the director's method of concentrating audience attention on important actions or characters. The second meaning refers to the actor's focus, or where the actor looks: You direct actors to "focus" on one character so the audience will also look there. The technique is no more complicated than the simple practical joke in which several people on a crowded street corner stare intensely at a building top, making passersby look up at the same place.

"Direct focus" means all actors look at one place or character, as shown in Figure 18-11. The audience will look at the same place or character. Direct focus can be strengthened by having all actors also gesture toward the character, a device often seen in musicals for a major character's entrance, as for the title song in *Hello, Dolly* when the waiters are placed in lines leading to Dolly's entrance, all looking and pointing at Dolly.

Figure 18-10. Open and Closed Turns

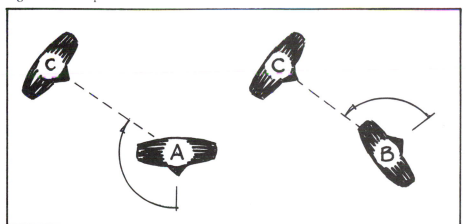

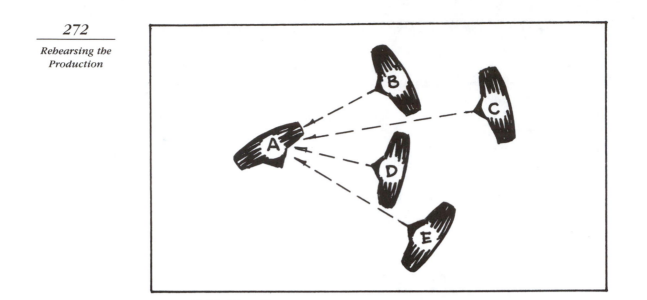

Figure 18-11. Direct Focus

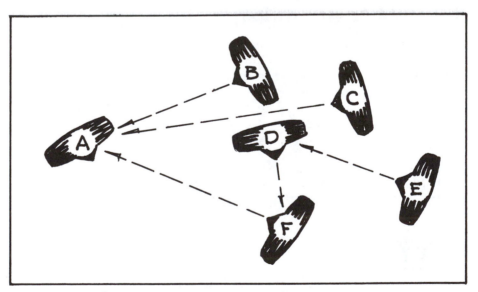

Figure 18-12. Indirect Focus

"Indirect focus," shown in Figure 18-12, is more subtle than direct focus. Instead of all actors looking at the significant character, several look at another character, who restores focus to the major character. Indirect focus allows artful variations; if many actors look at one character the result might be too blatant, lacking imaginative variety.

Director Louis Scheeder uses both direct and indirect focus techniques in this scene from *The Two Gentlemen of Verona* at the Folger Shakespeare Theatre. The three armed characters provide direct focus by pointing at the center two. The actor on the left uses indirect focus because he is looking at the character on the far right; if the audience follows the left actor's line of sight, the right actor's direct focus returns attention to the center. — *Photograph courtesy of the Folger Shakespeare Theatre*

USING SEPARATION

One actor separated from a crowd, surrounded by empty space, draws attention. The audience will focus on the single character standing or sitting alone. Although this focus device requires a fairly large cast — it is ineffective with fewer than, say, five characters — it can be highly useful because the individual character in effect "stands out in the crowd." Separation can help characterization. For example, if you were directing *Cyrano de Bergerac* you would consider using separation often to enhance Cyrano's characteristic desire to stand proudly alone, away from others.

USING CONTRAST

Contrast draws attention to the actor in the different body position, posture, or otherwise unusual situation. You can achieve this focus effect by having one character stand while all others are seated, sit while others stand, or sit on the floor or a table while others use more conventional chairs and sofas.

KEEPING ACTORS FREE OF FURNITURE DURING SIGNIFICANT MOMENTS

Characters trapped behind furniture become ineffectual, losing strength because in effect they are cut in half by the furniture that obscures them from the waist down. For example, imagine Hamlet giving his "To be or not to be" speech behind an overstuffed sofa, dodging tall table lamps, and caught upstage of an ornate dining table. The following photograph from *The Cherry Orchard* illustrates the weakening effect of bodies being cut off: Three of the upstage characters

In this scene from *The Cherry Orchard* at the Guthrie Theater, a number of focus techniques place attention on the seated character. The actor is center stage, a powerful area; he is facing full front, and most of the others are closed; he is both gesturing and speaking; four of the five other characters are focused on him, thereby instructing the audience to look at him; he is separated from the others, giving him more dominance; and because he is seated while most others are standing, contrast differentiates him and draws attention to him. The production was directed by Tyrone Guthrie. — *Photograph courtesy of the Guthrie Theater*

are less dominant because furniture or another performer obscures portions of their bodies. They would be badly placed if at this moment they were significant to the action; they are perfectly placed if they are subordinate to the primary interest.

USING LEVELS

Use of levels helps control focus. In general the higher the actor, the more dominant. Steps, levels, and platforms are significant aids. But even with a scene design that has no elevated platforms or steps, you have a wide variety of positions that will achieve variations in level. Characters may lie, sit, or kneel on the floor; sit or kneel on a chair or on the chair's arm; sit on a table; stand; or stand on step stools.

In this scene from *Hang on to Me* at the Guthrie Theater, director Peter Sellars uses levels inventively by positioning some actors in different positions on the floor, some actors in chairs, and one standing. All lead the eye to the highest level, the actress on the piano. Other techniques add to her dominance: All the other actors are looking at her, she is gesturing, she is full front, and she is separated from the others.
— *Photograph by Joe Giannetti*

The director's use of levels can be theatrical and vivid, as in this scene with actors leaping from covered platforms in the production of *Wind in the Willows* directed by John Neville-Andrews at the Folger Shakespeare Theatre — *Photograph by Julie Ainsworth*

USING THE TRIANGLE

Many apparently complex compositional and focus techniques are actually based on the simple triangle, and that formation is one of your more useful tools. The triangle configuration places focus on the character at the apex (see page 279). The basic triangle consists of two downstage actors looking upstage at the actor between them, but you can devise a number of variations.

STAGING ENTRANCES

Entrances of major characters change the action of the play, as discussed in Chapter Four, because the new character changes ongoing character relationships. Given the importance of entrances, each one should be appropriately dynamic. Move other characters away from the entrance area before the major character enters, and provide open areas into which the character can move; you may also position other characters in a triangle to focus on the entrance.

Think of the door as being some three feet farther on stage than it actually

Levels aid composition, as shown in this scene from *A
Sleep of Prisoners*, directed by the author at the
William and Mary Theatre. — *Photograph courtesy of
the William and Mary Theatre*

is: Instead of having the performer enter and stop in the doorway, tell the performer to enter, continue moving until well on stage, and only then stop. This
technique is especially helpful if the entrance area is UR or UL in a corner with
poor sight lines, if the area is crowded with furniture pieces or other performers,
or if the scenery design is busy and you want to pull the performer away from
the walls. Your lighting designer will appreciate your efforts to bring performers

Simple levels can be theatrically effective, as shown in
this scene from *Vanities*, directed by Bob Hall for the
Virginia Players at the University of Virginia. A number
of focus techniques emphasize the standing character:
She is separated from the others, she has center stage,
the other two are looking at her, and she is at the apex
of a triangle. — *Photograph courtesy of the Virginia
Players*

further on stage, away from scenic units, because it is difficult to light such areas
without casting unpleasant shadows on the walls.

STAGING EXITS

Exits of major characters are important actions, because the remaining characters necessarily establish a new set of relationships. You may wish to structure
a slight pause after an exit, rather as if the play had to take a deep breath to
prepare itself to continue; those left on stage may look after the departing character until the door closes, take a small pause, and then turn back to start the new
action.

One of the director's useful blocking tools is the triangle. Note the easy movement within the triangle in this series of scenes from *Hamlet*. Performers at the sides of the triangle focus on the performer at the apex, giving him stage, and his position is more powerful because he is center. You can freely move the actor within the triangle, allowing visual variety while maintaining focus on him. Frank Grimes is Hamlet in this production directed by John Neville-Andrews at the Folger Shakespeare Theatre.
— *Photographs by Julie Ainsworth*

Most exits should be timed so that the character's final words are said only a few steps before the actual exit. Block the performer close to the doorway for those last words, either in place before the exit speech or moving to the location during the speech. The timing is incorrect if the performer finishes the speech and then has to take a long trek across the stage to the door.

Overplayed exits can look hyperdramatic: The performer speaks, pauses to march to the door, stops, makes a sweeping turn to face the others on the stage, finishes the speech ("And so — farewell!"), and swirls around and out the door. Such exits, popular on Broadway in the mid-1930s and sometimes brought back to life by a theatre's self-proclaimed "star," have been replaced by more subtle technique that uses fewer dramatic effects.

In this variation on the triangle, the arrangement again
focuses attention on the performer at the apex. Hamlet
also has focus because of contrast; he is the only
character seated. In addition he is facing full front
while the other two are only partially open.
— *Photograph by Julie Ainsworth*

BEING CONSISTENT WITH THE PICTURE FRAME STAGE

The proscenium arch is a picture frame around the stage. It has generated a
number of theatrical conventions based on the concept that across the downstage
curtain line is a "fourth wall" through which the audience can see the stage although the people on stage do not know the audience is present. If the director
accepts the fourth wall premise — that is, if the play's action is set within the
frame — the production should remain true to itself and stay comfortably within
the frame from beginning to end.

Blocking a performer downstage past the curtain line is called "breaking the
curtain line" or "breaking the fourth wall." If your vision requires you to break
that fourth wall, you should do it relatively early in the production. Waiting until

Inventive directors can make an exciting stage moment from what might otherwise be a mundane entrance. In the top photograph, Peter Francis-James is Laurent in this production of *Tartuffe* directed by Lucian Pintilie. In the bottom picture, Len Cariou is Petruchio in *The Taming of the Shrew* directed by Michael Langham. Both productions were at the Guthrie Theater. — *Photographs by Joe Giannetti*

the play's climax and then having characters walk out of the frame and through the fourth wall changes the production's ground rules.

USING LARGE MOVEMENTS TO ENHANCE PERFORMERS' EMOTIONS

If a character has an angry speech but the actor cannot find the emotion, try reblocking the scene and giving the actor large sweeping movements that attack other characters. Use improvisations to add dimension to the scene. Work through the sequence several times, adding angry movements to help the actor convey the appropriate emotions. Then try eliminating all movement. In most cases the performer will not lose the emotion. Indeed the actor may even show additional depth because the emotions remain but there is now an obstacle to its expression; the effect may be that of a volcano ready to erupt.

BLOCKING TABLE SCENES

Scenes involving people sitting at a table are tests of the director's ingenuity. If there are only three people, the problem is lessened by placing two actors at the left and right of the table, and the third actor at the upstage side. Often directors place a fourth chair downstage of the table to make the scene appear realistic, but for staging purposes no one sits there.

But imagine you are directing a play like *Brighton Beach Memoirs,* which requires six people to eat a full dinner. Two actors can be placed at each side of the table, and two more in upstage chairs, but the remaining two characters are difficult to place. If those two are also placed in chairs upstage or at the side, all characters are likely to be open but the glaringly empty space downstage of the table will make the scene look unrealistic. If the two are in downstage chairs, they will be closed so that the audience will not see their faces or actions, and they will mask one or more of the upstage performers.

One alternative is to rake the table and the chairs and leave an open area that will keep all performers open, as illustrated in the photograph of *The Three Sisters* on page 283. Another choice is to place characters in downstage chairs and motivate them to leave the table early. Directing *Brighton Beach Memoirs,* I placed the two mothers in the downstage chairs. With careful attention to timing we were able to move them to the kitchen whenever an upstage person had lines; they returned with food to stand upstage of the table to talk to the others, and they returned to their chairs only when they would not interfere with the scene.

USING PERFORMERS' BACKS

Concern about keeping characters open should not lead you to conclude that it is wrong to block performers with their backs to the audience. Often such arrangements can add dramatic impact to the scene.

Dinner table scenes, such as this one from the Guthrie Theater's production of *The Three Sisters*, challenge the director's ability to solve problems. Here director Liviu Ciulei carefully positions the characters to leave a downstage opening for audience sight lines; raking the table also opens many characters. The inventive director will seek opportunities to have characters move from the table, stand in place, or otherwise open body positions for audience visibility. — *Photograph by Joe Giannetti*

Expect Blocking to Evolve during Rehearsals

Blocking that was effective in the early days of rehearsal may turn sour for a number of reasons, almost all of them indicative of the production's growth. As performers develop their characters, the changes may demand different blocking. As the performers grow more adept at displaying their characters, blocking must also become more communicative; and as more demands for perfection are placed on the performer, comparable demands are placed on the director. Blocking that was originally acceptable may simply not work later.

Your work evolves and changes no less than that of performers. Preserve your right to experiment, to abandon this blocking to try that, just as you insist that

The director can solve difficulties with table scenes by finding motivation for all performers to squeeze close together on the upstage side, as shown in this scene from *The Madwoman of Chaillot*, directed by Howard Scammon for the William and Mary Theatre. [As evidence of the educational theatre's ability to train actors for professional careers, note that Linda Lavin, then an undergraduate student at William and Mary, is on the left (wearing a makeup nose).] — *Photograph courtesy of the William and Mary Theatre*

your cast experiment and grow. Do not feel distressed if blocking frequently requires revision: As characters change and you get new insight, you can change any appropriate element.

Blocking will work out if you prepare yourself privately in advance, force yourself to keep in mind the essence of each scene and character, and tackle it in logical small action units. While quality blocking must be your goal, it cannot be your initial goal: Do not create frustration by expecting to achieve perfection with initial blocking. Look on the blocking process as an enjoyable test of your wits, a chess game, a chance to construct a new entity with living people, and especially an opportunity for you to express your creative storytelling instincts in aesthetically pleasing ways.

In this theatrically exciting scene from the New York
production of *42nd Street* director-choreographer
Gower Champion proves there is no rule demanding
that the director always place performers in an open
position. Indeed, the back often can be more dramatic
than a full front; in large cast productions, a visually
boring stage picture would result if all performers
faced toward the audience. A revolving stage increases
the dramatic impact. — *Photograph copyright 1986
Martha Swope*

Physical actions are the necessary balance for verbal actions. When the actor is truly
alive on stage there is an endless variety of interaction between verbal and physical
behavior. Ideally, the audience should be unable to differentiate whether he walks when
he is talking or talks when he is walking!

—UTA HAGEN
Respect for Acting

Exercises

Review the blocking of your play.

1. Does your blocking tell the play's story? Ideal blocking is pantomimic drama-

tization that expresses character relationships and the play's story. Examine your blocking as if watching a movie or television set with the sound turned off.

2. Have you given full stage emphasis to all key moments, including the point of attack, the protagonist's statement of goal, obstacles, plot complications, and the climax? Does blocking make these scenes vital and dynamic?

3. Does your blocking properly focus audience attention on the action?

4. Are you using a dynamic variety of techniques to focus audience attention? Examine your blocking to see if you are using such techniques as open or closed body positions, levels, areas of the stage, contrast, separation, and the triangle.

5. Have all distractions been eliminated?

6. Is all movement motivated? Is the motivation clearly communicated to the audience?

7. Is the blocking interesting to watch?

CHAPTER NINETEEN

Rhythm, Tempo, and Pace

Armed with a master vision of the play on imagination's stage, "hearing" and "seeing" the total theatrical effect, the director shapes the production both in *space* — as discussed in earlier chapters on blocking — and in *time,* which involves rhythm, pace, and tempo. For the former you are sculptor and choreographer; for the latter you become a symphony conductor. Your work in space demands a well-honed visual acuity; your work in time requires an equally sharp musical sense and concept of proper pacing.

Discussing the play-in-time is difficult: It is easy to illustrate the play-in-space with concrete examples, but time's abstract nature does not lend itself to such clear examples. Therefore it is necessary to use a number of less specific analogies. For example, to compare directorial work with driving an automobile, the play has one basic rhythm that is like the posted maximum-minimum speed limit on the interstate highway; dramatic sense requires various tempi within that speed as you travel hills and valleys, clear roads and confused intersections, fog and clear weather; and pace is like the changes from one tempo to another that you make with the gear shift, accelerator, and brake.

The play director has been compared to a symphony conductor. The latter, however, works from a score well-marked with the composer's concept of relative rapidity or rate of movement (*allegretto, allegro, legato, adagio,* etc.), volume (*diminuendo, crescendo,* etc.), and feeling (*con amore* etc.). Composers even indicate specific metronome settings to indicate desired tempi.

The director, on the other hand, works from a script that at best can only partially suggest the playwright's intent with directions such as *pause, silence,* and *quickly.* How, then, do you ascertain the proper use of time? Does the script's

The directorial vision of delightful, up-tempo fun permeates this scene from *The Merry Wives of Windsor*, directed by John Neville-Andrews at the Folger Shakespeare Theatre. — *Photograph by Joan Marcus*

lack of indication imply a lack of concern with rhythm? Does *pace* mean the performers are to say their lines and pick up their cues without pause? Of course not.

[A] sense of rhythm allowed [Tharon Musser, professional lighting designer] to move easily into musicals. "I always had the gut feeling it takes to do a musical in terms of cueing and timing and helping to create applause. What I had to learn was how to implement that feeling in lights. One light does not a scene make in a musical, whereas it can in a straight show." Her first hit musical, *Mame,* serves as an example.

"It took four weeks playing out of town before I got the 'Mame' number cued right. The first night it happened it stopped the show five times. Jerry Herman is a very difficult composer insofar as he builds a number not only in terms of volume but by changes of key, and so on. Finding ways with Jerry's stuff to pull back — in order to have something left for the final rideout — is very difficult. In the final rideout in the 'Mame' number everything but the kitchen sink was on. The trick, of course, is to build for those moments, pull back, change color, move forward again. You can really make that audience response where you *want* them to respond."

Rhythm in light need not only be a result of cueing; it comes from line and composition as well. For *Ballroom,* which employed a circular set by Robin Wagner, there was "not a straight line in the light plot," Musser claims. *A Chorus Line,* on the other hand, was nothing *but* straight lines.

—ARNOLD ARONSON
"The Facts of Light," *American Theatre,* January 1986

Rhythm

Rhythm refers to the total effect on the audience of the play-in-time: its sequential pulses created by such units as beats, action units, scenes, and acts and by dialogue, character changes, and stimulus-response cycles. Rhythm is the master control, a drum beat that dictates production effects such as performers' basic rate of line delivery, music, and lighting shifts. Each play has an inherent rhythm, just as art and life are played at different rhythms. Your task is to find the play's individual rhythmic qualities and apply them correctly to the production.

How do you recognize rhythm? Intuitive responses indicate rhythm in all life and art, and with training you can increase your sensitivity to the rhythms around you. An America's Cup yacht performs at a rhythm different from that of a small dinghy; football is played at a different rhythm from badminton; ocean waves in calm weather have a different rhythm from those that herald a hurricane; the hummingbird flies at a rhythm unlike the eagle's; a lumberjack's working rhythm differs from a computer hacker's; Sousa's "Stars and Stripes Forever" and Pachelbel's Canon in D have totally different rhythms; swing differs from rock; Robert Browning's poems differ in rhythm from those by T. S. Eliot; and a six-year-old boy's personal rhythm is not like his teenage sister's, and both are unlike the father's.

Alert to these inherent qualities, the director knows that *King Lear* and *Death of a Salesman* have basic rhythms that are quite different from those that characterize *A Comedy of Errors* and *The Importance of Being Earnest.* Apply *Earnest*'s rhythm pattern to *Salesman* and the effect is ludicrous; put *Lear*'s rhythms in *Comedy of Errors* and the production will die.

Tempo

Tempo refers to the impression of speed — fast, slow, moderate — within the units that create rhythm. Just as there is a basic rhythm to the *1812* Overture but varying tempi throughout, a play's overall rhythm is constructed of a number of tempi.

Within a broad overall rhythmic pattern that controls the whole, a play contains various tempi that are akin to the pattern but different. For example, *Macbeth* has a strong, pulsating, demanding rhythm with heavy stresses, but isolated scenes have different tempi. The Porter scene, for example, is brisk and flowing throughout; a start-rush-hesitate tempo characterizes MacDuff's speech after he discovers the dead Duncan; Macbeth's "Tomorrow and tomorrow" speech is slow and fatigued. All tempi are artistically unified to the pattern established by the rhythmic whole.

Pace

Pace refers to shifts in tempo. Pace is the dynamic and changeable factor of a production, in contrast to rhythm, which is inherent in the script, and tempo, which is a basic rate. The terms *slow-paced* and *fast-paced* appear too often in less-than-well-informed critics' comments about productions. In fact to pace a play is to seek variations in speed, from the smallest units such as speeches to larger units such as acts.

Pacing is not speed. A vital theatrical production demands intelligent and sensitive use of time's dynamic variations, pauses, accelerations, hesitations, and silences. One premise governs the entire theatrical production, whether dealing with volume, humor, or tempo: Whenever the production takes on a repetitive sameness, audience interest will decrease. If you play the entire production at unvaried high pitch and volume, it becomes boring; if you attempt to achieve comic effects with every line, humor vanishes; and if you make the tempo unchanging, the audience will find the production monotonous. Just as an actor who speaks in a monotone at the same rate and volume is a poor choice for a major role, a director whose productions lack dynamic rhythm, pace, and tempo is a poor choice for a major play.

A well-paced scene varies the volume and rate of speeches, pauses and silences, physical movements, and gestures. Pacing means that on a certain cross the character walks slowly but then increases speed; the character speaks deliberately in one speech and rushes the next; a character reacts quickly and angrily to one stimulus and freezes motionless for a long pause in response to another. Good pacing pits a deliberate delivery against a rapid-fire delivery, as director Elia Kazan did with Marlon Brando's Stanley and Jessica Tandy's Blanche in *A Streetcar Named Desire*.

A book is a part of life, a manifestation of life, just as much as a tree or a horse or a star. It obeys its own rhythms, its own laws, whether it be a novel, a play, or a diary. The deep, hidden rhythm of life is always there — that of the pulse, the heart beat.

—HENRY MILLER
The Cosmological Eye

Combining Rhythm, Tempo, and Pace: An Example

Discovering a play's inherent rhythm allows the director to unlock mysteries of characterization, mood, and dramatic impact. To cite a personal example, I was in the third week of rehearsals of Garcia-Lorca's moving poetic tragedy, *The House of Bernarda Alba,* and had not yet found a way to achieve the play's power. Although the cast (including Glenn Close, who was then an underclass student) was magnificent, our rehearsals were creating only a competent production, not a moving one. In particular I felt we had not found the essence of the play's opening scene, which is crucial to establishing the tenor of the production.

At one rehearsal of the first scene I began to drum my pencil against a desk to simulate the stage directions concerning the offstage tolling of a funeral bell: It tolls, stops, tolls again, stops. Against this tolling the maid delivers exposition about the death of the man of the house while townswomen enter in mourning. Then the widowed Bernarda enters from the funeral, a stern matriarch determined that her five daughters will be brought up within the established traditions.

My pencil-beat simulation of the funeral bell became slower and more compelling as my imagination played the sound of the bell. The rhythm dictated the entrance of the townswomen and the delivery of the maid's speech. More significantly, it dictated Bernarda's entrance.

Quickly we found a stick for Glenn to use as a cane, telling her that Bernarda would place it on the ground in rhythm with the bell. We did an improvisational exercise to awaken sensory recall of the proud Bernarda walking home from the church through the dusty streets and walls of noisy townspeople, always following the compelling beat of the funeral bell. Finally we played the opening scene with her entrance.

So effective was her entrance that the cast broke into spontaneous applause. From that moment of discovery came knowledge of the basic rhythm that governs the whole play; more importantly, the rhythm helped the performer snap Bernarda's character into brilliant focus. In fact all members of the cast found that the rhythm opened doors to characterization.

We did not use the funeral bell's rhythm for the entire play, of course. The tempo of the first scene was too slow to use for long, and other scenes had their own tempi. With attention to pace we found dramatic variations, but always the funeral bell's rhythm persisted.

Supposing you are an actor who is playing Hamlet. "To be, or not to be: that is the question: Whether 'tis nobler in the mind to suffer . . ." — those infinitely familiar lines. You have to find the inflection, that is to say the tone, to which they are sung or spoken, the pitch, the pace, the rhythm and the color.

—TYRONE GUTHRIE
Theatre Arts, November 1944

Study your play's inherent rhythms before rehearsals begin, and continue the searching process during rehearsals. Try tapping your finger or a pencil against a desk — the analogy to the symphony conductor returns to mind — to discover the rhythms of important scenes. Experiment with changes of pace for dramatic variation, and when you perceive a possible shift of tempo, try working it in at rehearsal. If a given shift is ineffective, discard it and try a different variation.

This process will not only reveal the rhythm, tempo, and pace of the play in rehearsal but also give performers a strong concept of the play's performance quality. The ultimate result will be a mental clock that paces the performers through the production.

Exercises

1. To help you become sensitive to rhythm, when you attend dramatic productions deliberately tap your finger against your leg at various speeds until you find the rhythm of the production. Movies and television programs can give you additional experience in discovering directorial rhythm. Do you discover faster rhythms in comedies and slower rhythms in tragedies? What kind of rhythm governs adventure stories? Suspense stories? Are there distinct changes of pace, with productions starting slowly and gradually increasing tempo?

   Carefully observe the key points in the story — foreshadowing, point of attack, complications, obstacles, climax — and note shifts in pace. Do the productions tend to move relatively quickly or slowly until such key points and then change pace? Describe the shift of tempo at each significant moment.

2. Work with a group of directors or actors to tap out the best rhythm for a production of *King Lear*. Then work together to find the rhythm for a production of *The Odd Couple*. What do you discover? Continue the experiment for productions of such diverse plays as *Medea, You Can't Take It With You, Death of a Salesman,* and *Lysistrata*. Are you able to discover certain standard rhythms depending on the play's genre?

3. Practice tapping a pencil against a desk until you believe you have discovered the rhythm of the play you are directing. Take that rhythm into rehearsals and communicate it to your performers.

4. Carefully rehearse pace shifts at key moments of the play you are directing. Explain to your cast that you will be experimenting with increasing and decreasing the performance's pace at those moments.

5. In rehearsals listen carefully to the performers' cue pickups. Ideally performer A will speak the first word at the conclusion of performer B's last word, but actors typically insert a pause before speaking, even taking a breath when they hear the last word of the cue speech. Experiment by working to eliminate all such pauses in a given action unit. What is the result?

   Now experiment by having performers *overlap* that last word of cue speeches, B speaking the first word at the same time that A is saying the last word. Do the given action unit at that tempo. What is the result?

Finally experiment by building in pauses before crucial lines, such as those involving the point of attack, complications, statement of goals, and the like. This means that A will complete the speech, and B will take a deliberate pause before speaking the important line. What is the result?

6. Working with all members of your cast, practice the play's rhythm by clapping hands.

7. Working with one performer at a time, practice each individual character's basic rhythm by clapping hands.

I rely greatly on rhythm. I think that is the one thing I understand: the exploitation of rhythm, change of expression, change of pace in crossing the stage. Keep the audience surprised, shout when they're not expecting it, keep them on their toes, change from minute to minute.

—LAURENCE OLIVIER
Los Angeles Calendar

CHAPTER TWENTY

Working with Actors, Part Three: Problem-Solving

As an actress I like everything concerning the production I'm in to be mapped out before opening night. But how can I expect this from directors who trust that improvisations will cure the problems created by their own inadequate homework? Six weeks after opening night [of the musical version of *I Remember Mama*] I am still forced to improvise. I miss the directors I knew who would want moments to be *clear*: this scene is about *this,* and this scene is about *this* — and here the violin is playing. Good directors know all about that and will make it happen. *They* use the actors, they are challenged by the fantasy of whom they work with.

See me! Use me!

—LIV ULLMANN
Choices

There is a certain logic in the fact that the final chapter of this book discusses the director as problem-solver. Here we look at problem-solving with actors, but in fact almost every aspect of your work as director requires a working methodology that will help you identify what's wrong and then search out possible corrective actions.

As you work with actors to bring your vision to life on stage, you continually diagnose their performance problems and seek solutions. The director has a mandate to take action: You use insight to perceive symptoms, logic to identify causes, and creativity to search for all possible alternatives that may solve the problem. When you are convinced you have found all the options, you select the alternative that you think will unravel the puzzle. When working with actors (or any aspect of play direction, for that matter) avoid shortchanging the process by using the first alternative that comes to mind; only after you have examined all possible alternatives will you be able to judge which one is best. If that option does not solve the problem, repeat the full process.

The following examples examine strategies for solving acting problems. These samples illustrate; they do not dictate; their value lies less in specific cures

"Less is more" is an important artistic dictum. Director
Mike Nichols used minimal blocking and business to
intensify the dramatic impact of Glenn Close and
Jeremy Irons in the Broadway production of *The Real
Thing*. — *Photograph copyright 1986 Martha Swope*

than in indication of a directorial method of identifying a problem and considering various solutions. The key words and phrases that are repeated in these
strategies include *experiment, try, if . . . then,* and *identify.*

The Cast Brings Nothing New to Rehearsals

SYMPTOMS

You are disappointed at the lack of growth. Although performers are recep-
tive to your comments, they return to rehearsals showing no evidence of having
worked on their characters since the last rehearsal. Each rehearsal merely repeats
the same old characterization and line readings.

IDENTIFYING THE CAUSE

A pattern of lack of growth may be caused by the director's failure to set specific goals at the beginning and end of each rehearsal. Actors need you to be specific, to prescribe a road map that will get everyone to the desired destination.

CORRECTING THE PROBLEM

At the end of every rehearsal, give notes to each performer, setting definite goals for the next rehearsal. To one actor you might say, for example, "Steve, tonight you showed a new aspect of your character. In Scene 2 you're beginning to show that Denton wants to help Anne. That's fascinating. Tomorrow night let's experiment to see how that will work in Scenes 4 and 7. Between now and tomorrow, I want you to make a written chart of Denton's emotions, by beats, in every scene with Anne. Bring the chart. We'll work through scenes tomorrow. Questions?" Set comparable goals for each performer.

At the beginning of the next rehearsal, restate the performers' goals. After rehearsal comment on their work on the goals set earlier, praising those who are achieving their goals. Set new goals for the next rehearsal. The process gives you and the performers viable targets for each rehearsal.

Setting directorial goals is no less important. After the cast has left, talk with your assistant about the rehearsal just completed, identifying problems and seeking solutions. Give yourself goals for the next rehearsal. Setting goals is arguably your most effective technique for focusing on planned improvements at each rehearsal.

The Performers Lack Conviction

SYMPTOMS

Performers are merely going through the motions without conviction; they deliver speeches by rote. The performers do not appear to be investing themselves in their roles; they seem dull and unimaginative.

IDENTIFYING THE CAUSE

If you perceive the fault in just one performer, you can conclude it is that individual's personal attitude or inability, but if a number of performers show the same lackadaisical attitude, you may be responsible for the problem. In either case you need to help the performers gain insight into the script and characters.

CORRECTING THE PROBLEM

Take all possible steps to awaken your own imagination. Show a personal investment in the play and production. Eliminate directorial communications that may be interpreted as noncommittal. Prepare more carefully for each rehearsal.

Consider changing your rehearsal schedule to incorporate techniques that make the play meaningful and relevant. If you are directing *The Diary of Anne Frank,* for example, you might invite a rabbi to discuss the history of the Jews, bring photographs of Anne, have an actor read aloud portions of Anne's diary, confine the cast within the actual dimensions of the Franks' hiding place and induce fear of discovery, and do improvisations to help the cast understand how the Franks had to find a way of life despite the dangers they faced.

Help performers see other dimensions of their roles. Ask "what if?" questions. Try having actors exchange roles in an action unit. Conduct improvisations that add extra layers to characters and situations. Take the cast on an imaginative walk through the community outside the world of the play. Be warmly supportive and encouraging.

You face two difficulties. One is recognition of your contribution to the problem. The other is inventing enough "what if?" questions and improvisations. Both difficulties can be overcome with careful planning and creative problem-solving.

A Performer Blurs Actions and Emotions

SYMPTOMS

As you watch rehearsals you feel that a performer appears to overlook vital portions of the character's actions and emotions. The character seems to lack motivation.

IDENTIFYING THE CAUSE

Watch the performer carefully during a simple action. Perhaps the assignment is to enter, cross to another character, and speak. Is the actor rushing through the actions and omitting reactions? Are the actions out of focus, a jumble of effects without visible motivation? If so, possibly the actor has lost sight of each component part of the given action or reaction during that simple assignment and thus is not showing the more complex aspects of the character.

CORRECTING THE PROBLEM

Do the action "by the numbers." You and the performer work out each piece of the action carefully. Do pieces one at a time, always fully completing one before starting the next and never anticipating the following action. For example, here is one sample set of numbers that might apply to a performer's entrance:

1. Open door; step in; get well on stage. Stop.
2. Look around the room; see Character A. Stop.
3. Show your emotional responses to A. Stop.
4. Disguise how you feel from A. Stop.
5. Look around the room further; see Character B. Stop.
6. Show emotional response to seeing B. Stop.
7. Project your emotional responses to B. Stop.
8. Show that you are deciding to cross to B. Show motivation to cross to B. Stop.
9. Prepare to go to B — that is, if you're reluctant to go, take a deep breath, raise your chin, and get yourself steeled to cross. Stop.
10. Cross to B showing one attitude, emotion, intention. Stop.
11. When you arrive, hold still. What is your emotion? Exaggerate it, show it. Stop.

Doing an action "by the numbers" isolates the individual pieces of the whole. The performer must completely finish one piece before moving to the next; the exercise forces the performer to think of objectives and obstacles. Expand the "by the numbers" drill from a single physical moment to other physical and emotional scenes. The simple drill can be valuable if you help the performers see how it pertains to other aspects of their work.

A Performer's Emotions Lack Clarity

SYMPTOMS

It is difficult to know how the character feels. You sense that the performer is showing emotions, but none are clear.

IDENTIFYING THE CAUSE

Watch the performer carefully during emotional scenes. Are the emotions blurred? Is the actor trying to show many emotions at once? Does it appear that the performer has not found a way to simplify the complex or perhaps believes that good acting shows many emotions at once? Another possibility is that the performer is overintellectualizing the role.

CORRECTING THE PROBLEM

Experiment with isolating emotions, asking the performer to play a single emotion at a time. For example, to help the actress find Kitty's emotions in Saroyan's *The Time of Your Life,* guide her through separate aspects of the character.

"In your encounter with the bartender, when he is trying to diminish you, try playing Kitty strictly as a street-tough, emotionless whore, nothing else." When she has done that successfully, ask her for a different isolation: "Now, in the same encounter, play Kitty only as a soft, vulnerable, frightened young girl." After she portrays that quality, a third experiment: "Now talk to Nick but really be focused on Joe; your objective is to ask Joe to help you." Continue to experiment, insisting the performer play only one emotion at a time. When the actress is able to play single emotions, ask her to do the scene with two selected emotions. Suggest that two is quite adequate.

Think of the performer's emotion as a sort of exotic stew. Your job is to help the performer find the ingredients. Isolate the various emotions that are combined. After you have identified the pieces, take the performer aside after rehearsal to discuss your conclusions. Seek understanding of what emotions the performer is trying to project and what you are receiving.

Two of the men responsible for the exciting production of *A Chorus Line* talk with the dancers of the prize-winning show: Michael Bennett (center, in striped shirt), who conceived, directed, and choreographed, and Marvin Hamlisch (right, gesturing), who composed the music. — *Photograph copyright 1983 Martha Swope*

The "by the numbers" drill discussed earlier can also be used for emotional development of characterization and motivation.

The fear of being phony has become one of the phoniest things in the theatre.

—ROBERT LEWIS
Method or Madness?

A Performer Makes the Character Emotionless

SYMPTOMS

The performer is not showing emotions. The character appears flat and dull.

IDENTIFYING THE CAUSE

Possibly this performer's inhibitions are preventing growth into the character's emotions. Observe the actor's physical behavior, looking for signs of muscular tension, which often accompanies emotional inhibition, or protective physical positions (arms crossed over chest, body turned away from other performers during emotional scenes, and so forth). These suggest that the actor may be worried about "overacting" or appearing "phony," common concerns with many performers.

CORRECTING THE PROBLEM

First be sure the performer understands the importance of the character's emotional range: Discuss interpretation and audience communication. Examine the character together according to the analysis discussed in Chapters 5 and 15.

Be supportive to overcome the performer's fears of being foolish during rehearsal, especially concerns about overacting. Explain that feeling "phony" is natural — after all, the actor is expressing the character's emotion in public for the first time. Be sure the actor knows that exaggerated acting in rehearsal is necessary in order to stretch emotional muscles; assure the performer that you will not let the actor overact in performance.

In "real life" many of us are unable to show our genuine emotions. We hide behind a series of masks. Don't be surprised to discover that some performers have difficulty expressing their characters' emotions. Be patient, but never stop exploring the emotional ranges of the character and the play because lively theatre is constructed primarily of emotions; audiences respond to emotions first, intellectual concepts later.

The Performers' Long Speeches Lack Clarity and Meaning

SYMPTOMS

The play seems to drag. There's a dull sameness to the speeches, and the characters' thoughts appear vague.

IDENTIFYING THE CAUSE

Listen to the performers' speeches, closing your eyes to concentrate more carefully. You will probably discover that performers are running thoughts together, resulting in a loss of clarity and meaning. While this melding of thoughts will be most evident in longer speeches, quite likely the problem exists in shorter ones as well.

CORRECTING THE PROBLEM

Guide performers through the thought units of speeches. Find the changes of topic, shifts of emphasis, and new attitudes. Separate each unit, and have performers read each differently, playing emotion and subtext in each thought unit. Create blocking at each shift to help the performer play the transitions.

The following speech by Abraham Lincoln in *Abraham Lincoln: The Giant Killer*, for example, would be dull if read without shifts for thoughts and emotions. Vitality will come with vocal interpretation based on insight into the character. Stage directions indicate one set of thought units the director could suggest to the performer:

This thing called success, I truly believe I don't know what to do with her if ever she did come 'round. [*Wryly, upbeat, with a bit of a grin, not self-pitying.*] Failure? Reckon I know his face. [*More gently. He's thinking of years past. Good memories.*] Times on the Sangamon, polin' our way down that brown muddy river, wavin' at folks workin' the fields either side or mebbe fishin' fer cat [*These are warm and happy memories.*], on those lazy summer afternoons I could look past the bend of that ol' River directly into my future. [*Almost hypnotically, very softly; the concept of "the world" is important here.*] Just driftin' through the world. [*Coming back to this world; bitterness creeps into his voice.*] Never knew then how hard findin' success was gonna turn out to be. She never got to be more visible than the bottom of that dirty brown muddy river. [*More brightly. He's pulling himself up.*] Ol' failure, now, that pesky critter's always there. [*He almost respects Mr. Failure.*] After a period of time, a body gets to know him so well you almost like him, warts and all. [*Laughs.*]

Vocal variations are easier when the performer is guided through beats and emotional dynamics of a speech. Detailed work on one speech will help the performer with other speeches.

Vocal variations and portrayal of strong emotions are necessary to bring Shakespeare's plays to dramatic life. In this scene from *Measure for Measure*, directed by the author at the College of William and Mary, Brent Harris is Angelo and Anne Tyler is Isabella.
— *Photograph courtesy of the William and Mary Theatre*

Performers Lack Vocal Life

SYMPTOMS

The performers appear to understand their characters, have dutifully divided speeches into communicative thought units, and are projecting emotion adequately. Still, there is a lack of vocal fire.

IDENTIFYING THE CAUSE

Decide which cast members most need improvement and in what areas. Try looking away from the actors in order to concentrate on voices, noting performers' rate, pitch, volume, and timbre, mentally or literally charting each individual's vocal inflection on a musical staff.

CORRECTING THE PROBLEM

First you must make the cast believe you are seriously interested in improvements. Perhaps because they have so much on their minds, actors typically do not hear a director's initial requests for more vocal variation. Repeat your requests. Praise the individual who is vocally alive. Stop the cast when they turn vocally dead. Show them your charts. One director tapes a rehearsal, edits together the most telling illustrations of poor vocal variation, and plays the recording to the cast. Other directors ask the performers to "sing" the lines as if in a musical.

Conduct exercises before each rehearsal, insisting on vocal variation. Try having the cast read passages in unison, changing rate, pitch, volume, and timbre. Experiment with readings from selections such as the King James translation of the Bible, which has powerful language that often stimulates dynamic readings.

Emphasis on verbs, which carry the speeches' action, helps bring sentences to life. Because performers may run out of energy by the end of the sentence, and vocally drift off, try having performers emphasize the final syllable or word of each sentence.

Performer Does Not Communicate Meaning of Speeches

SYMPTOMS

The character appears pleasant enough, but without fire or intensity. Speeches seem to lack meaning.

IDENTIFYING THE CAUSE

Listen carefully to the character's speeches. Do they make sense? Can you hear hidden meanings? Are the meanings clear?

CORRECTING THE PROBLEM

Because the actors may not fully understand their lines, try having them put the speeches into their own words. You might also try asking questions such as "What does that mean?" and "Why does the character say that?" As you work through this experiment, check to be sure the actors know the meaning of obscure or difficult words.

Ask each actor to state the subtext of his or her speeches. What is the character actually saying underneath the assigned text? What is the character feeling? What is the character thinking? What does the character want?

Given even a simple line like "Good morning everyone!" a good actor can convey such subtext as, "Although I feel perfectly horrible this morning and would prefer to curl up and die in a quiet corner, no one in this room will catch me acting like I've got a hangover!" But before that richness can be communicated, the performer must learn how to look for subtext. Try having the performers go through an action unit speaking both the assigned lines and the subtext. Have each actor read the character's speech, then speak the subtext; go to the next character's speech and repeat the process. Continually ask questions such as "What is the character thinking?" and "What do you want?" to encourage them to dig under the character's lines.

The Performers' Bodies Deny the Context of the Speeches

SYMPTOMS

The performers are vocally expressing the meaning of their lines but their physical statements are counterproductive. For example, one character has an impassioned speech about freedom, but the performer's body language speaks of being indifferent; another's character is angry but the actor's body signals boredom; a third's body inclines forward, like a skier's, on every line, then returns to plumb when the line is completed.

IDENTIFYING THE CAUSE

Consciously set aside rehearsal time to observe your cast's physical communications, as if watching television with the sound turned off. If you see only small problems, corrections will be easy; if one or more performers have physical problems with virtually every line, corrections will take time.

CORRECTING THE PROBLEM

If the problem is a minor one, simply tell the performer what you observe. Be casual to avoid magnifying a minor incident into a problem. If the problem is major, increase your attention to physical warmups, especially relaxation exercises, and experiment with having performers go through an action unit in pantomime to focus their attention on bodily communication. Be certain your performers know this is a major priority. Try working on individual problems outside of the group rehearsal.

A performer with severe problems will not eliminate them overnight. In fact your comments will probably aggravate the problem at first; with work the problem can at least be made less distracting. Be patient and considerate throughout. No doubt you and the performer will find the process frustrating, even at times confrontational, but your worst error would be inaction.

The Performers' Gestures Are Ineffective or Distracting

SYMPTOMS

The performers appear stiff and wooden with few physical communications. You note ineffective gestures that weaken character or distracting mannerisms that will irritate the audience.

IDENTIFYING THE CAUSE

Force yourself to watch performers' gestures. Mark the ones that seem especially effective or ineffective. Pay special attention to gestures that are counterproductive.

CORRECTING THE PROBLEM

Begin mentioning gestures in your notes to help the performers think of their own gestures. Make special reference to highly effective gestures and have the performer repeat the gesture to show what you mean. Often this process alone will improve overall gestures.

Ignore infrequent errors, but if a performer has a number of counterproductive gestures, watch them carefully to find the pattern. Work only on gestures that are repeated, not on those that occur infrequently.

There are a number of helpful generalizations for dealing with poor gestures. One common piece of advice is "no gestures below the waistline," which speaks to the problem of small and ineffective hand twitches: Get the performers to raise their hands higher. Another axiom is "keep the elbows away from the body," which addresses the problem of awkwardness caused by gesturing with the forearms while keeping the elbows clamped close to the ribs: Have performers spread their arms more freely. You may also wish to urge performers to use proper stage techniques such as "use the upstage hand instead of the downstage one."

To analyze a gesture, divide it into four component parts. *Preparation* raises the hand in position to gesture, *stroke* is a firm movement of the hand and arm from preparation position to an emphatic stop, *point* holds the hand in position for a recognized pause, and *return* brings the hand back to preparation. You might wish to spend fifteen minutes having the cast go through this kind of drill. This approach is only a mechanical device; ideal gestures appear to be motivated by the character.

The Performer Makes a Large Role Small

SYMPTOMS

A classic tragedy is failing to achieve greatness; the performers minimize the size of the roles. For example, a Lear or Oedipus seems somehow more contemporary and less "classic," thereby failing to elevate the audience to the necessary level of tragic response.

IDENTIFYING THE CAUSE

Examine your rehearsal techniques. If you use improvisations, are they carefully planned to elevate the actor into the character or do they pull the character down to the actor's personal level? The mistake lies in the latter approach. Many directors mistakenly lead actors to look at the character through the performer's personal dimensions.

CORRECTING THE PROBLEM

Find ways to help the performer grow into the role, and carefully avoid all implications that might decrease the dimensions of the character. For example, do not let the performer ask, "If I were in Lear's position, what would I do when my daughters take away my trappings?" That puts Lear into the performer's position, shrinking Lear to the actor's size and contemporary attitudes. Instead, encourage the actor to think "if I were Lear" and to ask such questions as — What does it feel like to be king, to have been the absolute ruler for years, to have had the responsibility for the life and welfare of all of the citizens? What would it feel like to believe that I rule by divine right? How would I give orders and how would I carry myself if never once had I been disobeyed?

The glory of characters such as Oedipus, Medea, Hamlet, Cleopatra, and Willy Loman is not that they are "like us" but that through them we perceive a greater aspect of humanity than we can see in ourselves. A great character demands great size, and an actor must be encouraged to grow to the role's dimensions, not consider it as himself or herself in a similar situation.

Actors Lack Contact with Each Other

SYMPTOMS

During rehearsals the performers seem to be distant from each other. Actors appear emotionally separated.

IDENTIFYING THE CAUSE

Look at the performers' physical contacts. Do gestures indicate receptivity, saying in effect, "I am open to you," or are they more closed with, for example, the arms folded over the chest? Do actors have large territorial spaces into which they will not let others enter? Do they play intimate moments in a distant manner?

CORRECTING THE PROBLEM

Try looking for motivation for the characters to touch. If, for example, you are directing *Fiddler on the Roof* and Golda and Tevye don't really seem married, the solution may be a simple touch, a hand on the shoulder, a hug. Physical contact should be enhanced by a look across the room, a smile, a wink. Even when physical touches may not be appropriate in performance, they can break territorial space barriers in rehearsals.

Trust exercises during warm-ups may help overcome the problem. One such exercise has the cast stand close together in a small circle with one actor in the center. Eyes closed, that actor allows himself or herself to fall gently in any direction. The others support the actor so there is no fear of landing on the floor. Have each cast member repeat this action until all are comfortable and secure with fellow cast members. Other trust exercises can be found in your favorite acting book.

Actors Are "Onstage," Not in Their Characters' Environment

SYMPTOMS

Rehearsals appear artificial or stagey. Characters do not relate to their environment.

IDENTIFYING THE CAUSE

Observe performers carefully. Possibly they seem highly aware of the stage — that is, they pose carefully full front or with the upstage foot advanced or they overproject their voices — or they always seem very aware of your location in the auditorium.

CORRECTING THE PROBLEM

Try awakening the performers' creative imagination to the physical environment. Tell them to ignore the stage and all of its trappings, forget about the audience being in one particular place, and discard all concepts of upstage and downstage. To help them think of the environment and not the stage, move yourself from "front and center of the house" to an upstage location so they stop playing to you in the auditorium.

Characters entering an environment for the first time must react to their surroundings. Take each performer through an entrance "by the numbers," looking at various parts of the room; finding a route through the furniture; and reacting to the sights, smells, sounds, and overall feeling of the room as if these are all new to them.

Help performers establish physical contact with the environment; have them touch the sofa, the table, the doorway, and so on. Help them make emotional contact by asking such questions as — Do you like the furniture? Is there a chair you bought at an antique sale that is precious to you? Is there a painting you'd like to burn? Are there pleasant smells? Do the neighbors make too much noise? Help performers concentrate on the environment's psychic influence by asking such questions as — Does this room make you happy or distressed, comfortable or ill-at-ease? What is on the other side of the entrance door? Down the street? Experiment with having the performers go through a rehearsal speaking their thoughts about the environment, interspersed with the dialogue, when they enter the room and use furniture and properties.

The Production Seems Overrehearsed

SYMPTOMS

Rehearsals have lost momentum. There is a dull sameness to performers at every rehearsal. The cast is losing interest in rehearsals. Performers are saying, "What this show needs is an audience." Your assistant gently remarks that the production looks overrehearsed. The well seems to have run dry.

IDENTIFYING THE CAUSE

The above symptoms are usually considered, incorrectly, evidence of an overrehearsed production. In fact the problem is that growth has stopped. It is the director's well that goes dry, not the performers'. Unless the director brings new ideas to rehearsals, there will be few if any improvements.

CORRECTING THE PROBLEM

Your corrections depend on your acceptance of two basic premises:

1. Bringing rehearsals back to creative life is the director's responsibility, not the cast's.
2. There has never been a dramatic presentation so perfect it could not be improved with thoughtful creative work.

You must bring new creative sparks to rehearsals. Before the next rehearsal carefully plan new improvisational exercises, warm-up techniques, concepts of the characters, and sensory exercises. In particular search out new obstacles for the characters, complications for the scenes, and conflicts of the play. Cancel as many complete production run-through rehearsals as you can — they probably contributed to the problem — and instead work on individual scenes, taking them apart to add new strengths.

Because most casts enjoy the relative comfort of keeping scenes as they are, they may meet changes with negativity or even hostility. Pretend you do not perceive those reactions, and press on with good-natured determination. If your new materials have creative sparks, the cast will reverse its attitude.

The Cast No Longer Seems to Care

SYMPTOMS

Cast members are arriving late. You have difficulty getting them to begin rehearsals. They socialize more, rehearse less. Although at first the cast appeared committed to the production, now you sense a lack of drive, perhaps even irritation with you.

IDENTIFYING THE CAUSE

Examine your own work habits. Are you communicating, consciously or unconsciously, a lack of commitment? Are you wasting their time?

CORRECTING THE PROBLEM

There is a good possibility that the director, not the cast, is responsible for the problem. Quite often a cast's apparent lack of caring is actually a reflection of their perception of the director's attitude. There are a number of ways that directors can communicate a lack of commitment to the production.

Perhaps the director tries to make the cast "like" him or her. Beginning directors are often preoccupied with getting their casts' affection, and they may waste half an hour or more at the beginning of rehearsals with social chitchat and playfulness. No wonder actors arrive late: They know nothing will be happening. No wonder performers show a lack of commitment: They sense their director does not care about the show but simply wants a party atmosphere.

Perhaps the director just doesn't get down to work. Beginning directors often want to avoid working their casts. But in years of advising directing students and evaluating experienced directors' work, I have never heard one cast complain that the director overworked them; I have often heard complaints that the director did not *direct,* which meant that the director followed paths other than making rehearsals profitable.

Actors want to know that the director is leading them in pursuit of excellence. If the director appears willing to accept less, quite possibly the performers will retreat from investing themselves into the production. Show your own serious commitment: Always arrive early for rehearsals, be well-prepared, insist on starting rehearsals on time, continue to experiment with new ideas and staging concepts, and suggest ways actors can improve characterization. Respect your own and the company's artistic abilities; remember that actors deeply want to grow and improve. Continually set fresh and higher goals for yourself and the cast. Don't worry about whether the company "likes" you — that's a secondary concern (and besides, affection is much more likely to come if they respect your dedication to achieving the very best production possible). Possibly you will want to tell them, "Come on, get serious" — but *first* say that to yourself.

A Principle of "Benign Neglect"

Often during rehearsals you may see this or that not going correctly — perhaps one performer has lost concentration, another is off-stride, properties aren't being used correctly — and you stop rehearsals and step in to correct the problem. As more elements seem to misfire, you stop the action more often to make corrections. Stop! You are on your way to overdirecting the play.

Do not assume that the director must address every problem. Often your best action is to do nothing. To encourage performers to develop without directorial interference, try applying a "principle of benign neglect." The phrase has its origins not in theatre but in politics: One night, following a tiresome rehearsal in which nothing seemed to go right and I was exhausted from trying to solve each problem, I heard a U.S. Senator on the late news suggest an American policy of "benign neglect" so that countries could develop independently without this nation's "help." The next night I applied the concept to rehearsals; I stepped back in the hope that performers would be stimulated to solve problems themselves. Whatever the phrase's merits in a political context, I found that the policy can be effective in play rehearsals.

By benign neglect I mean an active, not passive, directorial action, deliberate and planned, not adopted by accident or default. You examine the situation, measure its dimensions, and judge its effects. And then you consciously decide whether you or the performer is the best person to find the answer.

We who direct must admit frankly that often we do not know how to solve a problem. Often we sense that something is wrong but we cannot identify the cause. The concept of benign neglect is applicable. Before we try to remedy the situation, we need to ask if our surgery might do more harm than deliberate inaction would. It may shock actors to discover that we do not know all the answers, but there it is.

Exercises

The following questions are designed to help you plan problem-solving strategies before problems occur, thereby making each setback easier to handle. The process always involves identifying the problem, listing all the possible solutions, and selecting and applying the one that experience indicates is most likely to succeed.

1. Recalling productions in which you have acted, what particular problems seemed endemic to the casts? Did performers have difficulty with concentration? With physical communication? Were many unable to perceive subtext? Describe general major problems that affected those casts.

2. How did the directors attempt to correct those problems? Which directorial techniques appeared most successful, and which seemed ineffective? Why? Judging from your observation of those directors' attempts to solve problems, which techniques will you adopt if you encounter similar problems in the play you are to direct?

3. What are the problem-solving techniques of a director whose work you know well? What techniques strike you as especially effective? Why? Does the director address problems directly, indirectly, or both? Does the director solve problems by benign neglect, encouraging performers to seek personal solutions? What directorial problem-solving techniques do you most admire? How will you seek to employ those techniques in your play?

4. Based on your analysis of characters and situations in the play you will direct, what problems may members of your cast encounter in bringing characters to life? Does the play contain passages that are unusually difficult to memorize? Do you expect that performers will need to battle to express wide-ranging emotions? Must a fast tempo be maintained throughout? Does the play depend on communication of the subtext? Every play has unique difficulties; describe potential problem areas in your play.

5. How will you attempt to solve each problem? What techniques will you use to help performers through these problems? List several possible solutions for each problem.

A . . . student once asked me, *"What is the worst thing that happens to a director?"*

My answer was: "You see from all I've told you how thoughtfully, how painstakingly, how sincerely and how knowledgeably I labor on a production. Yet for all that my efforts to bring about the hoped for results may be in vain. The magic doesn't happen. I fail."

"What do you do then?" the candid youth asked.

"I forgive myself."

—HAROLD CLURMAN
On Directing

A Final Note: Successes and Failures

All of us who direct will have our failures. And our successes. Most often we will feel that our productions are a bit of both. Experience helps us learn to live with either extreme.

With a failure, loud and painful, we are badly bruised and battered. A theatre failure is hurtful because it happens in public, but a worse torment comes from believing we are responsible for the distress our colleagues, on- and offstage, also feel. We seek comfort in knowing that our favorite directors and our mentors have also had their failures, but personal culpability looms high in our minds.

When failure strikes, we know that we have an alternative: We don't have to direct. After all, we don't have to work in theatre.

We can avoid aiming high because that has its drawbacks and frustrations.

But we won't quit.

Despite the pain and disappointment, we must settle down to study the process that led to failure. We figure out what we did wrong. We know that denying the reality, scapegoating, accusing others of not following our lead, or blaming the audience won't help us learn.

With a failure, we do well to follow Clurman's advice: "I forgive myself."

And we go on to the next project.

With a success, we rejoice that our colleagues, on- and offstage, were well served. We are delighted with the acclaim they receive. Publicly we credit our playwright, actors, designers, technicians, management, producers, publicists, box office personnel, ushers, and especially the audiences. Secretly, away from the crowd, we smile.

The thrill of a theatrical success is overwhelming.

Aiming high has its rewards.

Most of us settle down to study the process that led to the success. We figure out what we did right.

And we go on to the next project.

Success or failure, you forgive yourself. And you go on.

One must love the art in oneself; not oneself in art.

—STANISLAVSKI

Appendices

From the first it has been theatre's business to entertain people as it also has been of all the other arts. It is this business which gives it its particular dignity; it needs no other passport but fun.

—BERTOLT BRECHT
Short Organum

APPENDIX A

Royalties, Permissions, and Play Publisher–Leasing Agents

Play publisher–leasing agents offer you a number of valuable services. Such companies as Samuel French and Dramatists Play Service, among others, are your major source for acting editions of the plays or musicals you direct (the "publisher" part of their label); and they also have the playwrights' authorizations to handle all copyright legalities and collections of royalties (their "leasing agent" duties) necessary for you to produce the play.

The companies distribute copies of catalogs describing the plays they handle. Listings are in convenient subdivisions, such as full-length royalty plays, full-length nonroyalty plays, plays for women, one-act plays, and the like. Descriptions of the plays contain information about the number of males and females in the cast, interior or exterior settings, the story, and selected reviewers' comments. The catalogs also detail the costs for royalties, scripts, and postage for mailing scripts to your theatre. Some companies offer other secondary services, such as publicity kits, posters, or books.

The publisher–leasing agent works for the playwright, charging theatrical producers for the right to present the playwright's work. Those charges, called *royalties,* are paid to the publisher–leasing agent, which then forwards the money to the writer or the writer's heirs according to contractual agreements specifying percentages for writer and publisher.

The arrangement is financially advantageous for the playwright because the company's promotional effort increases the number of productions of the playwright's work and therefore increases the writer's royalties. The arrangement also frees the playwright from time-consuming correspondence and the mechanics of supplying playscripts to directors.

The arrangement is more convenient for the director than a process of searching out the playwright's address, writing the author, and waiting until he or she has time or is in the mood to answer inquiries about rights and royalties and how to obtain copies of the script.

Rights

The basis of all arrangements is the copyright. The playwright *owns* the play no less than you own a car, an inventor owns an invention, or a landlord owns an apartment house. The play is the playwright's investment for his or her future and heirs. The copyright laws protect the playwright, preserving his or her ownership of the work. They give the writer control over what is done with the play, just as a deed gives a landlord control of an apartment.

Public Domain

For one reason or another, a play may not be protected by copyright and therefore "belongs to the public" or is in the *public domain*. Most often a play is in public domain because of age: The play was written before copyright regulations became effective, or the copyright has expired. A play written before 1910, even if copyrighted then, is apt to be in public domain now (unless the author later revised his or her plays, as G. B. Shaw did, in which case the date of the revision may keep the play out of public domain). All plays by Sophocles, Shakespeare, and Molière are in public domain, and you can present them without securing rights or paying royalties. Indeed, you can revise them, turn them into musicals, or mangle them heartlessly, as is so often done to Shakespeare.

But even though the original play is in the public domain, translations may be protected by copyright. For example, Edmond Rostand wrote *Cyrano de Bergerac* in 1897, so it is clearly in the public domain. You can present it royalty free providing you perform it in its original French version, translate it yourself, or use one of the translations made at the turn of the century that are in public domain now. However, if you use the Brian Hooker translation — a viable dramatic choice — you must obtain permission because the Hooker translation is protected by copyright. Dramatists Play Service handles the rights to the Hooker *Cyrano* and will charge you $210.00 in royalties for an amateur eight-performance run.

What plays worth staging are now in public domain? It is not practical to list many here, but a sampling might encourage you to search out other plays of value to you. *The Contrast* (1787) by Royall Tyler and *Fashion* (1845) by Anna Cora Mowatt Ritchie are two early American plays with good theatrical values that have held up well in recent productions. The Joseph Jefferson version of *Rip Van Winkle* (1865) has had successful adaptations. *Madame Butterfly* (1900) was a short play by David Belasco and John Luther Long before it was transformed into an opera. Oscar Wilde died in 1900, so his plays such as *Salome* and *The Importance of Being Earnest: A Trivial Comedy for Serious People* are in the public domain. The classic one-act, *Riders to the Sea* (1904), the once-controversial, richly poetic *The Playboy of the Western World* (1907), and all other plays by John Millington Synge are also in public domain.

Legal and Ethical Concerns

All of us in theatre share a legal and ethical obligation to the playwright. The copyright is legally absolute. The director who participates in presenting a play in violation of the playwright's expressed conditions — who produces the play without first obtaining permission — is, simply, a thief.

"But we can't afford to pay the royalty" is an invalid excuse and worthless in a court of law. Often that excuse is heard from theatres that expend funds liberally for costumes, scenery, equipment, travel, advertising, and even lavish cast parties. For most theatres, royalty expenses are but a small portion of the overall production cost. If you are directing in a theatre that cannot afford to pay royalties, you should look for plays that are in the public domain.

"But we aren't charging admission" is also an invalid excuse. Permission must be obtained, and royalties paid if required, regardless of the theatre's admission policies.

The playwright is the cornerstone on which the living theatre rests. We who work in theatre have an ethical obligation to honor, encourage, and support the playwright. We should do all we can to increase the number of playwrights to keep our theatre healthy and active, and our payments of royalties significantly help playwrights continue writing. Cheating the playwright cheapens the art, and the director involved in such unethical behavior will, at the least, have to face his or her private question of moral obligation to the art.

Finding the Publisher–Leasing Agent for a Specific Play

When you select a play to direct, you have typically studied a version printed in an anthology with a dozen or more other plays. After you make your choice, you start looking for the play publisher–leasing agent that handles this specific script. Credit lines in anthologies are often misleading. For example, assume you want to direct David Rabe's *Streamers* and you find it in an anthology of thirteen plays. When you look for credit lines in the anthology, you find clear instructions: All rights, amateur and professional, must be obtained from the author's agent.

But writing the agent only delays the process. The agent will either forward your letter to the correct publisher–leasing agent or simply return it to you. Samuel French is the publisher–leasing agent that handles *Streamers,* and you will find all the information you seek simply by looking in the French catalog. So when you find a play you wish to direct, your first step is to examine the catalogs of the various publisher–leasing agents.

Dealing with Publisher–Leasing Agents

Your business with the play publisher–leasing agents will be eased by the application of a certain amount of ordinary good sense. Here are a few pertinent guidelines.

1. Be sure you have obtained rights before you advertise the production. Not all plays are available even though they are listed in the publishers' catalogs. If a professional revival is scheduled or a road company will be touring the play, you may not receive permission to present the play.
2. Plan ahead to allow ample time for mail delivery, and do not expect immediate attention to your request for scripts. Most companies work rapidly, but you should allow a margin of two weeks or so.
3. You must have permission to produce the play whether admission is charged or not. Permission usually requires paying royalties.
4. If you feel you have an honest reason to request lowered royalties, by all means make your case to the leasing agent. Depending on circumstances, companies may honor requests for lowered royalties.
5. Do not expect to return acting editions to the publisher–leasing agent for a refund. Once you have ordered the playbooks, they are yours.
6. Do expect to be required to return all scores, books, sides, and other material for a musical. Most companies will rent, not sell, musical materials. A few companies sell materials. Check the catalogs.
7. Payment of royalties is due in advance of production. You would violate agents' rules if you opened the show without having first cleared all necessary requirements.
8. Keep copies of all correspondence with the company. Your letters and the company's, copies of checks or money orders, invoices and receipts, and post office insurance forms should all be carefully saved. They will be valuable if you become entangled in the company's computerized web and receive repeated incorrect demands for payment.

CONTRACTUAL OBLIGATIONS

The play publisher–leasing agent will describe a number of specific requirements in the catalog and in the contract you sign. You can expect obligations such as the following.

1. You must not change the title of the play. Why would a theatre revise the play's title? The logical answer, in the agents' view, is that the producers are attempting to hide the fact of the production from the watchful eye of the leasing agent.
2. Posters, advertisements, and publicity stories for the production must give credit to the play's author(s).

3. The printed play program must include a statement to the effect that "(*Play Title*) is produced by special arrangement with (Name of publisher–leasing agent)." It usually is printed in small type at the bottom of an inside page of the program.

4. The author's name must appear on the program. For a musical you may be required to list a number of creators, including composer, book author, first Broadway choreographer or producer, and the like.

5. The play must be performed as written. In some cases you will note that the acting edition is markedly different from the anthology version. You are required to follow the acting edition. You are expressly forbidden to make "substantial" changes.

Calculating Royalty Charges

The leasing agent's catalog specifies royalty charges. A description for a typical full-length play might indicate royalties of $50–$35. The first figure is the charge for the opening performance, and the second is the charge for each successive presentation. For a total of six performances, royalty charges would be $50 for the first night plus five times $35 for the rest of the run: $50 plus $175 or a total of $225.

Royalty charges for musicals are a shock to the uninitiated. An amateur theatre might pay $175 ($50–$25) for six performances of *A Streetcar Named Desire* but $1700 for six performances of *Fiddler on the Roof.* Be prepared to negotiate royalty costs because most musical publisher–leasing agents base their charges on factors such as ticket prices and auditorium size. Often you can convince the company to lower their charge. In addition to royalty charges for the musical, you will need to budget rental costs of $100 to $200, and another $25 for postage and insurance. Because all materials must be returned to the company, you must remind members of the cast and orchestra to treat scores and books carefully.

Nonroyalty Plays

If you are on a tight budget, you may consider presenting a nonroyalty play. Some publishers offer such plays, listing them in their catalogs as "nonroyalty" or "budget" plays. Usually you are required to purchase as many playbooks as there are characters in the play. Read carefully the catalog conditions that apply to nonroyalty productions. Read the play even more carefully: Often the royalty-free script is simply not a quality play. Remember that for performers, director, and audience, a well-written play can be a delight well worth the royalty expense; the nonroyalty play seems free but there may be intangible costs. High schools in particular often fall into the trap of trying to save royalty expenses by selecting a nonroyalty play; all involved may labor in vain until they become weary with the script, the effort, and theatre. With the nonroyalty play you probably receive a script worth what you are paying. A good play is far easier to direct than a poor one. If your budget is tight, prune expenses elsewhere or try looking for a good play that is now in the public domain.

APPENDIX B

Names, Addresses, and Descriptions of Play Publisher–Leasing Agents

The following list of play publisher–leasing agents describes the variety of plays you can find. These descriptions, however, are generalized and you will want to study the catalogs carefully to make up your personal descriptions of the offerings.

1. *The Anchorage Press, Inc.* Box 8067, New Orleans, LA 70182. (504) 283-8868. Materials for children's theatre, ranging from one-act to full-length plays, including comedies, dramas, adaptations, and musicals.
2. *Aran Press.* 1320 S. Third Street, Louisville, KY 40208. (502) 636-0015. Materials for dinner, professional, university and college, and community theatre. Full-length and one-act plays and adaptations.
3. *Atre Publico Press.* Revista Chicano-Riquena, University of Houston, University Park, Houston, TX 77004. (713) 749-4768. Hispanic writers only. Full-length, one-act, children's, and musical plays.
4. *Baker's Play Publishing Co.* 100 Chauncy Street, Boston, MA 02111. (617) 482-1280. Plays for high schools, community theatres, and university touring productions of children's plays. The company says it is the largest publisher of chancel drama in the world.
5. *Broadway Play Publishers, Inc.* 357 West 20th Street, New York, NY 10011. (212) 563-3820. Specializes in publishing new plays that have been produced on Broadway, Off-Broadway, Off-Off Broadway, and in regional theatres. The company says the focus is not on play publishing but on play discovering. Full-length, one-act, and musical plays.
6. *I. E. Clark.* St. John's Road, Box 246, Schulenburg, TX 78956. (409) 743-3232. Full-length, one-act, and children's plays and adaptations.
7. *Contemporary Drama Service.* Box 7710 Elkton Drive, Colorado Springs, CO 80933. Plays for junior high and high schools, colleges, and churches of all denominations. One-act, full-length, musical, and holiday plays; reader's theatre; monologues; and comedy sketches from Carol Burnett and Saturday Night Live.

8. *David McKay Co., Inc.* 750 Third Avenue, New York, NY 10017. One-act and full-length, dramas, farces, and religious and children's plays. Among the playwrights represented are Robert Sherwood, Ferenc Molnar, Owen Davis, Ayn Rand, and Anita Loos.

9. *The Dramatic Publishing Co.* P.O. Box 109, Woodstock, IL 60098. (815) 338-7170. Plays and musicals for nonprofessional productions. Full-length, one-act, and children's plays. Among the playwrights represented are Brian Friel, Edward Bond, Eugene O'Neill, Peter Weiss, and A. A. Milne.

10. *Dramatists Play Service, Inc.* 440 Park Avenue South, New York, NY 10016. (212) 683-8960. Established by members of the Dramatists Guild. Full-length and short plays, musicals, and children's plays. Among the playwrights represented are Lanford Wilson, Marsha Norman, Sam Shepard, Lillian Hellman, Preston Jones, Arthur Miller, and Tennessee Williams. Most of the plays have had Broadway productions.

11. *Eldridge Publishing Co.* Drawer 216, Hill Avenue, Franklin, OH 45005. (513) 746-6531. Plays for smaller high school and church groups. Skits, one-act and full-length plays, musicals, and operettas. Language and subject matter are wholesome.

12. *Heuer Publishing Co.* 233 Dows Building, Box 248, Cedar Rapids, IA 52406. (319) 364-6311. One-act and full-length plays for junior and senior high schools.

13. *Lillenas Publishing Co.* Box 527, Kansas City, MO 64141. (816) 931-1900. Materials for church productions, Sunday School plays, and skits or readings. No secular works.

14. *Meriwether Publishing, Ltd.* 885 Elkton Drive, Colorado Springs, CO 80907. (303) 594-4422. Full-length and one-act plays, adaptations, children's plays, musicals, and revues.

15. *National Publishers, Ltd.* 1310 Chardonnary, Houston, TX 77077. Plays for student audiences.

16. *New Plays.* Box 273, Rowayton, CT 06853. (203) 866-4520. Plays intended for adults and teenagers to perform for young audiences; the company says it seeks to avoid children's theatre stereotypes such as cute dragons and the premarital problems of princesses.

17. *Performance Publishing Co.* 978 North McLean Boulevard, Elgin, IL 60120. Now part of Baker Plays.

18. *Pioneer Drama Service.* 2172 South Colorado Boulevard, Box 22555, Denver, CO 80222. (303) 759-4297. Plays with simple production needs; the company aims at junior and senior high schools, community theatres, children's theatre, melodrama theatre, park and recreation groups, and youth groups.

19. *Samuel French, Inc.* The address if you live in the "western states" is Samuel French, Inc., 7623 Sunset Boulevard, Hollywood, CA 90046. (213) 876-0570. If you live elsewhere, address Samuel French, Inc., 45 West 25th Street, New York, NY 10010. (212) 206-8990. Both locations handle plays for all groups; only the New York office handles musicals. Its catalog lists plays; nonroyalty plays; children's drama; high school, community the-

atre, and university theatre plays; and plays from London's West End and New York's Broadway.

20. *West Coast Plays.* Box 7206, Berkeley, CA 94707. (415) 841-3096. Full-length and one-act plays, children's plays, and musicals.

Musical Publisher–Leasing Agents

Musical publisher–leasing agents usually rent materials instead of selling them, and all musical material must be returned after the production or you face a hefty fine for missing materials. The companies insist that producers erase all marks in books or scores or pay another fine, but one often receives badly marked books.

To the following list of names and addresses you will want to add those companies under the heading of play publisher–leasing agents who also handle musicals: Anchorage, Arte, Broadway, Baker's, I. E. Clark, Contemporary Drama, Dramatic Publishing, Dramatists, Eldridge, Meriwether, Performance, and Pioneer.

1. *Centerstage Press.* 4638 East Shea Boulevard, Suite B-150, Phoenix, AZ 85028. (602) 996-2982. Sixty-minute musicals for family audiences. Royalties include a fully orchestrated performance tape. Scripts do not have to be returned. Sample musicals include *Heidi, Wizard of Oz,* and *Tom and Huck.*

2. *Music Theatre International.* 1350 Avenue of the Americas, New York, NY 10019. (212) 975-6841. In all my dealings with musical publisher–leasing agents, MTI has consistently been the most cooperative. Sample musicals include *Annie;* the Joseph Papp/Wilford Leach *Pirates of Penzance; Fiddler on the Roof; Guys and Dolls; The Fantasticks; Seven Brides for Seven Brothers;* and *Sweeney Todd: The Demon Barber of Fleet Street.*

3. *The Rodgers and Hammerstein Theatre Library.* 598 Madison Avenue, New York, NY 10022. (212) 486-0643. As the title of the company suggests, you find here musicals by those giants of musical theatre, but the company also handles musicals by other composers. Sample titles include *Oklahoma!; Annie Get Your Gun; Show Boat; Pal Joey; The Sound of Music; The Boys from Syracuse; Lost in the Stars;* and *Carousel.*

4. *Samuel French, Inc.* (Address given above.) Sample titles include *The Wiz; The Best Little Whorehouse in Texas; They're Playing Our Song; Chicago; Grease; The Desert Song; Of Thee I Sing; Purlie;* and *Raisin.* Unlike some companies, Samuel French will sell you the libretto of the show.

5. *Tams-Witmark Music Library, Inc.* 560 Lexington Avenue, New York, NY 10022. Toll Free, (800) 221-7196; in New York state, (800) 522-2181; in Canada, (800) 841-8408. Free perusal service. Sample titles include *Bye Bye Birdie; My Fair Lady; Brigadoon; Camelot; No, No, Nanette; Cabaret; Man of La Mancha; A Chorus Line; Li'l Abner; Oliver!*

6. *Theatre Maximus.* 1650 Broadway, New York, NY 10019. Primarily known for handling *Grease.*

APPENDIX C

Glossary

Above. The upstage area away from the audience; the opposite of *below.* To "cross above the table," the actor crosses upstage of the table. (See also *downstage* and *upstage.*)

Act Call. The final warning before the beginning of an act, the stage manager calls *places.*

Act Curtain. The theatre's main curtain, which separates stage from audience.

Act Warnings. The stage manager warns performers and crews that the curtain will rise in thirty minutes, then fifteen, then five. This is followed by the *act call.*

Action. A play's major events and character's changes in response to stimuli; the play's forward progress shown to the audience by dialogue, character development and relationships, movement, and gesture.

Action Unit (also "motivational unit"). The smallest measurable piece of a single action, containing its own beginning, middle, and end.

Ad Lib (from the Latin ad libitum, *"at one's pleasure").* Spontaneous dialogue not specified by the script.

Antagonist. The protagonist's opponent, the character who actively interferes with the protagonist's efforts to achieve a goal.

Apron (also forestage*).* The geographic area of the stage between the front curtain and the audience, in front of the proscenium arch or main curtain.

Area. A portion of the stage for playing a scene. Areas are such locations as down right, up left, and so forth.

Arena Stage (also central staging*).* "Theatre in the round," a round or square stage surrounded by audience.

Aside. A theatrical convention calling for a line to be heard by the audience yet unheard by other performers near the speaker. Typical of nineteenth-century melodrama. (See also *soliloquy.*)

A Vista Change. Shifting scenery in full view of the audience.

Backdrop. A large hanging scenic unit, usually canvas and often painted, hanging at the back of the stage set.

Backing. A masking drop or flat behind an opening in the set (such as a window or door) to hide the backstage area from audience view.

Back Lighting. Light from upstage directed onto the set and performers to contribute dimensionality and plasticity.

Backstage. The areas behind the stage not visible to the audience, such as wings, shops, and dressing rooms. Opposite of *house.*

Balance. (1) A factor in designing a floor plan, scenery, actor placement on the stage, or composition; typically symmetrical or asymmetrical. (2) An abstract concept regarding the competing conflicts of characters.

Batten. A metal pipe, sometimes a strip of wood, hung above the stage parallel to the proscenium, on which are hung lighting instruments or scenic units.

Beat. A performer's unit of measurement describing the character's thoughts, goals, or desires; the beginning to end of a single intention or state of mind. (See *action unit.*)

Below. The opposite of *above,* the area closer to the audience. To "cross below the chair" the actor moves downstage of the chair. (See also *downstage* and *upstage.*)

Black Box Theatre. So named because typically it is painted a nonintrusive black; usually a second theatre or lab theatre prized for its highly flexible staging and seating, which encourage experimentation.

Blackout. (1) Quickly extinguishing all stage lights, leaving the stage dark. (2) A short scene, usually comic and part of a series of sketches, that ends with (1).

Blocking. The directorial process of assigning performers' movements.

Body Position. The performer's physical angle in relation to the audience. A full front body position squarely faces the audience; other positions are three quarters open, profile, three quarters closed, and full closed.

Border. Above the stage, a curtain hung parallel to the proscenium to prevent the audience from seeing lights, battens, and the stage loft.

Border Lights. Lights hung above the stage on a *batten* and focused down.

Box Set. A stage set with walls on three sides and, at times, a ceiling. The *fourth wall* is imaginary, between the audience and the action.

Breakaway. Costumes, scenery, or properties designed to fall apart, collapse, or break on cue.

Build. To increase the tension of a speech or scene, using energy, emotional key, pitch, volume, and intensity.

Burlesque. (1) An evening of entertainment popular at the turn of the century. (2) A broad performance style, typically involving exaggerated facial expressions, increased volume, and stylized comic technique.

Business. Pantomimed action developed to enhance characterization.

Call. Announcement of the time performers are required to be present for rehearsals or performance.

Call Board. A backstage bulletin board for posting calls and messages for cast and crews.

Casting. The end of the audition process, the assignment of a given performer in a particular role.

Center Line. A line on the stage floor, used for blocking rehearsals and setting the floor plan on the stage, running along the stage's exact center from up-stage to downstage.

Center Stage. The area in the middle of the stage.

Central Staging (also **arena stage***).* A stage surrounded on all sides by the audience.

Characterization. The performer's complex acting process of using dialogue, movement, business, makeup, and costume to bring to life all aspects of the character.

Cheat. An actor's subtle move that does not attract audience attention; directors may ask actors to "cheat to left" or "cheat open."

Chorus. (1) Singers and dancers in a musical. (2) A group of cast members speaking lines in unison.

Clear Stage. Before curtain, the stage manager's order to performers and crews to leave the stage unless they are to be seen by the audience at the beginning of the act.

Climax. The highest dramatic tension in the play; the answer to the *major dramatic question*; the end of the play's conflict.

Close. To turn away from the audience.

Closed Turn. A performer's turn in a direction away from the audience, thereby presenting his or her back; generally considered a poor movement. The opposite *open turn* usually is preferred.

Continuity Rehearsal (also **run-through***).* Rehearsal of a scene, act, or play from beginning to end.

Comedy. A broad generic term referring to an effect designed to make the audience laugh. The term includes a number of forms, such as high comedy, low comedy, satire, comedy of manners, drawing room comedy, and sentimental comedy.

Comic Relief. A comic scene in an otherwise serious play, such as the Porter's scene in *Macbeth,* which is designed to release audience tension.

Company. The performers and crews engaged in the production.

Convention. Any production premise commonly accepted by the audience, such as the *aside* or *fourth wall.*

Counter (also **dress***).* A shifting of weight or small semicircular move by one performer in the opposite direction of another performer who is crossing in front. The move corrects composition and also helps the first performer avoid being covered.

Counterweight System. The major device for flying scenery (that is, raising it up out of the audience view). The system includes ropes, pulleys, a fly loft, and stage weights to balance the scenery. (See also *flies.*)

Cover. Obscuring an actor or piece of business from the audience's view. For example, in *King Lear* one or more actors may be placed downstage of those involved in blinding Gloucester to make the effect more dramatic. (See also *masking.*)

Crisis. In the playscript an event that establishes the conflict's resolution.

Cross. The performer's move from one area of the stage to another.

Cue. A specified signal to performer or crew; it may be a word, movement, or gesture. For performers *cue* typically refers to the preceding performer's last words; for the crew, *cue* usually refers to a signal to initiate sound, a shift in lighting, curtain, and the like.

Curtain Call. The final portion of performance when the performers bow to acknowledge the audience's applause.

Curtain Line. (1) An imaginary line on the stage floor generally considered to be the place the *act curtain* contacts the stage. (2) The final speech of an act.

Curtain Time. The assigned time for a production to begin.

Cyclorama. A canvas drop, sometimes curved, along the farthest upstage portion of the stage; in theatrical shorthand, the "cyc." Many theatres consider it the sky drop; in use it is the target for colored lights.

Denouement. Part of the play's *resolution* that wraps up the loose ends of the plot following the climax. Not present in all plays.

Dialogue. Exchange of speeches between performers.

Dimmer. An electronic system that controls the intensity of stage lights, from full bright to darkness.

Downstage. A term originated when stages were raked with the highest point furthest from the audience (hence "upstage"), the stage area nearest the audience or footlights. Opposite of *upstage*.

Dramatic Question (also **major dramatic question***).* The focus of the play; the play's question posed at the *point of attack* and answered in the *climax*.

Dress. (1) A semicircular move by one performer in the opposite direction of another performer crossing in front of him or her. The move corrects composition and also helps the first performer avoid being covered. The movement is also called a *counter*. (2) Often theatrical shorthand for *dress rehearsal*.

Dress Parade. A time in the latter stages of rehearsals when director and costume designer sit in the auditorium to observe cast members in full costumes for the first time as they "parade" across the stage, illuminated by production lights and viewed within the set. The goal is to check artistic unification of the costumes within the context of other production values; costume alterations or replacements are likely, so dress parade must be held enough before dress rehearsals to permit changes.

Dress Rehearsal. One of the final rehearsals before opening. Usually a dress rehearsal is run as if an audience were present, although some theatres prefer to distinguish a "modified dress" rehearsal (perhaps makeup will not be used) from a "full dress" rehearsal (run as if it were a performance).

Dress the Stage. Adding pictures, properties, flowers, ornaments, and comparable decorations to complete the environment; usually the scene designer's responsibility.

Drop. A scenic unit, usually constructed of canvas, that can "fly in" or "fly out" (be lowered onto the set or raised out of audience view).

Dry Up. For the actor, to forget lines.

Effect Machine. A special lighting device for projecting visuals; also fog machines and other unusual effects.

Emotional Memory. A Stanislavski technique in which the performer evokes a personal memory of an emotion similar to the emotion the character feels.

Emphasis. Placing stress on a line, speech, action unit, or any other production aspect.

Ensemble Acting. A close-knit team built with trust and respect. Each actor responds spontaneously to immediate (not anticipated) stimuli.

Entrance. Coming on stage into view of the audience.

Exit. Leaving the stage.

Exposition. Material in the playscript designed to inform the audience of necessary background events prior to the current action.

Extras (also **supernumeraries** *or* **walk-ons***).* Actors who have no lines and little assigned characterization. Spear carriers, members of the crowd, etc.

Fantasy. The unreal, often romantic. The term applies to both playscripts and design.

Farce. A low form of *comedy* stressing exaggeration and ludicrous events. The term applies to playscripts or performing.

Flat. A scenic piece usually constructed of a wood frame covered with canvas.

Flattage. A number of *flats* used to create a set.

Flies. The area above the stage where lights and scenery are hung or "flown" (raised by a system of ropes, pulleys, and counterweights). (See also *counterweight system.*)

Floodlight. A lighting instrument that cannot be focused but is used to illuminate an area; in theatrical shorthand, a "flood."

Floor Cloth (also **ground cloth***).* Canvas securely attached to the stage floor, typically padded to absorb sound and painted to prevent light reflections.

Floor Plan (also **ground plan***).* A scale line drawing of set and furniture from the perspective of the *flies*.

Fluff. An actor's missed line or comparable mistake.

Fly Gallery. An elevated catwalk at the side of the stage. Here the *flyman* operates lines to raise or lower light and scenery battens.

Flyman. The member of the rigging crew who operates the lines that raise or lower scenic pieces and lights.

Focal Point. A term used in composition; the major point of interest in any scene, drawing the viewer's eye.

Focus. (1) Directing audience's attention to the focal point. (2) The actor's visual point of reference, as in "focus on the protagonist." (3) Controlling the intense spot of light from a lighting instrument.

Follow Spot. A high-powered spotlight, typically located in the rear of the auditorium and operated by a lighting technician to focus on an actor moving about the stage. A follow spot is virtually mandatory in musical productions.

Footlights. A row of low-wattage lamps on the stage floor at the edge of the *apron*.

Foreshadowing. Actions or dialogue that creates suspense by indicating an action to occur later; valuable to guide audience response, *foreshadowing* usually applies to the script but infrequently may also refer to a performer's preparation for later action.

Forestage (also **apron***).* The geographic area of the stage between the front curtain and the audience.

Fourth Wall. A concept inherent in proscenium arch stages, referring to an imaginary downstage wall that completes the three-wall *box set.* The fourth wall is transparent to the audience but not to the performers.

French Scene. A unit, originated in French neoclassical playwriting, that divides acts into smaller pieces. The French scene begins with a major character's entrance and ends with a major character's exit.

Front Lights. Spotlights located in front of the proscenium arch.

Gelatin. A thin sheet of colored transparent material, originally gelatin but now a cellophane-type material, placed in front of a lighting instrument's lens to add color; in theatrical shorthand, a "gel."

Gesture. The performer's expressive movement of head, shoulders, arms, or hands to communicate emotion or attitude.

Given Circumstances. A term popularized by Stanislavski, referring to the dramatic events affecting the performer's playing of the scene.

Give Stage. A director's request for one performer to assume a weak position (facing upstage) to emphasize another who therefore becomes more dominant (typically facing downstage); opposite of *take stage.*

Grand Drape. A drapery unit hung downstage of the act curtain and upstage of the proscenium arch.

Green Room. A backstage lounge, not always green in color, normally near dressing rooms, where actors await cues before and during a performance and receive visitors after the final curtain.

Gridiron. At the top of the *stage house,* a strongly constructed structural framework of beams supporting blocks through which lines raise and lower lights and scenery; in theatrical shorthand, the "grid."

Grip. A stage technician who handles scenery.

Ground Cloth (also* floor cloth*). Canvas covering for the stage floor; used to deaden sound and to prevent light reflections.

Ground Plan (also* floor plan*). A scale line drawing of set and furniture giving a bird's-eye view of the stage.

Ground Row. A low constructed scenic piece often cut to show the outline of a landscape. Usually a ground row is used to mask or cover the lights at the base of a *cyclorama.*

Guillotine. A curtain that moves up and down, taking its name from the action of the well-known instrument of execution. The curtain would fly up to disclose a scene or lower to hide it, rather than moving from side to side like a *traveller.*

Heads! A warning call indicating that an overhead object is falling or being lowered.

Height. In scene composition, the distance between the top of an actor's head and the stage floor. For variety, actors are placed with varying heights, using chairs, platforms, body position, etc. (See also *levels.*)

Hold. To delay, as in "hold the curtain" or "hold for laughter."

House. All parts of the theatre in front of the footlights: auditorium, lobby, box office, and the like. Opposite of *backstage.* The actor's typical question about how many seats are filled is "How's the house tonight?"

House Lights. Auditorium lighting.

House Seats. Tickets the management saves for its own use.

Illusion of the First Time. The overall performance's communication that all of the events are happening spontaneously, never rehearsed.

Illusion of Reality. The audience's acceptance of story, people, and setting as a real experience involving real people in a real environment. Akin to Coleridge's statement that poetic faith involves "a willing suspension of disbelief."

Improvisation. Elimination of written dialogue and plot to create a role without rehearsal; in theatrical shorthand, "improv." Usually an exercise to open the performers' concept of character and situation.

In. Toward the center of the stage.

Inciting Incident. An event before the play begins that lights the fuse that will explode at the *point of attack*.

In One. A geographic location on stage below the first set of wings. In musicals, a scene played "in one" takes place downstage in front of a drop while a scene shift takes place upstage.

Intention. The character's real reason for being in the scene regardless of dialogue.

Interlude. In earlier theatre a short farce between the acts of a major play; also called *entr'acte*.

Kill. (1) In performance, lose the desired effect of a line, as in "kill the laugh." (2) In production, turn off, or eliminate, as in "kill the light."

Left Stage. The actor's left while facing the audience. Often *stage left*.

Leg. A narrow drop hung from a batten, used for masking in place of wings on the side of the stage. Frequently called a "leg drop."

Levels. (1) Platforms or steps. (2) The actor's vertical relationship to the stage, such as lying on the stage floor, sitting on the floor, sitting in a chair, etc. (See also *height*.)

Light Booth. A small room, usually at the back of the auditorium with a direct view of the playing areas, from which crews control lights (and often sound).

Light Plot. A chart of lighting instruments.

Lines. (1) Actors' speeches. (2) A set of ropes attached to battens and used to raise and lower scenery.

Major Dramatic Question. A key to interpretation of the play; in theatrical shorthand, the "MDQ." The question is generally posed early in the play close to the *point of attack* and answered at the climax.

Masking. Concealing from the audience's view some action or some part of the stage not designed to be seen. (1) A piece of scenery concealing backstage areas. (2) One performer's position obscuring another. (See also *cover*.)

Melodrama. A style of playwriting that emphasizes plot and action at the expense of characterization. Characters typically lack plausible motivation and are often stereotypes (hero, villain, etc.); good triumphs over evil.

Method. A school of acting, evolved from the teachings of Constantin Stanislavski, that stresses an actor's internal development to motivate the character.

Mise-en-Scène. The total artistic effort of the director.

Monologue. One character's long speech uninterrupted by others.

Mood. The dominant emotional quality of a character, play, or scene; the primary atmosphere created by all elements of production or performer techniques.

Motive. The character's basic desire through the play. (See also *spine*.)

Motivation. Reasons for a speech or action.

Move On. To move toward the center. *Move off* is to move away from the center to the side. *Move up* is to move upstage away from the audience. *Move down* is to move downstage toward the audience.

Naturalism. A "slice of life" style of playwriting. Often considered a more extreme form of *realism,* the approach seeks an exact reproduction of life. It differs from realism by attempting to be nonselective. The term applies to both writing and acting.

Objectivity. An actor's focus on outward ramifications of reality; the opposite of *subjectivity,* which deals with inner feelings and thoughts.

Offstage. The areas of the stage not seen by the audience.

Onstage. The stage area visible to the audience.

Open. To turn the body to play more directly to the audience.

Open Turn. A turn that keeps the performer's front to the audience. (See also *closed turn.*)

Orchestra. A seating area for the audience, usually the front section of the main floor of the auditorium.

Out. Away from the center of the stage.

Overlap. To speak one's lines while another performer is speaking.

Overplay. To exaggerate, place greater emphasis than the lines, movement, or character demands.

Pace. Overall speed of a scene or a speech; control and change of tempo.

Pantomime. Storytelling action without words.

Parallel. A platform that folds up when not used.

Pick Up. A director's command to performers ("pick it up" or "pick up cues"), most often used to indicate acceleration; more accurately the intent is to decrease the interval between cue and next speech. The performer is to begin speaking immediately after receiving the cue or even to overlap the cue.

Pin Rail. In the *fly gallery* a heavy steel beam to which are attached the lines that raise or lower scenery or lights.

Pit. An area in the auditorium for musicians, between the front row of seats and the stage.

Places. A call to performers to get in position for the beginning of the act or scene. (See also *act call.*)

Plant. To establish a property or an idea that later will become significant.

Play Up (also pointing*).* To emphasize a given word, line, or piece of business.

Plot. (1) The playwright's arrangement of the events of the play. (2) A schedule of items, such as a *light plot* or *properties plot.*

Pointing (also play up*).* Emphasizing a word, line, or piece of business.

Point of Attack. The beginning of the play's plot; the play's first complication; the moment when existing equilibrium is first broken.

Practical. A stage unit that can actually be used. A practical window is one that can be opened.

Precasting. Casting performers before auditions.

Presentational Staging. Nonrealistic staging that emphasizes theatrical devices.

Producer. The owner of the production.

Projection. (1) For the actor, intensifying dialogue so it will be audible to the audience. We think of projection as a mental desire to communicate with people in the back row of the auditorium, not a mere increase in volume. (2) For lighting, casting scenic images by a lighting instrument.

Prologue. An introductory scene in a play.

Prompt Book. The director's book containing a copy of the playscript and all production information.

Prompter. A person who helps performers remember lines.

Properties. (1) Small objects used by the character, such as cigarettes or a purse; in theatrical shorthand, "hand props." (2) Larger objects found on stage, such as furniture; in theatrical shorthand, "stage props."

Proscenium. A picture frame separating audience from stage, an architectural opening through which the audience looks at the stage.

Protagonist. The central character, who both initiates and receives action. The protagonist consciously strives to achieve a goal.

Rake. A slant or angle. A "raked set" is angled, not parallel to the footlights; a "raked stage" is slanted, rising gradually from footlights to upstage wall.

Ramp. An inclined platform, often replacing steps.

Read. To convey to the audience. (1) A performer's emotions or motivations that are too small or internalized do not "read" or communicate to the audience. (2) Technical effects, such as makeup or scenic effect, as "that wallback design is too small to read in the middle of the house."

Realism. A selective representation of the objective world. The term applies to both script and performance techniques.

Representational Staging. An attempt to reproduce life. (See also *presentational staging.*)

Resolution. The part of the script that follows the climax and resolves the conflict of the play.

Revolving Stage. A circular unit that turns, allowing quick scenery changes.

Revue. A performance composed of music, dances, songs, and sketches, with little characterization and plot, often loosely organized along a general theme.

Rhythm. A regular or irregular pattern of beats.

Rigging. Lines and pulleys that are attached to the *gridiron* and run from the *pin rail* to the *battens.*

Right Stage. The actor's right while facing the audience.

Ring Down. To call for lowering the curtain, as in "ring down the curtain."

Romanticism. Dealing with different times and places, a representation of life as the playwright believes it should be, rather than as it is.

Royalty. A fee charged by playwright or play publisher–leasing agent for the right to present the play.

Run-Through. A nonstop rehearsal of a scene or act.

Satire. One of the forms of *comedy,* satire ridicules its subject.

Scenario. The playwright's outline of the play.

Scene. (1) A part of a play's act. (2) The locale of the play, as in "the scene is a living room."

Scrim. A curtain, usually made of gauze or net, that is opaque when lights strike it from the front but becomes transparent when the primary light source is behind it. The designers can paint on it without damaging the transparency. Its goal is to allow audiences to see through a wall or fixed area.

Set. (1) To fix lines or business permanently. (2) A production's scenery.

Setting. Similar to *scene*; the place where the action happens.

Share Stage. To position two or more performers so that each receives equal emphasis.

Shift. Move or change scenery.

Sides. Greatly abbreviated pieces of the playscript, sides contain only a given actor's lines and cues.

Sight Line. The visibility of the stage's acting area from the audience; the angles of vision from the audience to the rear of the set, usually measured from the far left and far right portions of audience seats. In most theatres the director must be concerned about sight lines to the upstage corners of the set.

Skit. A short episode with little characterization and minor plot, usually comic.

Soliloquy. A solo speech by the performer, usually alone on stage (in contrast to the *aside,* which is spoken while others are on stage); an extension of the character's thoughts, most often depicting the character's inner turmoil.

Sound Booth. A room, located either in the auditorium or on the stage, in which technicians operate equipment to play recorded sound over speakers.

Spike. To mark on the stage floor with tape or paint the location for a specific piece of furniture or scenic unit.

Spill. Leakage from a lighting instrument; spill light is unplanned light.

Spine. (1) For the actor the character's single motivational theme or drive throughout the play (also *superobjective*). (2) For the director spine is the play's single motivational driving force or theme, often called the through line of action.

Spotlight. A lighting instrument that can be focused.

Stage Directions. Instructions in the playscript for scenery, properties, movement, lighting and sound effects, and so forth. Not all stage directions were written by the playwright; some refer to the play's first professional staging in conditions likely to be unique and therefore of limited value to subsequent performances elsewhere.

Stage House. All of the area above and to the sides of the stage, from the proscenium arch to the rear wall, the side walls, and the roof. Typically the term is used to describe the very tall structure that contains the *flies.*

Stage Left. The actor's left when facing the audience.

Stage Manager. The authority figure in charge of performers and crews during performance.

Stage Right. The actor's right when facing the audience.

Static Scene. A scene with little action, slow pace, and no compelling drive. Seldom a virtue.

Steal. (1) The process of one actor's improperly taking attention from another actor who should have emphasis. (2) More positively, an actor's subtle move that does not attract audience attention, as "steal open" (also *cheat*).

Strike. To remove setting, furniture, or props from the stage. To "strike a set" means to take it from the stage.

Style. The overall atmosphere of the production.

Stylization. A directorial emphasis on style that becomes one of the dominant elements of the whole.

Subject. Part of the play's master *thought,* which is subdivided into *subject* and *theme.* The subject is a very brief (preferably one-word) description of what the play is about.

Subjectivity. An actor's focus on inner feelings and thoughts; the opposite of *objectivity,* which deals with the outward ramifications of reality.

Subordinate. The directorial process of treating a given production element as minor in order to emphasize a different element.

Subtext. The meaning underneath the existing lines; what the character feels or believes that is not spoken directly in dialogue; the character's intention perhaps disguised by the lines. The lines are the text; the underlying meaning is the subtext. An approach to characterization based on "subjectivity." (See also *intention.*)

Suggestivism. A production technique, the setting is suggested by use of highly simplified realism.

Supernumeraries (also **extras** *or* **walk-ons***).* Characters without lines; members of the crowd or chorus; in theatrical shorthand, "supers."

Superobjective. The character's motivating drive from first entrance (actually, even before that first entrance) to final exit. Similar to *spine.*

Suspense. Highly charged uncertainty about the outcome of action; a key portion of dramatic excitement, suspense comes from playwright and director.

Switchboard. The theatre's master electrical (or electronic) console that controls all lighting instruments.

Symbolism. A theatrical style; playwright and/or directorial focus on life's inner meanings and symbols, often spiritual; in sharp contrast to *realism* and *naturalism.*

Tableau. A composition of performers, typically motionless and speechless.

Tag Line. (1) The final line of the act or play, as in *curtain line.* (2) A character's last speech as he or she exits.

Take Five. Slang for "stop working and relax for five minutes"; usually understood to be a ten-minute break.

Take Stage. A director's request to a performer to get into a more dominant body position (usually by opening more) in relation to other actors in order to be the focus of attention; opposite of *give stage.*

Teaser. Part of the stage's physical masking devices, an adjustable horizontal border drape that masks the flies, located upstage of the *act curtain* and downstage of the *tormentors.* The teaser can be raised or lowered, thereby in effect determining the height of the stage opening.

Technical Rehearsal. A period specifically devoted to allow designers and technicians to interweave technical elements into the production.

Tempo. The performance's general rate of playing; the production's rate of speed. Tempo depends on cue pickup, the rate lines are read, and often projection levels and intensity.

Theme. Part of the play's master *thought,* which is subdivided into *subject* and *theme.* The theme is the playwright's attitude toward the subject as expressed in this play.

Thought. The play's intellectual concept, best expressed by examination of *subject* and *theme.* Thought is the play's message, the playwright's major reason to select the particular characters going through the designed actions.

Throw Away. To underplay or deemphasize a line or speech. It may be done deliberately to place greater emphasis on a different line or speech.

Thrust Stage. A stage that projects into the auditorium so that the audience sits on three sides.

Thunder Sheet. A sound effect device; a large piece of tin hung backstage, which is shaken to create a thunderous noise.

Timing. A carefully planned rate of line reading, movement, or business, designed to achieve maximum effect.

Tonality. A specific mood, tone, or quality that is projected by a performer or scene.

Top. To make a speech more dynamic than the preceding speech by speaking with more volume, speed, or intensity; topping builds tensions and displays character emotions.

Tormentor Lights. Lighting instruments hung above the stage just upstage of the *tormentors.*

Tormentors. Permanent or temporary masking units on either side of the stage upstage of the teaser; in theatrical shorthand, "torms." As the *teaser* adjusts the height of the stage opening, torms adjust the width.

Trap. An opening in the stage floor for special entrances and exits, important for magical appearances or disappearances.

Traveller. A stage curtain that divides in the middle to open to the sides of the stage.

Trim. To adjust a scenic unit, such as a *tormentor* or *teaser,* to the correct position.

Turn In. To face or move toward center stage.

Turn Out. To face or move away from center stage.

Understudy. An actor-in-waiting, prepared to step in to play a major role if the principal performer is unable to perform.

Unit Setting. A design technique; a setting that is not changed during the performance even though locales change in the course of the action. This is a popular approach for production of Shakespeare's plays, which otherwise would demand dozens of scene shifts.

Unities. A classic concept of dramatic construction holding that stage time should be congruent with real time, that the place of action cannot change, and that the action must all relate to a single plot.

Upstage. (1) The stage area furthest from the audience, in contrast to *downstage,* which is the area closest to the audience. The terms date back to older theatres with raked stage floors that sloped up away from the audience. (2) For a performer, to move further to the back of the stage than another performer, forcing the second performer to *close* in order to face the upstage actor. This can be a viable directorial device to focus attention on the upstage actor; done out of a performer's whimsical desire to *take stage,* however, it creates illwill as well as poor focus.

Vaudeville. A variety show of nonrelated specialty acts.

Vomitoria. Entrance-exit ways from the downstage areas of proscenium or thrust stages; actors can enter or leave by means of ramps underneath the front rows of the audience.

Wagon Stage. A platform on wheels for quick scene shifts; in theatrical shorthand, a "wagon."

Walk-Ons (also **extras** *or* **supernumeraries***).* Performers without lines.

Wing and Drop. A set consisting of several pairs of wing *flats* on either side of the stage, each upstage pair jutting further onstage than the pair just downstage. The *drop* is usually a painted *backdrop* upstage.

Wings. (1) *Flats* set in pairs on either side of the stage to mask offstage areas. (2) The right and left sides of the playing area.

Selected Bibliography

Acting

Alexander, F. Mattias. *The Resurrection of the Body*. Edited by Edward Maisel. New York: Dell, 1971.

Benedetti, Robert L. *The Actor at Work*. 3d ed. Englewood Cliffs, NJ: Prentice-Hall, 1981.

Berry, Cecily. *Voice and the Actor*. London: Harrap, 1973.

Chaikin, Joseph. *The Presence of the Actor*. New York: Atheneum, 1972.

Cohen, Robert. *Acting Power*. Palo Alto, CA: Mayfield, 1978.

———. *Acting Professionally*. Palo Alto, CA: National Press, 1972.

Cole, Toby, ed. *Acting: A Handbook of the Stanislavski Method*. Rev. ed. New York: Crown, 1947.

Cole, Toby, and Helen K. Chinoy, eds. *Actors on Acting*. Rev. ed. New York: Crown, 1980.

Crawford, Jerry L. *Acting in Person and in Style*. 3d ed. Dubuque, IA: Wm. C. Brown, 1983.

Delgado, Ramon. *Acting with Both Sides of Your Brain*. New York: Holt, Rinehart & Winston, 1986.

Funke, Lewis, and John E. Booth. *Actors Talk About Acting: Fourteen Interviews with Stars of the Theatre*. New York: Avon, 1973.

Grotowski, Jerzy. *Towards a Poor Theatre*. New York: Simon & Schuster, 1968.

Guthrie, Tyrone. *Tyrone Guthrie on Acting*. New York: Viking, 1971.

Hagen, Uta, and Frankel Haskel. *Respect for Acting*. New York: Macmillan, 1973.

Lessac, Arthur. *Body Wisdom: The Use and Training of the Human Body*. White Plains, NY: Lessac Research, 1978.

———. *The Use and Training of the Human Voice: A Practical Approach to Speech and Vocal Dynamics*. 2d ed. New York: Drama Book, 1967.

Lewis, Robert. *Method or Madness*. New York: Samuel French, 1958.

Linklatter, Kristen. *Freeing the Natural Voice*. New York: Drama Book, 1976.

McGaw, Charles. *Acting Is Believing*. 4th ed. New York: Holt, Rinehart & Winston, 1980.

Redfield, William. *Letters from an Actor*. New York: Viking, 1967.

Saint-Denis, Michel. *Theatre: The Re-Discovery of Style*. New York: Theatre Arts, 1969.

Shurtleff, Michael. *Audition: Everything an Actor Needs to Know to Get the Part*. New York: Walker, 1978.

Spolin, Viola. *Improvisation for the Theatre*. Evanston, IL: Northwestern University Press, 1963.

Stanislavski, Constantin. *An Actor's Handbook*. Edited by Elizabeth Reynolds Hapgood. New York: Theatre Arts, 1963.

————. *An Actor Prepares*. Edited by Elizabeth Hapgood. New York: Theatre Arts, 1936.

————. *Building a Character*. Edited by Elizabeth Hapgood. New York: Theatre Arts, 1949.

————. *My Life in Art*. Translated by J. J. Robbins. Boston: Meridian, 1956.

Ullmann, Liv. *Changing*. New York: Knopf, 1977.

Costuming and Fashion

Barton, Lucy. *Historic Costume for the Stage*. Boston: Baker's Plays, 1938.

Boucher, François. *20,000 Years of Fashion*. New York: Abrams, 1967.

Contini, Milia. *Fashion: From Ancient Egypt to the Present Day*. New York: Odyssey, 1965.

Davenport, Milia. *The Book of Costume*. New York: Crown, 1948.

Hill, Margot H., and Peter A. Bracknell. *The Evolution of Fashion, 1066–1930*. New York: Drama Book, 1967.

Kohler, Carl. *A History of Costume*. New York: Dover, 1963.

Laver, James. *Costume and Fashion: A Concise History*. New York: Thames & Hudson, 1985.

————. *Costume Through the Ages*. New York: Simon & Schuster, 1963.

Russell, Douglas A. *Stage Costume Design: Theory, Technique and Style*. Englewood Cliffs, NJ: Prentice-Hall, 1973.

Wilcox, R. Turner. *The Mode in Costume*. New York: Scribners, 1958.

Direction

Albright, Hardi. *Stage Direction in Transition*. Encino, CA: Dickenson, 1972.

Brook, Peter. *The Empty Space*. London: MacGibbon & Kee, 1968.

Cohen, Robert, and John Harrop. *Creative Play Direction*. Englewood Cliffs, NJ: Prentice-Hall, 1974.

Cole, Toby, and Helen K. Chiney, eds. *Directing the Play*. New York: Bobbs-Merrill, 1953.

————. *Directors on Directing*. New York: Bobbs-Merrill, 1964.

Clurman, Harold. *On Directing*. New York: Macmillan, 1972.

Dean, Alexander. *Fundamentals of Play Directing*. New York: Rinehart, 1953.

Dietrich, John, and Ralph W. Duckwall. *Play Direction*. 2d ed. Englewood Cliffs, NJ: Prentice-Hall, 1983.

Engel, Lehman. *Getting the Show on: The Complete Guidebook for Producing a Musical in Your Theater*. New York: Schirmer, 1983.

Glenn, Stanley L. *A Director Prepares*. Encino, CA: Dickenson, 1973.

Grotowski, Jerzy. *Towards a Poor Theatre*. New York: Simon & Schuster, 1968.

Guthrie, Tyrone. *In Various Directions*. New York: Macmillan, 1965.

Hodge, Francis. *Play Directing: Analysis, Communication and Style*. Rev. ed. Englewood Cliffs, NJ: Prentice-Hall, 1982.

Houseman, John. *Front and Center*. New York: Simon & Schuster, 1979.

Kirk, John W., and Ralph A. Bellas. *The Art of Directing*. Belmont, CA: Wadsworth, 1985.

Prince, Hal. *Contradictions: Notes on 26 Years in the Theatre.* New York: Dodd, Mead, 1974.

Roose-Evans, James. *Directing a Play.* New York: Theatre Arts, 1968.

Spolin, Viola. *Improvisation for the Theatre: A Handbook of Teaching and Directing Techniques.* Evanston, IL: Northwestern University Press, 1963.

Staub, August. *Creating Theatre: The Art of Theatrical Directing.* New York: Harper & Row, 1973.

Wills, J. Robert. *The Director in a Changing Theatre: Essays on Theory and Practice.* Palo Alto, CA: Mayfield, 1976.

Lighting

Bellman, Willard F. *Lighting the Stage: Art and Practice.* 2d ed. New York: Crowell, 1974.

Bentham, Frederick. *The Art of Stage Lighting.* 2d ed. New York: Theatre Arts, 1976.

Bergman, Gosta M. *Lighting in the Theatre.* Totowa, NJ: Rowman, 1977.

Jones, Robert E. *The Dramatic Imagination.* New York: Theatre Arts, 1941.

McCandless, Stanley. *A Method of Lighting the Stage.* 4th ed. New York: Theatre Arts, 1958.

———. *A Syllabus of Stage Lighting.* 11th ed. New York: Drama Book, 1964.

Palmer, Richard H. *The Lighting Art: The Aesthetics of Stage Lighting Design.* Englewood Cliffs, NJ: Prentice-Hall, 1985.

Parker, W. Oren, Harvey K. Smith, and R. Craig Wolf. *Scene Design and Stage Lighting.* 5th ed. New York: Holt, Rinehart & Winston, 1985.

Rosenthal, Jean, and Lael Wertenbaker. *The Magic of Light.* Boston: Little, Brown, 1972.

Rubin, Joel E., and Leland H. Watson. *Theatrical Lighting Practice.* New York: Theatre Arts, 1954.

Sellman, Hunton D., and Merrill Lessley. *Essentials of Stage Lighting.* 2d ed. Englewood Cliffs, NJ: Prentice-Hall, 1982.

Warfel, William B. *Handbook of Stage Lighting Graphics.* New York: Drama Book, 1974.

Makeup

Buchman, Herman. *Stage Make-up.* New York: Watson-Guptill, 1971.

Corson, Richard. *Stage Makeup.* 6th ed. Englewood Cliffs, NJ: Prentice-Hall, 1981.

Management

Farber, Donald C. *From Option to Opening.* 3d ed. New York: Drama Book, 1977.

———. *Producing on Broadway.* New York: Drama Book, 1969.

Langley, Stephen. *Producers on Producing.* New York: Drama Book, 1976.

———. *Theatre Management in America.* New York: Drama Book, 1974.

Newman, Danny. *Subscribe Now! Building Arts Audience Through Dynamic Subscription Promotion.* New York: Drama Book, 1977.

Reiss, Alvin H., ed. *Market the Arts!* New York: FEDAPT, 1983.

———. *The Arts Management Handbook.* New York: Law-Arts, 1970.

Wolf, Thomas. *Presenting Performers.* Cambridge, MA: New England Foundation for the Arts, 1977.

Playwriting

Bentley, Eric. *The Playwright as Thinker.* New York: Atheneum, 1967.

Busfield, Roger M., Jr. *The Playwright's Art: Stage, Radio, Television, Motion Pictures.* New York: Harper & Row, 1958.

Catron, Louis E. *Writing, Producing, and Selling Your Play.* Englewood Cliffs, NJ: Prentice-Hall, 1984.

Cole, Toby, ed. *Playwrights on Playwriting.* New York: Hill & Wang, 1961.

Egri, Lajos. *The Art of Dramatic Writing.* New York: Simon & Schuster, 1960.

Gallaway, Marion. *Constructing a Play.* Englewood Cliffs, NJ: Prentice-Hall, 1950.

Grebanier, Bernard. *Playwriting.* New York: Crowell, 1961.

Lawson, John Howard. *Theory and Technique of Playwriting.* New York: Hill & Wang, 1960.

Matthews, Brander. *The Principles of Playmaking.* Freeport, NY: Books for Libraries Press, 1970.

Smiley, Sam. *Playwriting: The Structure of Action.* Englewood Cliffs, NJ: Prentice-Hall, 1971.

Production

Burian, Jarka. *The Scenography of Josef Svoboda.* Middletown, CT: Wesleyan University Press, 1971.

Burris-Meyer, Harold, and Edward Cole. *Theaters and Auditoriums.* 2d ed. New York: Van Nostrand Reinhold, 1964.

Dolman, John, Jr., and Richard K. Knaub. *The Art of Play Production.* 3d ed. New York: Harper & Row, 1973.

Heffner, Huburt C., Samuel Selden, and Hunton D. Sellman. *Modern Theatre Practice: A Handbook of Play Production.* 4th ed. New York: Appleton-Century-Crofts, 1959.

Promotion and Publicity

Ashford, Gerald. *Everyday Publicity: A Practical Guide.* Law-Arts, 1970.

Capbern, A. Martial. *The Drama Publicist.* New York: Pageant Press, 1968.

Melcher, Daniel, and Nancy Larrick. *Printing and Promotion.* New York: McGraw-Hill, 1956.

Skal, David J. *Graphic Communications for the Performing Arts.* New York: Theatre Communications, 1981.

Levine, Mindy N., and Susan Frank. *In Print.* Englewood Cliffs, NJ: Prentice-Hall, 1984.

Scenery and Stagecraft

Bablet, Denis. *The Revolution of Stage Design in the Twentieth Century.* New York: Leon Amiel, 1977.

Bay, Howard. *Stage Design.* New York: Drama Book, 1978.

Burris-Meyer, Harold, and Edward C. Cole, *Scenery for the Theater.* 3d ed. Boston: Little, Brown, 1972.

Craig, Edward G. *On the Art of the Theatre.* New York: Theatre Arts, 1957.

Gillette, Arnold S. *An Introduction to Scene Design.* New York: Harper & Row, 1967.

Jones, Robert E. *The Dramatic Imagination.* New York: Theatre Arts, 1941.

Mielzinger, Jo. *Designing for the Theater: A Memoir and a Portfolio.* New York: Atheneum, 1965.

Motley. *Theatre Props.* New York: Drama Book, 1976.

Pecktal, Lyn. *Designing and Painting for the Theatre.* New York: Holt, Rinehart & Winston, 1975.

Simonsen, Lee. *The Art of Scenic Design.* New York: Greenwood, 1973.

———. *The Stage Is Set.* New York: Theatre Arts, 1963.

Sound

Collison, David. *Stage Sound.* New York: Drama Book, 1976.

Reference Guide to Finding Plays

Chicorel, Marietta, ed. *Chicorel Theater Index to Plays in Collections, Anthologies, Periodicals and Discs.* New York: Chicorel Library, 1972.

Connor, John M., and Billie M. Connor. *Ottemiller's Index to Plays in Collections: An Author and Title Index to Plays Appearing in Collections Published between 1900 and Early 1975.* 6th ed. Metuchen, NJ: Scarecrow, 1976.

Keller, Dean H. *Index to Plays in Periodicals.* Metuchen, NJ: Scarecrow, 1979.

Plummer, Gail. *Dramatists' Guide to Selection of Plays and Musicals.* Dubuque, IA: Wm. C. Brown, 1963.

INDEX

Page numbers in boldface type refer to photographs and/or photographic captions.